TRIUMPHING OVER BUREAUCRACY

REBEL

— TO ADOPT TWO ORPHANS —

DAD

BORN WORLDS APART

DAVID R. I.
McKINSTRY

 FriesenPress

Suite 300 – 990 Fort St
Victoria, BC, V8V 3K2
Canada

www.friesenpress.com

I have tried to recreate events, locales and conversations from my memories of them. In order to maintain their anonymity in some instances I have changed the names of individuals and places, I may have changed some identifying characteristics and details such as physical properties, occupations and places of residence.

Edited by Lynn Cunningham

ISBN
978-1-5255-2955-9 (Hardcover)
978-1-5255-2954-2 (Paperback)
978-1-5255-2956-6 (eBook)

1. BIOGRAPHY & AUTOBIOGRAPHY

Distributed to the trade by The Ingram Book Company

Several people contributed to this manuscript, directly or indirectly, and I'd be remiss if I didn't thank them for their efforts. My husband Michael Rattenbury and our two sons, Kolwyn and Nicholas for their encouragement for me to write my story, Lynn Cunningham for editing, Maureen Gallagher for punctuation/proof-reading and the courageous parents of adopted children for whom we offered hope and encouragement during the writing of this book.

REBEL
DAD

Chapter One: The Search 1

Chapter Two: "They Should Kill Those F'ing Homos" 23

Chapter Three: Coming of Age 31

Chapter Four: The Confession that Didn't Happen 41

Chapter Five: The Lake 57

Chapter Six: Vancouver 1979 – 1987 63

Chapter Seven: Finding My Birth Parents 73

Chapter Eight: Our Wedding 95

Chapter Nine: Goodbye, Nick 109

Chapter Ten: Michael 125

Chapter Eleven: Maggie and Catherine 139

Chapter Twelve: A Commitment 147

Chapter Thirteen: The Other In-laws 155

Chapter Fourteen: Canada's Gay Adoption Test Case 163

Chapter Fifteen: Stranded in Bangkok 171

Chapter Sixteen: Waiting 179

Chapter Seventeen: Ellen 'Comes Out' and Mohini Offers Me a Son . . 187

Chapter Eighteen: August 1998 Susan's Legacy Arrives 195

Chapter Nineteen: Susan's Farewell to Kolwyn 211

Chapter Twenty: Bringing Nicholas Home to Canada 227

Chapter Twenty-One: What a Difference a Year Makes 235

Epilogue 263

About the Author 285

CHAPTER ONE
THE SEARCH

EXHAUSTION FROM THE CLOYING HEAT made lying in bed with the blanket over my head seem almost necessary during that first day in India: January 22, 1998. I slept soundly until 10:30 a.m., when I was startled awake by the ring of a telephone. Janice McCann, from the Canadian High Commission in Delhi, had tracked me down. "How about coming over after lunch?" she suggested. We chatted about my luggage being rerouted to Moscow, the expense of the hotel room and being scammed by the airport taxi driver. Janice laughed upon hearing I'd flown on the Russian airline Aeroflot from Bangkok to Delhi and they had sent my luggage onto Moscow.

"Typical of that airline. You must put in a claim for the luggage immediately and hope it is returned to Delhi before the end of this century," she said half-seriously. Janice said a consulate car would be dispatched to bring me to the Canadian Embassy, so we could review the names on the list of Canadian-approved adoption agencies in Delhi. I had been warned by the Ottawa law firm I'd hired to prepare my immigration paperwork that I needed to keep my sexuality a secret, never mention my husband Michael and to tow the 'company line' as suggested by Immigration Canada. I'd been forewarned and told to tell Indian officials I was a widower looking to adopt children. The debacle over my original adoption inquiry paperwork, stating clearly that I was a gay applicant, being sent to thirteen international agencies resulted in none of those countries offering me access or clearance to investigate available children in their orphanages. It had been a long-fought battle to get the officials at Immigration Canada to change my home-study to present me as a widower, rather than as a gay man, wanting to adopt internationally. Homosexuality in India was illegal and a taboo subject, and I was told not to tell any Indian, nor anyone at the Canadian High Commission, that I was gay.

Janice asked if all my paperwork was in order and I told her not yet, but that I had come anyway to do the necessary fact-finding and introduce myself to the executive directors of orphanages in Delhi. I reminded her about Blair Hart, an employee who had worked for the Delhi Canadian High Commission until a year ago, and how Blair, his wife and two young daughters had providentially arrived as guests to my small country inn called Woodhaven Country Lodge. Over supper one evening we'd chatted about our lives and upon hearing I was in the process of having my international adoption paperwork finalized, they encouraged me to send my paperwork to India. While in India they had adopted an infant daughter and said the process wasn't difficult for Canadians interested in adopting a child in New Delhi. I had asked if they thought my being a gay applicant would be an issue for the Indian government. Blair said India remained as homophobic as any country in Southeast Asia and strongly suggested I keep my sexuality a closely guarded secret but the fact there were so many children up for adoption he didn't think the Indian officials would ask many questions. I told them my paperwork was still in the process of getting a 'Letter of No Objection' from the Canadian Immigration Department (* this document is required to show a foreign adoption agency that Canada had done its due diligence and approved someone to adopt internationally and bring said child home to Canada) and that was the last hurdle to me applying to adopt internationally. "Forget waiting for that piece of paper from the Feds. You already have 90% of your paperwork approved so just go to India and let your presence be proof to the Indian adoption authorities of your desire to adopt children. By the time you return to Canada you'll have the last of that paperwork approved and you simply forward that official document to the orphanages and Indian authorities with whom you made contact," they suggested. Janice nodded and confirmed I'd heeded wise advice from Blair about coming to check out Canadian High Commission approved orphanages in Delhi. As much as I felt an instant connection with Janice, I made no mention of being gay or my husband Michael and let her believe I was a widower in search of adopting a child.

I returned to the hotel and began arranging meetings with personnel at the eighteen orphanages on my pre-approved list. Four were operated by Catholic missions and the rest were a hodgepodge of state-run and privately-operated institutions. Several had been established by kind-hearted, wealthy Indian matrons. Most of these orphanages had one particular country with which they had a special arrangement. In exchange for donations, that country would get first dibs on the orphans deemed acceptable by international standards. Children with deformities or those in poor health were considered undesirable candidates for international adoption because no country wants to take on the costly burden of health-care for such children. Without question, lighter-skinned orphans would be offered for adoption to infertile Indian couples domestically, then to off-shore Indians. Darker-skinned children were always offered to non-Indian international families. Of India's population of nearly one billion people, 160 million are untouchables, or the lowest caste of people. They do the menial jobs of cleaning out public washrooms, sweeping streets and removing animal and human corpses discarded around every shantytown. Many orphans from this caste end up in orphanages and are first on the list to be adopted internationally. Muslim refugees from Bangladesh and Pakistan live in makeshift camps around the city. If very young refugee children became separated from their families and were unable to look after themselves, they would die or be placed into public or privately-operated orphanages. Medical care for refugees was practically non-existent. Therefore, if a single parent of three children died in a back alley, those children would either live on the streets as beggars, perish from hunger or, if very fortunate, become wards of an orphanage with a long list of international couples desperate to adopt children.

My interviews were to begin the next day and continue until I had seen every possible orphanage approved by Immigration Canada. Around suppertime I hailed a taxi and headed into the center of Delhi to check out some inexpensive hotels in the Connaught Circle district.

Connaught Circle is the hub of the Delhi business and financial district, and a well-known shopping and tourist destination for over a century. It has over-the-top five-star hotels for business people, small hostels used by backpackers and everything in between. India's Republic Day celebrations would be happening on January 26, making New Delhi alive with revelers. Many of the hostels I viewed were full and those that had rooms looked so seedy that I couldn't trust the locks on the doors. The Jagoso Inn seemed slightly more secure; it was $50 U.S. per night for a bedroom with a TV (two Hindi and one English-language channels), a bathroom with cockroaches and an open-air hallway that ran across the side of the building. The bed looked comfortable enough, but the slate floor needed a good scrub with disinfectant. I paid a deposit and said I would be back the next day to check in around noon. I decided to meander and explore this area for a few hours before wanting a meal. Connaught Circle had a glut of eateries to choose from, but I wanted something familiar. My options were Indian-style Kentucky Fried Chicken or Pizza Hut. Being vegetarian I chose Pizza Hut.

The Pizza Hut line-up was ten people long when I put my name in the reservation book. Standing in line gave foreigners an opportunity to find someone who spoke their language for a shared dining experience. The waiters were all fair-skinned young men who resembled a group of happy university students working their way through college. There were no women on staff and it brought home the strangeness of this land where women's rights remain draconian and constrained.

I saw no sign of anyone gay in the streets, shops or restaurants. But shortly after being seated at a table I noticed a group of male students from Australia wearing T-shirts that read "The King's Cross and so is This Queen." They were overtly rebellious in their demeanor and several of the young men glared about the restaurant, as if challenging the patrons or staff to take umbrage with their behaviour. One Indian family dressed in Western clothes seated near my table just stared at them as they sashayed past our section of the restaurant, leaving many of the waiters chuckling. I smiled at the thought of their youthfulness and cheeky attitude.

One of the waiters introduced himself to my table of six people. Santosh was fluent in English and barely had a noticeable accent. He made a special note of our being international visitors and told us about local attractions, shops to avoid, how to get to the zoo—he was a terrific ambassador for Delhi. The British couple seated with me at the table appreciated Santosh paying some attention to us and allowing them to ask him questions about Delhi. I told him his English was like a welcome mat as I was feeling like a lost foreigner unable to communicate with people on the street or in the shops. Santosh said he and most of the other waiters were university students who had attended private schools. I wasn't sure if he was telling me the truth when he said his family regularly went to Kashmir or to Switzerland to ski and he had been to Hong Kong, London and Vienna on holidays with his school. He was friendly to everyone and it paid off when we left him an oversized tip.

I left the restaurant and headed back to the hotel in a cab. It was only 6:30 p.m. and still sunny and hot outside. I asked the driver if he would take me on a tour of the city before we got back to the hotel. Vinod was thirty years old and had been driving a cab for three years. He said his brother had moved to the United States and was a computer technician in Seattle. Santosh was trying to save enough money to visit his brother. I chatted about my reasons for coming to India and he told me he had driven many times for foreigners in Delhi who'd come to adopt children. On the way to see the parliament buildings and the wealthier districts of Delhi, we passed numerous open-air markets in crowded alleys and along main thoroughfares. A mile further along, and we drove along a street with beautiful boulevards and lined with high-walled and gated compounds, each a foreign consulate.

Vinod stopped the car at a roadside bazaar and I got out to watch a snake charmer working his skills on a huge cobra. A small crowd of international tourists were mesmerized by his control over this venomous snake. After five minutes of teasing and taunting, the act was over and all of us in the crowd put rupees down on the blanket beside him. I returned to my taxi feeling weak from the heat and asked him to take me to the hotel without delay.

Vinod asked if I'd found any children to adopt. I explained that this trip was just a fact-finding mission and I had interviews arranged with orphanages in Delhi for most of the following three days. Vinod suggested I hire him as a personal guide and driver for my appointments, as it would be less costly and faster than hailing a new taxi to each destination. He also asked if I would be interested in meeting some of his friends who were government social workers and could facilitate finding children for adoption. I said I was very interested in any leads he could present, and I'd pay him handsomely for any introductions to people who could provide useful information leading toward an adoption. Vinod told me he'd be waiting for me at the front entrance of the hotel to help with my move to Connaught Circle in the morning and then he would transport me to my orphanage meetings. I asked him for a daily rate and he said 2,000 rupees—approximately $40 Canadian—would be fair. I shook his hand and we agreed he'd become my guide through the maze of neighbourhoods with orphanages I needed to visit.

Back at the hotel I packed my only bag and wrote out the addresses of my appointments for the following day in bold print. Earlier that day at breakfast I'd eaten fruit and toast, and during the day I had consumed two cups of coffee. I'd been told not to eat soft-fleshed fruit or drink water that hadn't been boiled. I bought bottled water to be safe but discovered later street-purchased water bottles were often tampered with, filled with unpurified water. I'd consumed four bottles that day and my guts were churning. I was sick all night. By morning I was exhausted, and my face had the pale look of someone who had not slept in days.

Vinod was standing outside my bedroom door when I emerged looking ashen. I handed him the list of five orphanages I had scheduled appointments with that day.

The first was a state-run facility, Delhi Council for Child Welfare. The building rose up in front of us as we drove into an upscale neighborhood with white stucco houses, each lot divided by rows of fifty-foot-high trees. The narrow streets of this cul-de-sac were cobblestoned; the laborers who swept the streets spotless would take home only a few rupees for their daylong effort.

Nisha, the director of this facility, was a stunningly beautiful thirty-ish woman with a kind and gentle manner as she greeted me and then led me to her office. She had just placed a child the previous month with a family in Ottawa and she was happy to see another Canadian inquiring about adoption. Scanning through my file, Nisha asked me thoughtful questions while frequently making encouraging observations about my readiness to adopt children. However, after thirty minutes, she announced that this orphanage's charter denied single people, widowed or not, from adopting their children. She suggested I visit Mother Teresa's Missionaries of Charity orphanage, just up the road and the next place on my list. Nisha asked if I was Christian and gave me a warm, bright smile when I replied, "Indeed I am." After a short walk around the compound full of nicely dressed and happy-looking children playing under tall shade trees, she bid me goodbye and good wishes for a successful adoption.

Vinod drove me directly to the Missionaries of Charity compound. A garden worker opened the gate for the taxi to enter and fifty preschool children and two nuns instantly surrounded us. Vinod spoke to the first nun, who motioned him to move the car forward and for me to follow her to the office. The taxi drove slowly through the crowd of excited children playing tag with the car. Once inside the building, I was directed to sit in a small waiting room at the far end of a dimly lit corridor. As we entered the hallway leading to the waiting room, I gazed into a large room on my right filled with cribs housing at least fifty cooing or crying babies. The dank, cool air of this old cinderblock building was a relief from the oppressive heat outside in the courtyard. I was left wondering if these babies had ever seen the moon and the sun or had the chance to breath fresh morning air.

Dressed in a full habit, the head nun, Sister Joyce, came to greet me. I mentioned Nisha's name and told Sister Joyce I'd come to see her about adopting children. She showed no expression and her locked-tight lips gave me the impression I was in the presence of someone who didn't waste time on niceties. She motioned for me to follow her into an office off the open-air courtyard. She sat down behind an oversized desk, quickly scanned through my portfolio of home-study documents and after five dead-silent minutes said, "What you want?"

I told her my well-rehearsed story, which the Canadian adoption officials had dreamed up: I was a widower, and my late wife, Nicci, had begged me prior to her death to go ahead with plans to adopt children from India. I told Sister Joyce that I loved children and was able to afford to give children a wonderful, loving home in Canada. After twenty minutes talking about my reasons for wanting to adopt she began to loosen up. However, she said that being a widower still meant I was a single man in the eyes of the Indian judiciary and very few orphanages would give me a child.

"Why not you get married again?" she asked. I just shrugged and handed her photos of my home, Woodhaven, and my life in Canada. After a quick gaze at the pictures and a chuckle over the dogs she said, "I think you good man. Want to see children?" I stood up and nodded eagerly.

She walked in front of me and led me into a room like the nursery I'd passed when I first entered the building. Sister Joyce informed me that three helpers were preparing lunchtime formula and Pablum for sixty babies and if I wanted to help feed one or more of them I could. I was overjoyed at being asked to help care for these youngsters.

"Are these babies available for adoption? Would I be able to adopt one or two of your babies?" I asked her wide-eyed with joyous anticipation of her saying yes. "These babies were orphaned at birth and it is okay for a Canadian to adopt our babies. Maybe you like one of these children?" she smiled up at me. My gosh! I had no idea it would be this easy. One of the helpers motioned for me to follow her into the kitchen and she put a bowl of Pablum in my hands. Sister Joyce handed me a baby from one of the cribs and told me to feed this little boy. I spent the next hour feeding children from the cribs amid the smiles and chuckles of the nuns and helpers. I wondered what they were saying to each other about this Canadian man who wanted so fervently to adopt children.

Vinod was brought into the nursery by the nun who had greeted us at the gates of the compound. While he stood there watching me, I had two or three youngsters crawling up my pant legs and another two scrambling up my arms. They just didn't want to let go of a prospective parent. As I fumbled to balance all the children, the supervising nun walked past me toward a young boy, who looked about three years old, trying to escape from his crib. She smacked him across the face and pushed him back into the crib. He didn't cry or flinch. I was horrified but knew if I confronted the nun, I risked being asked to leave and not return.

Vinod smiled as he stood beside me in the nursery and asked if one of these children was going to be mine? I could feel my smile widening from ear to ear and whispered that I thought Sister Joyce liked me because she had invited me to visit the children and help feed them. Vinod smiled and said, "You look happy with baby." He mentioned if we were still going to make the next appointments we had to leave within thirty minutes or be late.

As I placed the children back in their cribs, they shrieked and cried while reaching up to be held again. It was painfully obvious that they didn't have much tender time in human arms, except for ten minutes of feeding three times each day. I walked back through the long inner hallway past an office where Sister Joyce was talking with a blond-haired Caucasian man and woman.

"They from Norway," she said as I peeked into the room to say goodbye. I told her I had to go to another appointment but asked if I could come back later to help with suppertime. As I left the building and entered the compound, I was swarmed by 100 children all looking to be less than five years of age. They were playing in the dirt piles of the compound and when they saw me they rushed over and grabbed at me to pick them up. On one hand it was exhilarating to have all this attention from so many adoptable children, but Vinod came over and pulled them off, so I could get into the taxi.

"They want to go with you," he said. "These children always do this to white people who might adopt them." To experience clinging children trying to climb into my arms was gut-wrenching, and I could feel tears welling in my eyes. The taxi drove out of the compound amid wails from the children who hadn't yet touched me. I wondered how the nuns and helpers managed to be calm surrounded by orphans clamoring for constant attention.

By 6 p.m. I had visited five institutions. Only the Missionaries of Charity orphanage had given me any indication I might be considered as an adoptive parent. Two Catholic missions had curtly refused to consider me because I was single and male. Another state-run group told me that due to infertility on the rise in India, Indian couples and Indian nationals living abroad were given first right of refusal. One official apologized and said I would be the last person to be considered because they didn't give children to single men or women.

I returned to Sister Joyce's compound and told Vinod that I'd stay for a few hours feeding the children. He agreed to wait when I told him I'd treat him to supper on the way back to my hotel.

I entered the nursery and found several older nuns feeding the children and changing the diapers of those standing at the sides of the cribs. If a child wasn't being fed, he or she was crying alone. Some cribs held two or three babies. Without delay I grabbed a bib and a bowl of paste-like stew from a large pot in the adjoining kitchen area and began to feed babies in the row nearest me. Some of the nuns were quite brusque in handling the children. I watched one nun walk down a center aisle of cribs and slap eighteen-month-olds on the cheeks for standing up in their cribs. Appalled by this abuse, I again had to grit my teeth in silent indignation.

I cradled and sang to a pair of crib-sharing babies simultaneously. Two nuns walked by and smiled like angels looking down from on high. I was desperate to make a good impression on the nuns and Sister Joyce. As I looked into the eyes of the children, Elsbit and Lampai, cradled in my arms, I whispered, "I'd take the two of you home to Canada tomorrow if Sister Joyce would let me." Had I become a rebel with a cause? My cause being to return to Canada with multiple orphans from India to raise as my children. Imagining myself arriving home with children, greeting Michael and us becoming a family was the fuel that fired my defiant determination and had been at the root of my recalcitrant attitude toward changing the system for decades so I, as a gay man, could live out my dream to become a parent. My journey to fatherhood was not going to be a quick, easy sprint to the finish line, but instead a lengthy mountainous marathon.

The babies smiled up at me and then nodded off to sleep. Several attempts to put them back into the crib failed as they awakened every time. My arms were falling asleep and I knew Vinod was waiting for me. Finally, the babies were sound asleep, and I quickly placed them into the crib at opposite ends. I bent down and kissed them goodnight and told them I would like to be their dad. I said a prayer asking God if these two babies were to be mine would He please let me have a sign.

As I passed through the hallway leading out to the compound Sister Joyce walked around the corner, surprising me. We were both taken aback at almost running into one another. "You are good with babies. Someday you be good father," she smiled and walked past me into her office. I hopped into Vinod's taxi absolutely tingling with excitement and told him to head to a restaurant where we could share a grand meal.

Over supper, Vinod told me he had made some good contacts with adoption officials who wanted to meet me the next afternoon. He said they worked for the state and babies could be placed through any of the state-approved orphanages on my list. The catch was that it would cost me $3,500 U.S. up front to bribe the assistant of the man who would make the decision about me adopting a child. I was blown away by this suggestion I pay some unknown guy's assistant a bribe just to put my paperwork on the top of the daily pile of adoption papers. "Well, let's wait until I know if Sister Joyce will give me some children. Hopefully I will know by the end of tomorrow if I will get two of her children," I naively said to Vinod.

I was too excited to sleep right away so I wrote a two-page letter to Michael telling him of my adventures that day and how optimistic I was about getting Elsbit and Lampai. Details of my every encounter with the different orphanages, some religious groups and others state-run, flowed effortlessly into this message. I wished Michael could be here to experience how it was unfolding and to see first-hand what I was doing to find us a family of children to adopt. I knew he wouldn't be keen on me paying bribes to anyone, so I didn't mention Vinod's suggested baksheesh payments to officials in the adoption ministry. I went to the front desk clerk and paid to have this letter faxed to Woodhaven. My room wasn't air-conditioned, but it had a big ceiling fan that whirled constantly and kept me comfortable. The hot water taps didn't work so I shampooed my underwear, socks and shirt in cold water under the tub faucet. I had barely settled into bed and turned out the light, my mind reviewing the events of the past twenty-four hours, when my doorknob jiggled. I was stunned, and for a split second it seemed I must have been dreaming, but ten seconds later it rattled again, and I heard someone pushing against the locked door. I bolted upright and yelled, "Hey, stop that," in a loud, deep voice. Someone ran down the hallway and disappeared. I put a chair in front of the door and braced it under the doorknob to further decrease any risk that someone could break in during the night. I fell asleep wondering if $50 per night was worth it. Staying in a better hotel would give me a heightened sense of security unavailable here. I had to be prudent about money—there were potential adoption costs and the possible necessity of staying in Delhi for a month or longer. My luggage still hadn't been traced and I was skeptical about ever seeing my belongings again. Any thief would find it slim pickings in my room if he did break in.

Vinod drove me to three orphanage appointments the next morning. Not one gave me any hope of adopting children. Around lunchtime we drove into the compound of the Missionaries of Charity and were met by Sister Joyce alone in the courtyard. As if she had been waiting for us to arrive, she walked up to the taxi window and said, "You healthy man. Go find new wife and make babies. You don't get any of our children. Sorry, but you go now."

I was stunned. She turned to walk away. I flung open the door of the taxi and ran around in front of her and stood looking down at her face. I could feel a swell of anger rising in my throat. She halted immediately and looked up at me with an expressionless face, reminding me of the first time I'd met her.

"I want those two babies I cradled last night. My paperwork is good, and I have shown you my sincerity. Why won't you give me children to adopt?" I asked, trying not to appear too confrontational.

"You go find new wife. These babies for infertile people. You make babics of your own." Her brows furrowed as she repeated herself. "Now you go out in taxi." She slipped past me and into the side door and I could hear the latch lock.

Speechless and shocked, I stood alone in the compound staring at the closed door. Vinod put his arm around my shoulder, saying, "I will find you children to adopt." I allowed him to usher me back to the taxi and we drove off, leaving a cloud of diesel smoke behind. I was devastated. Even though God hadn't sent me a sign, I had hoped those two babies would somehow be mine today. Had I just been an extra pair of hands to relieve nuns on mealtime duty in the nursery? Had she somehow figured out I was gay? How could she be so dismissive? Didn't this woman have any compassion or humanity?

"You want to meet adoption official I told you about yesterday?" Vinod asked cautiously. He knew my emotions were raw and I was on the verge of a rage meltdown. I didn't even get to say goodbye to Elsbit and Lampai, I kept saying to myself.

Elsbit (third from right) and Lampai (far right), the two babies
I hoped to adopt from Missionaries of Charity.

I agreed to pay the $3,500 to get my paperwork into the hands of a state adoption official. We stopped at a State of India Bank and I took $3,500 from the $10,000 in traveller's cheques in my waistband wallet. Vinod drove me to a concrete low-rise near the parliament buildings and told me to bring my backpack full of paperwork. I was led into the air-conditioned lobby and we took the elevator to the sixth floor. Other than most of the people working behind desks being Indian, the elevator opened into an office area that could easily have been located in any downtown Toronto office tower. Vinod escorted me down a long corridor to a small lobby and told me to wait for him to return. The wad of money was in an envelope stuffed deep into a pocket of my trousers. Within a few minutes Vinod returned with a pleasant-looking man, about forty, who had a somewhat nervous smile. Vinod introduced me to Mr. Vasnani and said to give the man the envelope. I nervously placed the bulging envelope into his waiting hand. It disappeared quickly into his pocket as he smiled and waved us into an adjoining office. It took him several minutes to examine my documents and he asked if he could take copies of them, excusing himself and leaving Vinod and me alone to ponder what would happen next.

"How will this work?" I asked politely when he returned. "Can you guarantee me a child to adopt?"

Mr. Vasnani looked up and stopped writing on the documents long enough to say that I would get one chance on the pile for each $3,500 given to him. He explained that if his boss picked up my documents, one of only five or six sets he would examine on a given day, my chances were very good that I'd be given immediate clearance to adopt a child by the Indian Child Welfare office. He asked how long I would be staying in Delhi and I told him as long as it would take to find children. His facial expression took on a sinister, greedy smile that gave me the creeps, but I couldn't let on that I was nervous about being milked for more money. He told me he would contact Vinod by phone each day and tell him if I had won the prize. If my documents weren't chosen, Mr. Vasnani would put them on the top of the pile of a different official, and so on until someone gave me the clearance. This wasn't honest or above-board, but

I felt I had few options. I remembered being counselled by one of the immigration officials in Ottawa who said I must not pay bribes as that would nullify my adoption if discovered. However, in the next breath, I was told to take about $20,000 in small bills, as I might need it. Was Mr. Vasnani an example of what that official had implied?

Over the next week Vinod taxied me to the remaining orphanages on my list, as well as numerous others we discovered along the way. I decided to drop in rather than make appointments, as it didn't seem appointments were necessary. Many places on my list were unprofessional-looking dumps and I was almost glad to discover that they didn't have any available children for overseas adoptions. The last of the eighteen orphanages on my list was an hour's drive away. Vinod asked me if I wanted to continue and I told him we had to check it out. First, though, he called Mr. Vasnani. It didn't come as any surprise that once again I hadn't won the lottery, but Mr. Vasnani would continue to place my documents on another official's pile as long as I continued to pay another bribe each day. My options were dwindling, and I felt I had no choice but to keep trying with this supposed government insider. I agreed, and before we headed off to the last orphanage on my list, we went to a bank to exchange traveller's cheques for U.S. dollars, then delivered the money to Mr. Vasnani.

It was 3 p.m. and we were getting caught in heavy traffic. Stopped at a set of lights, I became riveted by the sight of the hundred or so beggars milling around the cars and taxis. Some young mothers carrying babies in their arms couldn't have been much older than thirteen or fourteen years of age. With horror I watched as one thrust the hand of her baby into the car window and waved the child's bloodied hand, missing the tips off two fingers, in front of my face. Vinod saw the look of horror in my eyes and told me that often these beggars mutilate the hands of their babies because foreigners will take pity on them and give a lot of money.

Reflecting on the contrast between my fight to get a child and the plight of these youngsters with babies who would injure their infants to get money to buy food for themselves and their children, I felt sickened. The situation of these young girls and women, marginalized by caste, birthright and gender, gave them few options other than surrendering their babies to orphanages, which would care for their children until new families could be found. The price of my bribes to Vasnani would have allowed one of these mothers to keep and feed her baby for years. Was I selfish to keep surrendering money to this parasite in hopes of finding a child? Should I just put that money into the hands of one girl at the streetlights? To whom of the many would I give the money?

Vinod swerved to avoid hitting a cow and it jolted me back from deep thought. He told me we were entering Vasant Vihar, a gated and very wealthy area. The orphanage office, located in the home of a wealthy matron, didn't take long to find. We rang the bell at the entrance and a woman appeared to open the gate. Vinod said he would stay with the taxi. I told the woman that I was here to see Mrs. Raghunath and she smiled and told me in broken English to follow her.

Mohini Raghunath had received her approval status from the Canadian Immigration department only one month prior to my arrival. She was thrilled to have her first Canadian consider adopting one of her children. A warm and lovely woman in her traditional sari, her greying hair cut short, she had draped a shawl over her shoulders. Catching me gazing at the garment, she explained, "I know you think it is hot today, but I find January weather in the late afternoons to be chilly."

From the moment we met, Mrs. Raghunath was kind, gentle and encouraging. Giving me an overview of the Indian adoption rules, she told me I would never be allowed to adopt more than one child at a time, unless they were siblings. She and two other social workers at her orphanage had been insurgents over the past few years, fighting to reform, standardize and legitimize adoption procedures in India. She had worked tirelessly attending tribunals and conferences, trying to cut the red tape and bureaucratic entanglements that caused needless delays in finalizing domestic and international adoptions. Mohini explained that she had received a slap on the wrist recently, basically being told to lie low and stop being a reformer or risk losing her orphanage status. She offered tea and asked me to tell her about myself. After I presented the cover story the Canadian adoption officials had helped me devise, she informed me that should I be eligible to adopt from India, she wouldn't be allowed to offer me a daughter, but perhaps a boy about five years old. I asked why I wouldn't get a daughter and she said too many wealthy businessmen from Thailand and Saudi Arabia had come to India over the years to adopt little girls who ended up working in the sex trade. The Indian government had recently enacted a law prohibiting single men, Indians or internationals, from adopting daughters.

While we chatted, she scanned through my documentation, making notes and asking many questions. "Would you consider adopting two brothers? How old a child would you consider? I have a little boy who is ten years old and his mother can't keep him. She has asked me to find him a home out of India. He is a nice-looking boy, lighter skinned and very smart. Would a boy like this interest you?" she inquired. I told her I really felt fate had brought me to her doorstep and I would follow her instinct. I said I had hoped for a younger child, but I'd entertain all options she'd suggest. After an hour her secretary came in and spoke quietly to her in Hindi. The meeting was over.

"I am glad you came to see me today. I can tell by looking into your eyes that you would be a great father. My best advice to you is to go back to Canada now. Don't spend any more time or money in Delhi this trip. Guaranteed, I will call you within three months about a son. Get your remaining paperwork in order and send me the notarized documents when you receive your Letter of No Objection," she said. I was dumbfounded by her candour, warmth and her promise that she would soon call me to come back for a son she would find for me. I thanked her profusely and for the first time since arriving in Delhi I felt assured, calm and happy. I was so dizzy with elation that I felt a tear form in the corner of my eye. Mrs. Raghunath came and put her arm on mine and walked me to her gate. As she paused she turned and repeated the words that I still hear so clearly in my mind, "Go home, David. I will call you. Be confident that I will call you soon. And one word of advice: Do not try to buy off public or government officials in India. You will lose your money and it could work against your efforts to adopt a child." I wondered if this woman had telepathic powers. I wanted to hug her but thought I shouldn't be too forward. I smiled and clasped her hand in mine and said I believed in her and I would go home and await her call. She turned and walked away, and I watched her return to her lovely house, awestruck by the peace I felt in my heart for the first time in longer than I could remember.

Vinod noticed the difference in my demeanor the moment I entered his taxi. I told him what Mrs. Raghunath had said and how good I felt about her.

Vinod quietly mentioned that Mr. Vasnani had just telephoned him to report that my paperwork was not among the pile chosen for his boss to read the next morning. If I wanted to continue it would require another bribe. Without talking, I stared directly at Vinod. A few seconds later it became obvious to Vinod, without me answering him, that my expression indicated that I was through with that rip-off artist, Mr. Vasnani, and his bogus efforts to help me adopt. Without another word being said between us, he turned back into his driver's seat and drove me back to my hotel. Looking into the rear-view mirror I watched Vinod nervously glance at me as he drove away from this wealthy and gated community of Vasant Vihar toward my hotel in Connaught Circle. Staring at his nervous eyes in the rear-view mirror, I wondered how much kickback from my bribes had gone into Vinod's pocket. From insult to injury, I'd trusted Vinod as being one of the only people, other than Mrs. Raghunath, whom I'd met in India that I had trusted to be honest with me. Mrs. Raghunath's farewell warning echoed loudly in my head. If only I'd started at the bottom of the list, I'd be returning home with $20,000.00 of unused bribe money in my wallet. Arriving back at my hotel, my exit from the taxi was purposefully slow and poised. Vinod neither looked at me nor spoke to me and it was implied that I wouldn't require his taxi services during my final few days in Delhi. Feeling duped, I wasn't going to put another rupee into Vinod's hand.

Back at the hotel, knowing that Janice McCann often worked late at the High Commission office, I telephoned her direct number. She answered and excitedly began peppering me with questions about the success of my inquiries at the various orphanages. I gave her a comprehensive update on the outcome of my visits and mentioned that my taxi-driver guide had some contacts at CVARA, the Indian ministry for adoptions, whom he thought might be able to expeditiously navigate the bureaucratic red tape to help me find an adoptable child. I didn't mention having met the man or having paid the bribes.

"Your taxi driver is just setting you up. Whoever he knows in some government job doesn't have any authority to facilitate speedy clearances. That isn't how it works in India. He is totally bogus, David," she said. "I'm surprised he didn't hit you up for an outrageous bribe." She laughed heartily, and I was relieved I had not divulged how easily I'd been swindled by Mr. Vasnani and Vinod. I really didn't care at this point. I thanked Janice for her warm and friendly help during my visit to Delhi.

I put in time walking around Connaught Circle and repeatedly making calls to Aeroflot's office at the Delhi airport about my luggage. Finally, I got through to an agent and was informed my luggage could be picked up on my next trip to the airport. What could be more fitting in this upside-down world of India —just as I'm leaving Delhi my lost luggage is found. How I longed to feel a different shirt on my back, to have clean underwear and be able to use medications. It suddenly hit me, that what I had experienced with only one shirt to my name was exactly the way many of the street people of India live life 365 days of every year. I felt a twinge of conscience at the opulence of having luggage full of clothing waiting for me at the airport.

I faxed Michael saying I was leaving Delhi within 48 hours for the return trip across the Pacific and gave him an overview of my meeting with Mrs. Raghunath. I decided to spend my last days in India visiting temple sites and other landmarks. I booked myself on an inexpensive bus tour to Agra, about five hours east of Delhi, and home of the Taj Mahal. The magnificence of the marble Taj Mahal juxtaposed with the backdrop of abject poverty all around the area was a bit confusing to me. Some Indians I'd met, like Mrs. Raghunath, were absolute angels on earth. I was in awe of her. On the other hand, the attitude demonstrated by most working people I'd met, like Vinod, toward beggars and those less fortunate than themselves seemed harsh and unsympathetic—such a mass of contradictions.

We left the Taj Mahal late in the afternoon and it was 10 p.m. before the bus wove through the city traffic and let me off at my hotel. I had one day left and decided to just walk around Delhi and take in the sights. I checked out of the hotel later that morning. It was a hot day and I didn't stray far off the shady, narrow winding streets. Over lunch I met a young Irish businessman also killing time before heading off to the airport for a late evening flight home. We decided to share a cab to the various temple sites. He was a computer specialist in Delhi to recruit university graduates for his company. He was intrigued by my adoption story and at 7 p.m. we stopped for supper in Connaught Circle at Pizza Hut being served and entertained by Santosh again. By 9 p.m. we were in a cab bound for the airport. It seemed as if most international flights were scheduled to depart Delhi after midnight.

My passport and other documents were hidden in my waist pouch. I claimed my bags from the Aeroflot counter and bid goodbye to my Irish friend. With three hours before my check-in time, I walked through the many terminals of this sooty, humid airport and looked at the airport personnel I passed and wondered what their stories were—if anything, India was a country with so many common stories, yet I was intrigued by the stamina and courage of these individuals to work so hard for so little. So many people doing the same jobs, day after day....to me mundane, to them it was survival. I wondered if they thought much beyond survival from day to day? It wasn't my place to judge them, but I was perplexed and disturbed by the juxtaposition of rich and poor. So many destitute people going on in the hope that in the next life they would come back in better circumstances. I felt saddened by their seeming resignation to surviving day to day the poverty into which they had been born.

Three hours passed quickly and finally I settled into the departures line-up. I gladly placed my ticket on the counter and the agent smiled and asked if I was happy to be heading home to Canada. She directed me to the departure gate a hundred feet away and told me to present my documents to the duty officer. I couldn't believe I was heading home.

After five minutes in the line, I handed over my travel documents and ticket, nervous about potential screw-ups. The official looked up and said, "Passport, please." I was sure I had handed it to him with my ticket—it wasn't in my document pouch. Beads of sweat immediately formed on my brow. I frantically looked on the ground around me and then ran back to the baggage check-in counter to ask the agent if I had left my passport with her by mistake. She immediately looked as distraught as I felt.

Without any further hesitation I yelled loudly, "Police! Police! Someone has stolen my passport!" Within seconds, everyone around me was double-checking to be sure they had their own passports. Two airport security officers quickly arrived and asked what had happened. I told them my flight was leaving in forty-five minutes and my passport had been stolen between checking in my bags and walking 100 feet to the departures gate. Several junior officers came running over and in Hindi the senior officer told them something that sent the junior officers off at high speed.

"Sir, you must retrieve your baggage because without your passport you won't be leaving tonight," the senior officer said. "We must file a report in the office quickly. Please follow me." He touched my arm and indicated that I should go with him. I couldn't believe this was happening to me. I had less than $50 in my wallet and my Visa card was well over its limit. My remaining funds wouldn't get me back into the city or cover accommodation for a few more days or pay for food and taxi fare to get around to the various offices I'd need to visit to have a new passport issued.

The senior officer escorted me silently and quickly to the airport security office. The officer behind the counter was speaking in Hindi and looking directly at me. A moment later, a burly man walked out of a side office and asked in perfect English, "Are you Mr. David McKinstry from Canada?"

"We found your passport on the floor of the terminal by the exit doors. It was probably dropped by accident by the thief," he said. He opened my passport and examined the photo for a moment and then told me I should be more careful and if I hurried I would still make my flight. I flew out of his office after thanking him and his staff. I made it through the departures gate and down the ramp onto the plane with ten minutes to spare. I was either the luckiest person in the world that day or it had been another one of God's tests to see how much more angst I could withstand.

The return trip across Southeast Asia and over the Pacific Ocean to Canada was physically exhausting but emotionally I was on a real high. Janice McCann said to be sure to communicate daily with Mrs. Raghunath. "Keep in constant contact with her office by fax or email to show them just how eager you are to adopt a son.".

Michael met me at Toronto's Pearson Airport. This trek to India had taken its toll on me and he hugged me and said, "Welcome home, sweetheart." Michael said he was thrilled to have me home again. JC, the hospitality student who had been running the lodge in my absence, greeted us at the door with our pack of dogs. I had missed everyone so much. My time away felt like an eternity. I was so glad to be home in Canada. I threw my bags in our bedroom and said goodnight to JC., Michael kissed me goodbye and left for the return trip to Toronto. It was a school night and as head of math at Crescent School and during exams, he didn't want to miss a day of school. The dogs swarmed around and, on the bed, and we curled up together.

I was a changed man. I was so glad I'd followed Blair's advice and just gone to India. Meeting up with Mohini Raghunath was tantamount to finding an earthly guardian angel. There was no doubt in my mind that I would be a dad. I sensed Michael finally understood that tenacity was my preferred fuel. As I fell asleep that first night back in Canada, I was emotionally confident that Michael was the partner with whom I was destined to march into fatherhood. I loved him more today than when I left for India, and I felt parenthood would soon be within the realm of probability.

I was asleep before my head hit the pillow, the dogs already snoring softly around me.

CHAPTER TWO

"THEY SHOULD KILL THOSE F'ING HOMOS"

I DON'T RECALL A MOMENT in my life when I wasn't preoccupied with thoughts of the children I would parent. When I played house as a young child I always wanted to be the dad. Returning home to Woodhaven, the exhilarating prospect of adopting a son was sufficient to compensate for the financial worries that the trip to India had created.

Adoption had resonance for me because I myself had been adopted. In 1954, when I was born, there had been no fanfare—no photos, no hollering for joy, just bright, antiseptic lights hovering over an unwed teenage mother, a nineteen-year old woman who bravely carried her fetus to term despite the public humiliation and shame. The emotional agony of being rejected by the love of her life after announcing she was pregnant—he had become engaged to someone else—and leaving her hometown to become a resident in a Toronto home for unwed women, was almost unbearable. Feeling destitute, alone and scared, she hated lying to her grandmother about why she couldn't come home for Christmas due to job commitments. In mid-January 1954 she gave birth to a full-term, healthy baby boy and relinquished me to the Children's Aid Society, to be placed and into the waiting arms of my family. I became David Ross Irlam McKinstry, son of Dorothy and Eric McKinstry.

Peterborough, known fondly by locals as Peterpatch, would later be compared to the 1980's tv show, *Happy Days*. It was a somewhat stable, industrial, conservative town. I remember horse-drawn milk and bread trucks delivering door to door and how Mr. Doig's flatbed wagon, from which he would sell fruit and vegetables, lumbered slowly up the side streets during the summer. The neighbourhood kids fed carrots to the horses and watched their tails lift to let out huge brown balls of scat, which splatted on the road.

I was raised in a three-storey home that my grandfather had built prior to the start of World War I on Orpington Road with a sister, two years my junior. We had a loving set of parents and were part of a large extended family of relatives who lived close by. It was a childhood wherein my sister and I felt we were the richest kids on the block. Although our father worked his entire life at the Canadian head office of Outboard Marine Corporation as the Director of Purchasing and never earned a big-city salary, we owned an island cottage with a ski boat on nearby Stoney Lake and our family regularly had weekends away at Toronto's Royal York Hotel. In the winter, we went on an annual ski holiday with two other families, and we had family memberships at the YMCA and a local ski resort. I grew up putting clothes and sports equipment on my dad's charge accounts around town. It was only later I learned that some of our privileges were due to perks from suppliers at Dad's work, like the brand-new Evinrude 150 horsepower motor each summer and complimentary theatre tickets and weekends at the Royal York in Toronto.

Mum, a homemaker, was an active member of United Church women's group, canvassed for every local charity, made me thick peanut butter and banana sandwiches for an after-school snack and then shooed me out the door to catch the bus to the YMCA. Jell-O with fruit was a staple in our fridge, bushel baskets of apples from Mr. Doig's orchard lined our cold cellar walls and gallons of Central Smith orange-pineapple ice cream were a staple in our basement freezer. Every Saturday morning Mum walked to Sturdy's Market and left her shopping list to be filled. John, one of the butcher's sons, would deliver that grocery order an hour later and always take the frozen meats and ice cream down to the chest freezer. It didn't matter if we were at home or not, as we never locked our doors.

All was not idyllic, though. A neighbor and his wife started sexually molesting me when I was six years old. He called me over to his house from my front yard while my parents, who knew this family well and often had them babysit us, were raking leaves in the back yard. I remember them taking me upstairs to a bedroom to play. The game was to undress each other and lie on the bed. I remember feeling this was wrong, but I felt powerless to stop them. They were adults and even at that young age I assumed responsibility and a cloud of guilt and shame blanketed me. I felt I couldn't say this activity made me want to tell my parents. The awkwardness of this situation and my mistaken assumption I'd caused this to happen somehow became like an anchor of shame – my unspoken dark secret. As the abuse continued, I felt more and more guilt, as if I was in some way the perpetrator instead of the victim. It was not a daily thing, but it happened probably a dozen times during an eighteen-month period. They were naked and forced me to touch and lie on their bodies. Thankfully, by the time I was eight, they moved away, and the abuse ended. I had a tough time handling this secret and desperately felt I should confess to my parents; I just didn't know how to start that conversation or even hint at what had happened. I remember wondering as I walked to school if I was the only one in the neighbourhood who had been their victim.

Despite carrying around this never-to-be-disclosed burden of shame, I had a great relationship with my parents, and sister and I was raised to be community-minded, respectful of others, especially our elders. Dad and Mum were supportive of anything I wanted to do. My father encouraged me to join the YMCA swim team, as I had no interest in hockey. He was on the board of directors at the local YMCA. The Y became our second home. I remember the look of pride in my father's eyes as I became a hotshot on the junior swim team. He and Mum were there to cheer my ten-and-under relay team to victory as we captured the Provincial record for our age group. But there was one thing I didn't think I could share with him. I'd seen guys at the Y taunting "girly" boys and bullying them in the locker room. My father didn't tolerate any kind of bulling behaviour, but I could sense disdain when he'd tell the boys to stop teasing the one or two effeminate boys on the swim team. I'd heard some of the fathers talking about one boy, swishing their wrists and remarking he would have a hard time in life if he didn't *man up*.

The YMCA was the sports hub of Peterborough and being a member of the swim team automatically garnered me respect from people I didn't know. Robertson Davies was the publisher of The *Peterborough Examiner* in the 1960s and he insisted on daily stories on sports and local sports heroes. I remember my father introducing me to him at a YMCA annual supper meeting and being told he was one of Canada's literary elite. The Peterborough Family YMCA swim team was ranked one of the top teams in the province and produced notable and nationally ranked swimmers and divers. Peterborough's rowing, gymnastic, lacrosse and hockey teams were nationally recognized as well.

I attended the Y daily for swim practice or life saving programs. The games room at the Y had three or four ping pong tables and many of our team would gather to play ping pong for thirty minutes prior to our practice.

Beside the locker rooms was the cage where old George handed out towels and a bar of soap to the health club members. It was his duty to push the secret buzzer to open the door to the adult facilities. Kids weren't allowed. Being told we could not go in there by old George was just the incentive needed to up the dare-quotient for us to sneak in. Every manner of diversion was used to get George away from the cage. We'd yell, "Toilets overflowing!" or "Fight in the shower!" and he would come running out. A scout was always hiding nearby ready to reach into the cage window and push the buzzer, so we could gain access while George was off dealing with the imaginary problem. Once inside we headed for the sauna that was off limits to kids. It was always hell to pay whenever we'd barge into the sauna and meet up with one of our fathers, relaxing in the sauna after games of handball or running around the indoor track.

In total, my hometown seemed peaceful and safe, insulated from the troubles that plagued other communities. Unfortunately, this perception was deceptive, as I learned when I was thirteen years old. A swim team friend and I were showering after our nightly practice. I finished and headed to my locker to get dressed, leaving Peter lingering in the shower. Since his father was waiting to drive us home, I returned to the shower room and yelled for him to hurry up. Through the steam I saw Peter talking to a strange man at the end of the room. It didn't mean anything to me at that moment, so I just walked back to the dressing room to wait for him. Peter entered minutes later, followed by this unknown man, and proceeded to get dressed. Our fathers alternated driving us to swim practices and it was his dad's turn to drive us home that night. As Peter got dressed he said that he'd met a man in the shower who was a talent scout for a Toronto magazine. Peter said the man told him he had a good body and asked if he could take some photos of him for an upcoming teen magazine. Peter asked me to stall his dad for a while, so he could go upstairs to the men's residence to have his photo taken. The man was going to give him $5 for the photo. I had a gut feeling this wasn't a good idea, but Peter was proud of his pubescent muscles and would do anything to show them off.

Finally, Peter arrived in the lounge twenty-five minutes later and said he was ready to go. His dad was ticked off and asked where he had been. His excuses were clumsy, and it was evident Peter was hiding something. By the time his dad dropped me off at our house fifteen minutes later, Peter had confessed that he had been in a talent scout's room at the Y having pictures taken of him in a skimpy Speedo bathing suit, and in the nude. Peter's dad was choking with fury as he sped off to the police station.

With an officer in tow, Peter and his dad returned to the Y and found the man who had taken the photos. He was arrested immediately because the officer found many developed photographs of young boys, pubescent girls and adolescent men in the nude or engaging in lewd behaviours. In his early thirties, this man was married with three daughters and had just been hired by the local TV station as a cameraman. He admitted to the police he was staying at the Y, as many travellers on meagre budgets did in those days. Since I had seen this man in the shower talking to Peter, I would become part of the prosecution team trying to convict him of sexual misdemeanors.

The police arrived to speak to my parents a few hours later. They asked if I could identify the man who had talked to Peter in the Y's shower room. After stating I could positively identify the perpetrator, I was told to go back to bed while the officer remained to talk to my parents. My mother cried for a week and my dad couldn't get the anger out of his voice whenever this issue had to be discussed. They were concerned about the impact this experience would have on two thirteen-year-old boys. My father kept mumbling something about "Shooting those damn queers." I heard his wrath and knew I never wanted to be one of "those queers."

Weeks later at the courthouse, I sat in the waiting room with my dad, Peter's dad, the attending police officer and Peter. We had taken the day off school to be in court. It wasn't the first case on the docket, so we sat together for an hour shaking with dread while we waited to be called into the courtroom. The rage of our fathers was palpable. Our dads talked about many things while Peter and I just stared at the ceiling or read from a stash of comic books. I was confused and anxious. Instinctively I was aware of the importance of presenting a solid, masculine, heterosexual showing in court against this man who had assaulted Peter. I will never forget the words uttered by our fathers that morning.

"They should kill those fucking homos and piss on them." I had not heard my dad swear, ever. I knew from the tone of their voices and the gestures they made about homos that being a homosexual was the *worst* thing anyone could be. It was clear to me then and there I certainly shouldn't/couldn't/wouldn't be a homo. My father was enraged by the assault on my friend Peter and I feared the wrath I saw in my father's eyes that morning. Twenty years later in a psychiatrist's office, I vividly recalled that courtroom and how I realized I could never be a homosexual. I didn't want to incur hate and disdain from my parents or society. It took twelve sessions for me to realize Dad's tirade about "homosexuals preying on innocent kids" was totally off base. Given the research findings of Kurt Freund and Robin Watson, that the ratio of heterosexual to homosexual pedophiles is eleven to one, my father should have said pedophile, not homosexual, when referring to the man who'd accosted Peter at the YMCA.

I thought I had become gay because of the early childhood sexual abuse I experienced. The psychiatrist pointed out that homosexuality did not result from being molested as a child. He mentioned the nature-versus-nurture argument and said being gay was the result of genetic programming, not the by-product of one's experiences.

By high school I knew I was drawn to men but refused to acknowledge those feelings. I dated girls, concentrated on being an athlete and popular with my peers. I consciously developed my swimmer's physique to attract women, but on another level buffed up in the hope that someday men would find me attractive.

CHAPTER THREE
COMING OF AGE

HIGH SCHOOL INTRODUCED ME TO many experiences ranging from exposure to world travels, multiple varied part-time jobs, singing in a pop group and heading my student council. In early September 1973 it seemed as if the next four years were preordained by providence. I was entering the University of Toronto, where I would be studying toward an Honours in Physical and Health Education and swimming varsity for Canada's number-one-ranked university team. Who could ask for more?

Then I ran into Marilyn, the sister of an ex-girlfriend, on campus one afternoon. President of Gamma Phi Beta sorority, she began extolling the virtues of the Greek fraternities. The fraternity lifestyle sounded incredible—lots of interaction with sororities, the best parties anywhere and the chance to meet all sorts of people who would be lifelong friends. Joining a fraternity seemed like my ticket into Toronto's inner society and the path to achieving my goal of becoming a big fish in a big pond. I longed to replicate the sense of familiarity I'd known in my small town growing up with Eric McKinstry as my dad and my own claim to swimming fame.

My biology class partner, Richard Woods, and I were exchanging notes at the end of a class one day when he saw the name Gamma Phi Beta scribbled at the top of my binder. "Do you know one of the Gamma Phi's?" he asked. That led to a discussion about fraternities and he invited me along to check out the Alpha Delta Phi fraternity, where he was being rushed. I agreed and later that night called Marilyn about being invited to lunch at the Alpha Delta Phi. She was full of information about the history of that fraternity and encouraged me to do whatever I could to become part of the rush program. Thus armed, I headed off to meet the guys of Alpha Delta Phi.

The fellows there seemed genuinely interested in me. Prior to sitting down to lunch, the fraternity's vice-president, Michael Chow, gave me a tour of the chapter house. It was a massive old building and lodged eighteen residents in single and double rooms. We were in the lower games room, being shown the antique slate-bottom billiards table, when a voice from behind me bellowed, "David McKinstry, the swimmer from Stoney Lake?" I turned around to face Jamie Anderson. His family had an island cottage near Juniper Island, just a few miles from the island my family owned. Jamie made a big fuss over my swimming reputation around Stoney.

"This guy always cleans up at the summer regatta's and never loses the Lech One Mile swim. Are you swimming varsity?" he asked. From that moment I knew this fraternity was to be my home-away-from-home. I was overwhelmed that someone in this amazing bastion of Toronto elite recognized me, knew my family's island, talked about my swimming background and made me the centre of attention. Now to convince Mum and Dad that I *had* to join this fraternity—I knew their main objection would be the time it would take away from my studies and the commitment I'd made to the varsity swim team.

I spoke to my family almost every day of that first semester in Toronto. Dad had never attended university and in some way, I felt he was experiencing university life vicariously through me. It didn't take long to convince him the fraternity would be good for me. My swim coach was less enthusiastic. He had been coaching varsity swimmers for ten years and said fraternity parties and sorority girls had been the downfall of many talented swimmers. In the end he acquiesced and said it was up to me.

In early November I was inducted into the history book of Alpha Delta Phi, Toronto Chapter, during an elaborate initiation banquet held in the Great Hall of Hart House. One hundred and fifty men from many generations, including illustrious Torontonians like Christie Clarke, Robert Laidlaw, Ian Scott, Bud Porter and Jack McClelland, dressed in black tie to witness our induction. I was so proud to be a member of this great society. My desire to carve a niche for myself among U of Toronto's young elite was coming to fruition. Subconsciously, I hoped once accepted into this community, my self-loathing over being homosexual would be exchanged with socially acceptable heterosexual urges, marriage, family.

Annually, the varsity swim team spent the Christmas holidays at a training camp. In 1973 the team went to Fort Lauderdale, Florida, to train with some of the best university swimmers from across the USA. I had worked hard to earn a berth on this team and was excited about seeing Florida and being part of an exclusive training camp. I became best buds with Scott Day, a fellow varsity swimmer. We discovered that we'd both been adopted as infants and that unique fact seemed sufficient to cement our friendship. We did a mean rendition of "Rock Around the Clock" and "California Dreamin'" on the bus home from swim meets, though none of the other swimmers seem to enjoy our singing as much as we did.

The training camp was to begin a few days after my last Christmas exam. A room in the fraternity house became available, and I was scheduled to move in as of January. My first Christmas holiday spent away from family, this two-week camp was the embodiment of independence. I felt I'd arrived at adulthood.

It was hot in Florida and we spent most of our days training with 500 other swimmers from across the continent. Early morning workouts were followed by mid-afternoon volleyball games on the beach, weight training, then we were back in the pool late afternoon for a two-hour fast-paced workout called the salmon run. This was our daily routine in Fort Lauderdale. However, when the sun set, and the coaches went to bed, we cavorted and danced in local night clubs along the beach strip. We had a blast day and night. The guys on the team were preoccupied with finding new locations to cruise and pick up girls. We'd walk down Ocean Boulevard seeking out new clubs and new flocks of ladies. On each block there was usually a mooning session in front of obvious queer bars. I'd become a master of optics: for most of my teenage life, while in the company of family, friends, strangers, I deliberately worked at presenting myself as overtly heterosexual and hostile toward anything perceived to be homo. Although I felt a deepening twinge of guilt over my hypocrisy, I was in survival mode and I went along with my teammates as we laughed at and taunted "those people" sitting on the patios of gay bars. My membership in this boys' club full of macho insensitivity was more important at that moment than was the ruse I created to cloak my identity as "one of them." I was still years away from consciously admitting to myself I was sexually attracted to men. But being amid all this macho bullshit was all that mattered in the moment—it gave me status as a straight man and I felt I'd go to my deathbed with this secret.

A few days before New Year's Eve, our motel was invaded by three carloads of young women, members of the University of Texas swim team. They were given rooms two floors above our ground floor suites. We made the usual remarks about this fabulous turn of events and after one late afternoon practice our varsity swimmers were greeted with invitations under our doors to join the Texas team upstairs later for a party.

We joined in with the festivities that night in the girls' rooms. They had been recruiting swimmers and beach volleyball players to their party, and there were a hundred-people crowding into four adjoining rooms. We were unable to drink booze because of training agreements. However, the coach had agreed to lift that restriction for one night only, New Year's Eve. I met Becki, a Texas swimmer, that night. Tanned and gorgeous, she said she was nineteen. Becki made it obvious she wanted the night to go on forever, but a strict curfew hung over my head and missing the next morning's time trials wasn't an option. I told her to come and watch me at the time trials after her team practice and we'd spend New Year's Eve together. She reached up and kissed me softly and romantically for everyone to see.

Time trials were over by noon and we headed back to the motel for lunch. We now had a full twenty-four hours off to enjoy the New Year's festivities planned on the beaches and at parties along the motel strip.

Becki was lounging by the motel pool when our team arrived home from the time trials. I was really looking forward to being with her that night. We spent the afternoon together at the beach with the rest of my teammates and their dates. We played volleyball, swam in the warm surf, had shoulder-deep piggyback fights in the surf with Scott and his date. By 5 p.m., our team headed back to their respective motel rooms.

Scott and I were sharing a room with two seniors who had been to previous training camps. While we were shaving in the bathroom, the seniors were telling us tales of nocturnal activities we could expect to see and hopefully participate in on the vast expanse of beach across the road from our motel. We decided that wherever we were at 12:30 a.m., we'd rendezvous on the beach with our dates and head for the sand dunes dotting the ocean beach landscape.

Shortly after the 9 p.m. buffet supper, throngs of swimmers from the motel headed down the strip to a dance club. Midnight came and went. It took just a few moments to finish the kiss with Becki, leave the club and head for the beach. Scott and his date were only feet away from us as we strolled arm and arm, all of us very aware of each other's expectations. We found a nice mound of sand to cuddle up into and then it all happened too fast. Becki was all hands. We undressed one another with remarkable speed and dexterity for two teenagers who had consumed as much alcohol as we had. We accomplished what we had set out to do with barely enough time to slip our clothes back on and pretend we had only been on the beach watching the stars. The cops flashed their lights on us and told us to and return to our motels or we'd be charged.

As we were approaching our motel, Scott and his date suddenly appeared behind us. By the time we walked the girls to their motel rooms and had smothered them with drunken kisses, I was ready for bed. My head was swimming and I just wanted to close my eyes and sleep.

Becki emerged from her room the next morning only minutes before our team headed for the pool. She ran over to me and gently nudged me with a hello and a kiss. She hugged me, smiled and asked how I was feeling today. Then she told me that her carload of juniors was going to leave for Texas later that afternoon due to the sudden death of her roommate's grandmother. I didn't want to part like this. I wanted more time with her and more sex on the beach. I liked this feeling of being a normal heterosexual guy. I gave her my address and phone number and told her to write me, which she promised to do once she got back to school. Scott overheard my goodbye to Becki and shook his head at me when I returned to the group walking to the mini-bus that took us to the pool.

"Why give her your address, jerk?" he whispered as we boarded the bus. "What if you knocked her up last night? She'll be sitting on your doorstep in a month and you'll be dropping out of school. Dumb move, my man." Although brash and insensitive, his remarks were further hetero validation for my ego. The possibility of Becki becoming pregnant from last night's drunken sex-capade on the beach was probably nil to zero. However, I did get a rush of adrenalin at the thought of being normal enough to impregnate her and become a father—being a father was something I wanted to be more than anything in life.

The unexpected phone call came two months later. It was the assistant coach from the University of Texas swim team. Becki had asked him to call and tell me she was pregnant. We didn't talk long before he asked me to copy down her telephone number, so I could call her later that night. He said very clearly to me, words I will never forget, "Did you know Becki is only seventeen? If you lived in Texas you'd be in big trouble, young man."

I telephoned Becki an hour later and she answered the phone on the first ring. We talked for thirty minutes. She wasn't going to quit school, as the baby wouldn't be born until after the summer. Southern Baptists, her parents were sad and furious. They didn't want her getting married at seventeen and ruining her life, but they were insisting she carry the baby to term then give it up for adoption, which Becki agreed was the best thing to do. I told her I had been adopted and how I was glad she'd deliver the baby and offer our child to a loving adoptive home.

"Let's face it, we just had fun. I don't love you, but I am pregnant with your baby. I don't want to quit school and this way I can go back to my sophomore year in September. Just a minute: my mother wants to talk to you."

In a thick, icy-cold Texas drawl I heard, "David, this most regrettable situation will be looked after by us. We felt Becki should let you know what you had done." Those words stung—as if I had been the lone culprit. She continued, "We don't want any more contact with you. This was just a courtesy call and hopefully you will both learn from this mistake. Sex before marriage only creates problems like this. Please don't call Becki again." Then she handed the receiver back to Becki.

"Becki, will you get word to me when you have the baby. I'd like to know if it's a boy or a girl and if it's healthy." Becki said she would but asked me not to call her. Her parents were being very old-fashioned about her pregnancy and she had enough problems with them without having to deal with me. We said goodbye in tandem and that was it.

I immediately felt a myriad of emotions. In a strange way the pregnancy validated my desire to be heterosexual. Yet I was heartsick I had just added to another generation of kids born out of wedlock. In the days that followed, I felt despair and anger that my child wouldn't be raised by me. In bed I'd lie awake wondering if my child would look like me, inherit my athleticism, be gay or straight, be a singer in the band? I was relieved Becki wasn't going to have an abortion, but I was also terribly conflicted. In one way, I was happy that I could father a child, "proving" I was a heterosexual. But the knowledge that my child would be born and adopted into a family without me being able to hold the baby or even see him or her because adoption files were sealed, created an ache in my heart that I'd never experienced. Eventually, the awareness that I couldn't raise a child alone at this stage of my life sunk in and I became at peace with Becki's plan to give the child up for adoption. I never told Scott. I couldn't tell my parents, nor anyone else. I was ashamed and vowed I'd keep this indiscretion top secret.

Becki honoured her promise. Her father called in mid-September to tell me she had given birth to a healthy boy. The phone call lasted only as long as it took for him to tell me the gender and health status of the baby. I was too embarrassed to share this news with my family—I knew it would deeply hurt my parents that I'd been reckless—and I felt shame, like a searing, secret scar I'd carry for life that my child wouldn't know me or be told how much I regretted not being part of his life.

Two decades later, I placed a series of ads in Texas newspapers seeking a baby boy born on September 16, 1974, who had been placed for adoption, and contacted adoption firms that help adoptees in search of biological parents. Finally, in the late 1990s the phone rang.

I had a long and wonderful telephone conversation with Drew from his home in Texas. He sounded well adjusted, had finished college and was working for a securities firm in Houston. Drew had married his high school sweetheart after graduation and within six months she was pregnant. He told me his life had been privileged and he had wonderful parents, three brothers, one sister, and both sets of grandparents were still alive. But he didn't want any ongoing relationship with me, as his parents had appeared really hurt and confused when he told them he was going to call. I understood his reason for not wanting to complicate their lives or his own. Most of our call involved Drew peppering me with questions about my background, my education, had I married, and did I have other children. Intuition told me he was writing down all I was saying. I told him I was gay, had lost a lover to AIDS and that I was HIV negative, that I had located my own biological parents just a few years earlier and how we had formed a bond without it confusing or threatening the relationship I had with my mother. I shared my personal history with him for his own interest. Knowing my biological family history, I was able to fill in the blanks of his genetic history going back three generations—facts he wanted to know and at some point, pass along to his offspring. He was happy with his life the way it was and not keen to add me to his definition of family. I could understand his desire to maintain the status quo and not bring some unknown person into his life. The call ended in an awkward fashion, both of us agitated by our feelings and the information we had shared and wondering if we'd ever speak again.

A new emptiness began to take root deep inside me. I was still adjusting to Nick's death from AIDS only a few years earlier and now, having spoken to the son I'd fathered as a 19-year-old university student, I was left feeling abandoned and alone. I had heard my son's voice, heard him talk about his life, learned that he had become a competitive swimmer and that I was about to become a grandfather. The timbre and tone of Drew's voice echoed in my memory for weeks after that conversation. I fell into an abyss of depression for several months. My desire to adopt children never waned—in fact, speaking to Drew became like a light in the fog, guiding and encouraging me on to fulfill my quest to become a father. Never having the opportunity to hold my biological son or look into his eyes became one of my deepest regrets in life.

CHAPTER FOUR

THE CONFESSION THAT DIDN'T HAPPEN

I HAD DATED MANDY OFF-AND-ON in high school and I'd often dreamt she'd be the perfect wife. She was a highly ranked Canadian aquatic athlete, personable and articulate, compassionate and beautiful. Mandy could walk into a room and all eyes would turn to watch her. We did *Dancing with the Stars*-style routines at our high school dances and continued to see each other after I left for university. I kept telling Mandy she would end up marrying me, but she'd laugh and say we made better friends than lovers. Still, she agreed to be my date for the Alpha Delta Phi winter formal in February 1976.

Doug, my fraternity roommate, confided that he was getting engaged prior to the formal. I was desperate to signal to the world that I, too, was the marrying kind. But a month prior, I'd experienced an anonymous sexual encounter with a man. I had arrived back at the fraternity house the day after New Year's and found myself alone, not exactly sure why over the Christmas holidays I'd become consumed with the question of whether I was a homosexual. I never really thought of myself as being like the gay people you'd see on the streets of downtown Toronto; I told myself I was just one of the unlucky men with the propensity to be bisexual. I'd travelled to Australia after Grade 12, determined to experience life and make my fortune. I had sex with a 20-year-old woman on a beach in Fiji, then sex with a man in a Sydney hostel. I buried this Australian gay liaison into the *deepest closet* of my mind, believing this dalliance had just been a chance encounter since he had come after me—it was only real, I told myself, if I was the pursuer, gunning for sex. I convinced myself that by picking someone up I'd find out if I enjoyed it enough to switch teams. I knew I was 'probably' gay but was clinging onto the denial card for as long as I could. Always hopeful that one morning I'd awaken and be 'normal;' consciously denying my sexuality had become all-consuming.

I sat petrified in the darkest corner of a back-alley gay bar off Yonge Street, waiting for Mr. Right—I hoped to meet someone handsome and athletic who would either wow me or gross me out. A tall, good-looking late-twenties man approached me. He was perfect. A St. Andrews College grad who attended U of Toronto and now working in his father's investment firm on Bay Street; he appeared the embodiment of an all-Canadian 27-year-old man, athletic, handsome and talkative. Naive, I didn't even know he'd suggested we go to a bath house, nor had I any interest in the sex games he aggressively preferred. What a neophyte I must have appeared! Suddenly I did an about-face, no longer flirtatious and sure-footed. I was out of my element, petrified and desperate to turn back the clock. I fumbled and apologised to Mr. Perfect, dressed in a panic and frantically searched for a way out of the maze of halls and rooms and naked men. Once outside in the fresh air, I wretched, and my entire body shook. Panic-stricken at the thought of being recognized in this socially outré neighbourhood, I ran back to the fraternity house and showered for hours to get that man's saliva off my body and his cologne out of my senses. I told myself if being gay made me feel this bad, then I obviously wasn't queer and pursued Mandy with a fervour to prove my point. I'd drive to Oakville to wine and dine her in hopes of shifting her platonic inclinations into a romantic passion. I convinced myself that if I asked her to marry me at the formal, she just might say yes, and I'd be normal. Thoughts of my little son in the arms of another father was a yoke of steel across my shoulders. My shoulders would develop a heavy nagging ache whenever I thought of my son who'd been given up for adoption. At that point, I had assumed I would never hear from, or meet, him. I never really gave much thought to Becki, as I knew she was a survivor at heart and probably just needed to put her loss behind her and move forward. I wondered if she felt some sort of ongoing agony or had thoughts of our son every September on his birthday like I did. I pledged to God that I'd never father a child to be given up for adoption a second time. I desperately longed for a forever-family of my own. I'd prove to myself I could do it, and in the process show the world I was straight.

To my surprise Mandy accepted the ring and said she'd think about it. Alas, a few weeks later she announced it wasn't in the stars for us to become a married couple. I was crushed and spent the remainder of that term concentrating on my studies.

After almost three years of swimming varsity, my coach Robin Campbell sensed I was ready to hand in my swimsuit. He suggested I try coaching at University of Toronto Schools, a private high school for the intellectually gifted, just off campus and close to my fraternity house. UTS needed a swim coach and someone to help part-time with physical education classes. It was a once-in-a-lifetime opportunity.

Coaching the students became my life. In fifteen months I built up the team from splashing hackers into dominant swimmers at the city championships. I put heart and soul into my studies and into my part-time position at UTS. It was there during March break that I met Matt, one of the Royal Life Saving Society swim instructors. He was a member of the varsity water polo team - I'd noticed him around the Hart House pool over the past year.

Matt had a look about him that I found intriguing—handsome, fit and rugged—and intuitively I knew he was a gentle soul. I knew I found him physically attractive. He had the look of my imaginary lover – the one I thought about only in my dreams. Every time I found myself staring over at him on the pool deck or thinking about him while in class, I'd consciously shut him out of my mind. I had become a skilled master at shutting the closet doors of my mind.

During swim practice one afternoon, Matt appeared on deck and seemed to deliberately walk toward me. He was exceptionally pleasant, convivial and never stopped grinning. He had the whitest teeth, which enhanced his wholesome surfer appeal. His appealing smile instantly broke down my barriers and I wanted us to become friends. One of my senior UTS swimmers had mentioned to me that Matt had recently broken off a relationship with the older sister of another student on my UTS swim team.

Matt introduced himself and told me he was a second-year physical education student. Within a short period of time, we shared our thoughts about teaching versus further studies in human kinetics or streaming into kinesiology or medicine after graduation. Over the next few weeks I found myself looking forward to his presence on the pool deck. He would ask me to watch and correct some of his students' strokes or fill in for him discussing lifesaving theory. But in April, once exam time arrived, neither of us seemed to be around the pool at the same time.

I didn't see Matt again until the end of August, a few weeks before the start of the fall term, when he walked into the almost empty Hart House weight room. Obviously surprised to see me, he walked over and gave me a bear hug and said, "I hoped you'd be here." We finished our workout and headed up the stairs together. Matt asked if I lived on campus. I told him I was a member of Alpha Delta Phi fraternity and lived at the chapter house. As luck would have it, his older sister was married to an Alpha Delt who had graduated four years earlier. Matt asked many questions about the fraternity, the commitment required and how many new members could join each year. He sounded ripe to be rushed during our fall recruiting season, so I suggested he follow me to the house and I'd give him a tour. It didn't take more than a few visits to the chapter house to convince Matt to join the fraternity.

Matt reconciled with his on-again/off-again girlfriend but they remained on shaky ground. One afternoon he shared with me that he wasn't sure if it was going to last much longer. Likewise, I shared with Matt that I'd asked Mandy to marry me last winter, but she'd turned me down. "She told me we would make better friends than lovers," I said. Over lunch one day, I casually mentioned that I was ready to move out of the chapter house after three years as a resident. I needed my own space. Over the next week, Matt frequently suggested I consider renting an apartment. Shortly thereafter, I leased an apartment on Walmer Road, in the aging heart of the student ghetto.

I met Matt for lunch at the fraternity house throughout the rush season. Every fraternity brother thought he was terrific and would be an asset to the house. Matt met me after classes several days each week and would come back to my apartment to study between mid-afternoon and early-evening classes. We'd cook together, talk for hours about spirituality and enjoy great meals. I had wanted to get a pet and on a whim one day telephoned a Welsh Corgi breeder in North Toronto to inquire if any pups were available. The breeder had one male left from a litter born ten weeks earlier.

I named my pup Toby. Matt was captivated by him and told me that if I was going to be late getting home anytime, he would gladly come over and walk or play with Toby. I gave Matt a spare key and told him to use my apartment whenever he wanted.

And so, our friendship grew. When I wasn't in class, coaching at UTS or attending various fraternity functions and meetings, I was in my apartment with Toby and Matt. I'd arrive home after late practice and Matt would have chili on the stove. Three nights each week Matt had back-to-back late-night classes and early-morning water polo workouts. He stayed overnight on a cot in my bedroom. I looked forward to those hours we spent together, talking late into the night. We were young, athletic, handsome and single. By conventional standards we should have been out dating women, but we preferred one another's company. There were many Saturday nights we'd sit on the floor of my apartment looking at one another and smiling endlessly. Matt told me he had grown to love me like a brother and really enjoyed our fellowship. I felt secure and comfortable enough to tell him I felt the same way. Night after night we would watch Toby racing around the apartment, smiling at one another with eyes that wanted to say we were falling in love.

Matt pulled his cot over beside my double bed one night as we lay talking about life. At one point he placed his arm over my arm and told me we'd be the best of friends for life. We ended up sleeping side by side, our arms touching, every night when he stayed over. Lying in bed at night talking to Matt on the cot next to me was the embodiment of my dreams—maybe as close as I'd ever get to my dreams coming true. Neither of us ever consciously touched one another sexually, nor did we ever talk about sex. However, on several occasions, lying beside one another, we were sexually aroused and didn't bother to hide it. One day I came back the apt earlier than planned and Matt was in the shower. I knocked and shouted through the closed door that I was back and would take Toby out for a walk. Matt said to open the door as he couldn't hear me. When the door opened Matt stood naked in front of me with the shower curtain open and shampoo suds cascading down from his head across his chest and groin. He smiled naughtily and said "Come on in. I'm giving free shampoo's?" We stared at one another for what seemed a lifetime, as if daring each other to make the first move. I allowed myself to think, if only for a moment, that we'd be in each other's arms in two seconds. As if on cue, Toby ran into the bathroom and broke the sexual tension by jumping up on the side of the tub. Matt laughed, and I grabbed Toby and said I'd be back from a walk in 15 minutes. When I returned to the apt. Matt was on the phone arranging lifeguard schedules for the pool with another guard. We didn't pick up where we'd left off, but Matt wore that naughty smile until he left a few hours later for his water polo workout at Hart House. I could hardly concentrate on my studies that night. It wasn't Matt's night to stay at the apt which gave me hours to wonder about what had almost happened. Was Matt just fooling around? When he stood in the shower looking at me it was obvious he was getting aroused. What if Toby hadn't jumped up on the side of the tub? Had I fallen in love with Matt? Was I letting my mind stroll to places I didn't want it to wander? How did I resist? What steely reserve was I calling on every time I felt the urge to give in to my desires? Matt's eyes and his smile kept teasing me and I wanted to believe he was giving me the signal to proceed into his arms, but it was if my feet were encased in cement boots. I was torn between my desire for him and my over-whelming dread that once pandora's box was opened, I'd never be able to deny my romantic love for Matt and there would be no going back in the closet and I'd have to admit I was one of those people my father had said, "should be shot and pissed upon." I felt spineless knowing Matt's naughty smile and staged overtures had opened that closet door a crack, so I could peak into the world beyond, yet I resisted walking into his embrace.

My parents noticed a change in me, as did several good friends at the fraternity. I just seemed very happy. Matt bought me an antique mantelpiece that Christmas, refinished it and had it installed while I was writing my last exam. We put up a tree and had our own little Christmas together days before I headed home to Peterborough for the school break. We sprawled on the sofa each on our own side and our bare feet touched in the middle or rested on each other's thighs. It was that night that Matt took my hand in his and said he wanted me to know how much I meant to him. How I'd become the kind of friend he had only dreamed about ever finding. We seemed to know each other's thoughts without talking. That night we curled up together on the sofa with a blanket and watched a movie and fell asleep. I don't think I reached rem sleep because I kept awakening and feeling Matt lying next to me and breathing into the pillow we shared, I knew in my heart that the do-or-die time was getting close. But it wasn't an urge I could give in to on the eve of me leaving to go away for Christmas week with my family and Matt going to his family farm in Caledon for their annual Christmas gathering of the clan.

I arrived back in Toronto for a party at the AD Phi House a few days before New Years Eve. Matt and a bunch of our Brothers had gathered to play poker and pool and play drinking games at the fraternity house. Matt was going to stay at my apt that night. A few hours into the evening, Matt and I were standing together talking and enjoying a good laugh over his tales of Christmas hijinks that had happened with his sister and brothers over the holidays. Out of the blue one of our regularly uncouth Brothers roared into the room looking for more beer. He saw us smiling and laughing together and made a loud disruptive comment about Matt and me always being together. He bellowed, "What are ya, a couple of queers?" I could feel my cheeks turn lipstick red. Had my most guarded secret suddenly been revealed? Even though everyone within hearing distance dismissed his drunken remarks as the rantings of a jerk, it was enough to make even me question why Matt and I were spending so much time together and then begin wondering if Matt was gay, could they tell he was gay, that I was gay? The mere thought of the word being attached to my name was enough to send me into a sickened frenzy and in an instant, I decided I had to put some immediate and observable distance between us, at least in front of our fraternity Brothers. I told Matt discreetly that I was exhausted and just wanted to have a night alone in the apt—the look I gave him plainly said 'people might get the wrong idea.'

He knew what I meant, and poignantly but quietly asked, "This isn't the Dark Ages. It's almost 1977. Do you really care what people think of us?" and winked at me. Feeling sick over someone thinking we might be homo's, I poked him in the ribs and snapped, "As long as they don't think we're queer, I guess we're okay."

I could see Matt was hurt by me recoiling from that asshole Brothers remark's and the immediate 'chill in the air' aura I intentionally created between us. Matt said he'd get a ride home with a Brother who lived down the street from his parents and I left soon after for my apartment.

I retreated into myself and didn't interact much with Matt when we'd be at the Frat house over the coming weeks. Matt was becoming progressively clingier, wanting to spend consecutive nights sleeping over at my place. He brought over a housecoat and left several changes of clothes in my closet. While I knew in my heart I wanted to wrap my arms around him and make love to him, I just couldn't let on I loved him in a physical way. After all I still wanted to believe he wasn't trying to be sexual with me. I had built such a high fence to protect myself that I doggedly refused to admit to the reality of my love for him. We had never even discussed one another's views on homosexuality and the topic never came up in conversations as we lay on the floor beside one another with our elbows or toes touching. He wanted to hug me when I arrived home to the apartment and I made a cursory attempt at a 'male bonding' hug but nothing more. I hated pulling away from Matt. I was being cruel to us both. I thought of him continually, but I also became more and more frustrated and guarded by the thought of anyone suspecting our friendship might be man-love. It must have been so unsettling for Matt to have me cold one minute and my old self the next. I'm sure it was upsetting him – in fact he said so on too many occasions. He'd give me that naughty smile and grab my arm and say, "come on, let's just be together at 'our' apartment after class and enjoy quiet times like we used to do." It took every ounce of resolve for me to resist him sexually – I'd usually cave to his hurt or confused expression and agree to us having supper alone or spending hours talking on the sofa late into the night.

Mid-winter exams were upon us and we both studied hard that spring. Once spring break finished, the sorority and fraternity formals began to crowd everyone's social calendar. For one, I had been set up with a sorority sister of a friend's girlfriend who attended the University of Western Ontario. I had dated her a few times in first year, escorting her to other formals. Liz was from a prominent London family and she could easily put on the air of an aristocratic socialite, which in a warped way was a turn-on for me. She had called two weeks earlier and asked me to accompany her to her graduation formal. Matt asked if I really wanted to go and I told him I was looking forward to it.

"Maybe I'll get lucky!" I could tell my jesting was lost on him.

All that week Matt was out-of-sorts. He asked me not to go to London for the formal, as he really needed me nearby because he was feeling depressed and wanted time alone with Toby and me, which was exhilarating but also unnerving. Not trusting myself to reveal to Matt my deepening feelings for him, I pushed him away emotionally and physically—no more arms or toes touching. These frequent and often blunt snubs were hurtful to Matt and I could tell he was upset by my ambivalence toward him and our spending quiet time together.

Every day, Matt left me poems he'd written about our friendship on the kitchen counter. He had never been allowed to drink coffee at home with his parents but became a coffee connoisseur at my apartment. In one poem he wrote: "In you I have a kinship—someone who completely understands me—someone who doesn't judge me and encourages me to talk late into the night. You've opened my eyes and my heart—you've given me hope for many more hours of conversation, COFFEE and precious moments with our Toby. Love, Matt.

I became accustomed to being greeted by his poems at the end of a day. One night we just spent the evening talking about the challenges that lay ahead for us after graduation, my desire to have a large family, and Matt's wish to just let life unfold naturally for him. I deliberately reconnected emotionally with Matt. He was happier than I'd seen him in a month and we were consumed in the toe and elbow touching passion that had been the core of our smouldering, unacknowledged love affair. We spent the entire weekend together, something I'd avoided doing for several weeks. I lay in bed watching him sleeping on the cot beside me and it was all I could do to not slither from my bed onto his cot to finally make love to him. Finding myself so dangerously close to this precipice petrified me and the next morning I reinstituted a conscious effort to pull myself away, incapable of being honest with myself or Matt about my sexuality and red-hot love for him.

When I awoke the next morning, Matt was off walking Toby in the parkade up the street. He'd left me one of his poems by my pillow, so it would be the first thing I saw when I awoke. This was so like Matt...and yet I remained reluctant to face the mounting evidence that he was in love with me.

"Have you ever felt alone? Have you ever lost something irreplaceable but suddenly found it again? Logic told me to trust God but, you cared—Why? You showed understanding...not with a thousand questions but with an open ear and open mind. Was I alone? NO! I can talk to you at any time of the day or night ... just the two of us sharing thoughts, baring our souls. In our silence your eyes tell me your heart understands the way I feel about you. More than anything else, I feel love for you and from you. Thanks for the love. You know in your heart it means everything to me. Love, Matt."

Upon his return with Toby, we ate breakfast and Matt's mood changed from happy to anxious. He implored me to forgo the Western formal in favour of staying behind and being with him. He said he really needed me and wasn't feeling very sure of himself these days. Feeling even more confused and tortured, I blurted out "buck up and get a life. You've got the apartment to yourself with Toby until I get back. I'll be home by 9 p.m. tomorrow night. I've got so much on my mind right now I can't think." In a desperate and bold moment of honesty, I grabbed hold of Matt and hugged him so close I could feel his arousal. "I want to talk to you about some important stuff, about us." I was building up my courage to tell him how much I wanted to make love to him. I wasn't sure I could even say those words out loud, but I felt the day was fast approaching when I'd stifle my fear and utter this confession. We had been hugging closely for a few minutes and he leaned in and kissed my cheek and brushed his lips by my nose. I pulled far enough away from his face to see a tear in his eye and quietly said, "We will have late night dessert and coffee when I get back. Let's talk then, okay?" Matt looked like a beaten soul and reluctantly agreed to stop badgering me about not going to the Western formal.

I bid him goodbye mid-afternoon Saturday, April 16. He'd borrowed his dad's car and drove me down to the train station. Typical Matt, he hugged me on the platform but this time when he pulled away, he gently kissed my neck and looked at me for a few seconds, as if waiting for me to react. For a long few seconds I felt in a trance as I looked into his face and fought the urge to embrace him with all my might, looking into his eyes and pulling slowly away. As I boarded the train I turned and shouted, "Have fun with Toby. I'll see you tomorrow night." For a very scary second, I wanted to yell, "I love you Matt," but with the platform full of people I couldn't muster the courage. I thought I could see the glisten of tears on Matt's face as he waved me goodbye. I wanted to jump off the train and run back toward him—too Hollywood, even for me. I'd have six hours on the train over the next thirty-six hours to figure out how to be honest with Matt, even if it meant he might rebuff me. Was it possible I'd misread his feelings toward me?

The formal was fun, and the music amazing and we danced all night. I knew several guys from other U of T fraternity houses. My date, Liz and I ended leaving early to go and set up for the after-party hosted by her sorority. We sat and laughed and talked about many things, mainly about life after graduation. I had told her I was seeing someone in Toronto when she had called to ask me to escort her to the dance. She told me she had broken up with a guy a few months earlier and how she missed him terribly. It was a moment of reckoning for me. I told her I was so in love back in Toronto that I really wanted to get home. Liz understood perfectly and at 11:30 I made the call to the bus terminal and train station to see about late buses back to Toronto. I had just missed the last bus and no trains were leaving until 2pm Sunday. I had booked into an inexpensive hotel near the university to stay the night and it was also where a bunch of other Toronto guys were staying. I spent much of the night in bed awake and wondering about Matt as I waited for dawn to arrive. Liz had been invited to a sorority brunch and we arrived with big appetites. Liz asked if I'd spoken to my girlfriend back in Toronto yet and I said I was going to see her when I got home. Liz told me to be sure and tell my girlfriend how much she appreciated being able to snag me for her date to the prom for the night. I told her I would.

The damn train was later leaving than expected and there were delays on the line between London and Toronto. Just after 8 p.m. on Sunday, I walked jauntily into my apartment expecting Matt to be there with a coffee in his hand, ready to reveal what we both knew we wanted to say. With a stride in my step and newfound confidence I felt ready to tackle this conversation and open myself to making love to Matt.

I was greeted by an exuberant Toby. No Matt. He'd left a note on the kitchen counter. I'd missed him by ten minutes. He had waited until 7:50 p.m. for me. On my pillow he'd left a series of poems written over the past few hours. I unpacked, giving him enough travel time to get to his parents' house, and was just reaching for the phone to dial his number when my door buzzer sounded. Charlie Bartlett, a good friend and fraternity Brother was dropping by with his girlfriend Jenny to have a quick coffee and to play with Toby. By the time they left at 9:15 p.m. it was too late to call Matt at home. His parents went to bed by 9 p.m. and didn't appreciate phone calls after 8:45 p.m. I was almost glad that I'd have another night to mull over how to muster the courage to confess my love to Matt.

An hour later I crawled into bed and re-read Matt's poems. They were unmistakably revealing about his feelings for me and somehow, I felt a calmness after reading his words. Maybe a bit of remorse was bubbling to the surface of my soul—I realized I should have spoken to Matt about my deepening feelings for him. I'd been a cruel coward, unable to be honest with my potential lover and best friend. I'd make it up to him by preparing his favourite chili supper. I'd finally find the nerve to talk to him honestly about my own feelings for him and hopefully hear him say he loved me too.

The next morning, I headed off to write my last open-book exam, returning two hours later, and was just putting my key in the latch when I heard the phone ringing. It was Matt's brother-in-law, Bill.

"David," he asked, "did you notice anything odd about Matt on the weekend? Was he feeling all right?"

I told Bill I had been away in London at a formal while Matt stayed at my apartment for the weekend to look after Toby, adding that Matt had seemed a bit depressed since mid-term exams. "He's coming over for supper tonight and I'll find out what has been upsetting him. Bill, why the call about Matt? What's wrong?" Trying to make a joke, I said, "Did Matt meet some floozy last night, get drunk and not show up at home?"

After a few seconds of silence, Bill told me that Matt had been discovered dead in the backseat of his car hours earlier by his mother. "Is this for real?" I asked, trying to mask the earth-shattering horror I was feeling. "Matt's dead?"

Bill assured me Matt was dead and asked me to inform our fraternity Brothers.

Still dazed, I asked, "But how did he die?" Bill told me that the body had been taken away for an autopsy just thirty minutes earlier and it would be a day or two before they'd get the results. He said Matt's mother, a surgeon, suspected it might have been a brain aneurysm.

I don't remember how our phone call ended. Twenty-four hours later, Bill called to ask me to be a pall bearer at Matt's funeral. I asked if the autopsy results had come back but he just said it wasn't the aneurism, but no one wanted to talk about the cause of death and it wasn't going to be discussed outside of family. I had read and re-read Matt's poems, recalled all the 'near misses' at intimacy we'd shared, the long nights holding hands as we lay in separate beds sleeping, aroused but never talking about it or taking it a step further. I sensed I had been the cause of Matt's death – he must have killed himself. Why had I been such a fucking coward!!! My heart and whole body ached minute by minute and I wondered if I could keep my emotions in check at the funeral.

Three days later, Matt's funeral was held at a Presbyterian church in Don Mills. I felt numb and stunned: his death was my doing. I read the notes and poems he'd left me over and over and there was more than a hint of recognizable depression in his writings. Matt wrote that meeting me had changed his life, how in knowing me he felt love and acceptance as never before and how insignificant life was without my love.

My mind overflowed with regrets. If I had only called him Sunday night; if the train hadn't been delayed, if I'd hitch-hiked back earlier in the day instead of waiting for the train I would have seen him at the apartment and he probably would have stayed overnight and once I revealed my feelings, we would have been lovers, inseparable and ready to tackle the world and anyone who would oppose us. The letters he left behind for me became clearer and clearer. Matt had left notes about our deepening friendship and his love for me and how he wished we could keep things like they were forever. Did he commit suicide because I'd pushed him away?

After the funeral, I was the last one to leave the graveyard. Alone with my thoughts, I fell to my knees and asked God why Matt had killed himself. I desperately wanted to crawl inside the coffin to keep him company. The story circulating around after Matt's funeral was that he must have suffered a brain aneurysm during the night, yet suspiciously his family never released any official information from the coroner's report. I felt sure in my heart that Matt killed himself because I'd spurned his love.

A few weeks later I visited his mother in their garden. She made us tea and sat quietly as I told her I felt responsible for Matt's death. I became so overwhelmed with grief my shoulders shook and I just wept into her hands. I told her I knew he'd been depressed and how he had asked me to stay behind that weekend, so we could just talk. I told her about the letters he left behind for me the night before his death.

With tears streaming down her cheeks, Matt's Mom gently placed her hand on my shoulder, looked directly into my eyes and said, "You will cherish those poems from Matt just as I will cherish the letter he left for me. He shared some very personal thoughts about life, his special friendship with you and how happy he was spending time together with you at your apartment. Understand that I don't want this conversation to go out of this yard." I nodded, and she continued, "You and my son obviously shared a very special love. Other than I, his dad and sisters, you were the most important person in his life. I know now that Matt couldn't put that love into any context he could live with. My hope that you'll find peace within yourself and be content knowing God made you and Matt the way you are …and God doesn't make mistakes, David. You must accept this challenge and be happy. I don't have it in me to discuss these matters ever again."

I could feel my heart break all over again in that moment. She knew her son loved me, and I had rejected him because of my lack of courage to accept what Matt was saying by look, action and deed. We hugged and cried openly over the grief we shared. She was letting me know that Matt had been in love with me, but he couldn't deal with it and how she hoped I wouldn't fall prey to a similar fate.

In the months after Matt's death, I graduated, isolated myself in a new job as an insurance agent with London Life, and spent weekends at the cottage alone with Toby. I talked to an imaginary Matt twenty times each day. I constantly apologized for not recognizing how emotionally fragile he had been. I apologized for not holding him in my arms, as I had wanted to do many times, and making love to him. I apologized for lacking the courage to tell Matt that I loved him the way he loved me. I told Matt I was too afraid to let myself say the word "gay" and I hated myself for being so gutless. What would it take to awaken the rebel hidden deep within my soul?

CHAPTER FIVE
THE LAKE

I'D TOLD MATT NUMEROUS TIMES, prior to his death, that I wanted to swim Lake Ontario at least once in my life. He encouraged me and said he'd be there by my side coaching me on to victory. I was determined to train hard to reach this goal of not only swimming across Lake Ontario but to break the record and become the fastest swimmer to have made this crossing.

Emotionally, I felt confident knowing Matt, in spirit, would be by my side cheering me on. I spent hours each day in the Hart House pool developing better stroke technique and building up my endurance. By the autumn of 1977 I was mentally prepared to do whatever it took to turn this dream to swim Lake Ontario into a reality. I would swim up and down the pool talking to Matt every stroke of the way. It was easy to get lost in the pool and swim for hours at a time, conversing with an imaginary Matt. He never talked back but that didn't stop me from engaging in a continuous monologue with him under the water.

At Christmas 1977 I spoke to family and friends about my obsession with training in the pool every day. Genuine support and encouragement were mixed with joking remarks about my sanity. I knew I had to rachet my conviction up a notch and focus 500% on this goal.

I trained morning and night, seven days a week. My body quickly responded to this intense training regimen and I became somewhat obsessive about my ever-improving musculature. Since my early teens,

I'd had a competitive swimmer's body but now my physique was fine-tuned and chiseled. I was training up to seven hours a day by the end of April, and on alternate weekends I would do an eight-hour stint to pace myself and get used to long periods of straight swimming.

By January 1978 I knew I'd need to find a good coach to forge ahead with my desire to swim Lake Ontario. I sought out well-known Toronto marathon swimming coach Art LaFontaine and, after a grueling four-hour try-out practice, he agreed to become my personal trainer. Socially, Art was a bit off the rails and uncouth; nonetheless he knew about marathon swimming and how to prepare swimmers for an assault on Lady Lake.

In May, Art sent out a press release telling Toronto's media that I was training to swim Lake Ontario in July. He wrote, "David is steadfast and focused on his goal to become the fastest person to swim across that huge body of water – and he will do it in record time!" Art's press release coincided with an announcement by the CNE administration of the Pepsi Challenge Lake Swim for the middle of August. Lake Ontario swim fever hit Toronto! Art's press release said that I was going to be the first man to swim the lake in twenty-two years. I was photographed and interviewed by most Toronto newspapers and stories appeared weekly about my upcoming swim. The *Toronto Sun* printed a photo of me clad in a skimpy Speedo bathing suit as their Sunshine Boy of the Week, just days in advance of my swim date. After it appeared, I was both pleased and offended by the numerous phone calls I received from men calling to comment on that photo. I was still so in love with Matt (a feeling that had intensified during my year of training) that I was offended by this gay attention, but at the same time oddly turned on by it—something I couldn't possibly share with anyone but Matt.

I managed to put together a supportive crew of fraternity brothers, friends and family to accompany me across the lake for support. Three thirty-five-foot lake cruisers (one aptly named the *Fore Sure*) were hired to accompany us across the lake. Finally, the day came when conditions were perfect; our flotilla of boats left Toronto harbour at 7pm and I headed toward the starting point at Niagara-on-the-Lake. At 3:30 a.m.

on Saturday, July 22, 1978, I jumped into the warm seventy-six degrees Fahrenheit water. Greased up from head to toe, I'd never felt faster or sleeker than I did that night, making record time through the water. No one knew of my shark phobia. In a moment of insanity, I'd seen the movie Jaws just weeks before the start of my lake swim. I dove into the dark night and pitch-black water freaked by the 'possibility' a rogue shark had managed to swim up the St Lawrence River, ending up hungry in Lake Ontario. I effortlessly kept an image of Matt in my mind all the time I was in the water. I'd look down into the fathoms of black water beneath me talking to Matt, while simultaneously asking Jesus Christ not to let the teeth of some wayward rogue shark rip me apart halfway across this lake.

I had entered the water a lean one hundred sixty-four pounds of muscle and swam to a pace of eight-eight strokes per minute. The owner of the *Fore Sure* had purchased new direction-finding equipment a week before the swim, but it malfunctioned, and we veered eight to nine miles off course, toward Hamilton. Still, after eleven hours in the water, I was five miles from landing at Ontario Place and despite the added mileage, I remained two hours ahead of the existing record. I could see Art in the dingy, his face tightening with worry as his fingers massaged his forehead. He shouted, "Fifty thousand people are lining up along the shoreline to see you swim to victory." But I could tell by the look on my team's faces that they were worried. I was, too: from my throat down to my toes felt like one heavy block of ice. Kicking my legs took every ounce of concentration. Every time I looked up and paused for a moment, Art would shout, "Are you okay? Do you feel cold?" What I suspected but refused to acknowledge to Art or myself was that hypothermia already had its grip on me. Breathing in deep breaths of air felt like someone was squeezing my ribs and the sharp pain had become unbearable, forcing me to breath shallower and shallower breaths of air each time I raised my head to get air.

Just a few miles from shore we were in the deepest and coldest pocket of the lake. I knew my breathing was compromised but I couldn't stop to complain as it would alert Art that I might be in trouble, or worse. My lungs felt unable to inflate to receive the air I attempted desperately to suck in. During those last few miles, as my body cooled, and hypothermia gripped my chest like a steel vice, I vividly remember talking to Matt as casually as if we were sitting in my apartment. His warm smile and calm eyes were signaling everything would be fine and that he and Christ wouldn't let anything happen to me. I didn't worry about anything and kept my focus on those images of Christ and Matt only inches beneath my face.

I didn't have an ounce of fat to ward off the inevitable cooling of my core temperature. I had been stupid during the last month, refusing the advice of experienced marathoners telling me to fatten up to fend off hypothermia. While being tested at the Downsview Canadian Forces Base I was immersed in a cold-water tank to determine at what core body temperature I'd become incoherent and risk becoming hypothermic. I had refused to gain weight and during the cold-water tests it was all I could do to lie and say I was feeling chilly but fine. The truth was I'd never been so cold or being on the verge of passing out. My motivation was pure vanity: I wanted to be photographed as the hot swimmer emerging from this lake swim, not some fat-ass walrus crawling out of the water at Ontario Place.

"You're doing great. Keep kicking, David," Art and others kept shouting. I saw them through a haze, my eyes not focusing on much other than the image of Matt swimming face-up right below me. Art's shouting became monotonous. I put my face in the water and just rolled my eyes wishing I could be alone with Matt in Lake Ontario.

Thirty minutes after my eleventh-hour feeding, my heart was beating painfully, and it felt like it was trying to push through my chest wall. I imagined I must be having a heart attack. My breathing had become laboured. Unexpectedly, I felt as if my body was floating and I was strangely warmer. Matt was reaching out at me through the dark water. I knew something wasn't right but being this close to Toronto aborting this swim wasn't an option. I remember telling myself just to focus on pulling my heavy arms through the water. In my hallucinatory state, I asked Matt to stay beside me and help me make it to shore. A sense of rapturous inebriation enveloped me as I imagined him snuggling up beside me in the cold, black water. Part of my mind understood the image of him beside me was a dream, yet the closer I allowed myself to be swallowed up into this state, the warmer and more peaceful I became.

"David's sinking. Dive in and get him!" shouted my coach as I sank beneath the surface during one of my strokes. According to Gordon, my oldest friend and the scuba diver along on this swim, my disappearance happened so unexpectedly, everyone in the Zodiacs beside me was taken by surprise as I sank feet-first; initially those nearest me thought I was just undoing my bathing suit to slip beneath the surface to go to the bathroom. I wasn't afraid as I slid beneath the black water. I vividly remember feeling warm and relaxed, Matt beside me and Christ hanging suspended in the darkness in front of me. There wasn't a sense of fear.

I had, of course, succumbed to hypothermia. The *Fore Sure* had raced ahead to dock at Ontario Place, feeling confident I'd be swimming into the history books within an hour or so. Art used the walkie-talkie to alert the Fore Sure to the emergency and its crew swiftly returned to the swim scene with emergency medical personnel and equipment, who managed to stabilize me for transfer to the ambulance and well-trained hypothermia team waiting for me at St. Michael's Hospital.

After many hours being warmed slowly in the hypothermia tank, I spent the next twenty-four hours in hospital sleeping off the fatigue, awaking and expecting to see Matt sitting by my bed. What had happened? I tried to gather my thoughts. The bitter reality of my failure to walk into the history books, immobilized me like a straight jacket. I'd tried to make my parents proud by doing something extra-special. It wasn't long afterward that my family arrived to buoy my spirits and congratulate me for being a winner in their eyes. How condescending of them, I thought.

All sorts of thoughts raced through my head as I spent several days recovering quietly at home. Why had I not finished the race? Had Matt let me down? Why had Christ been with me and then abandoned me? Would being a winner not be as comfortable and familiar a state as being a loser was for me? What had I gained for all my training but to heap embarrassment upon my family? I surrendered to thinking of myself as "David the quitter."

One week later I announced I'd make a second attempt in a few weeks. Art wasn't keen on me trying so soon after having succumbed to hypothermia and tried to convince me to wait another year. But I wasn't going to spend another twelve months training as I had the previous year. Four weeks later, again featured in all the newspapers, I made another stab at the lake. Unfortunately, the waters of Lake Ontario had already started to cool by the end of August – I got twelve miles out before hypothermia once again ravaged my fatless body.

A dear older family friend was dying of breast cancer that summer. After my second attempt Betty said to me, "Maybe you'll be a better man for not making the lake. You have experienced a lot of humility in the past few weeks and that might end up being the essence of who you are to become in the future. You learn more from adversity than through victory."

It was sage advice from a wise woman. I will always remember her words, but it was a long time before I truly understood their significance.

CHAPTER SIX

VANCOUVER 1979 – 1987

VANCOUVER WAS A GREAT PLACE to come out. I didn't have to look over my shoulder to see if someone I knew was watching me enter a gay bar. Matt had been dead three years. I felt I needed to move forward with my life but still grieving him, I quit my job and moved west to re-enter university life at UBC. I was now a science/pre-med student at the University of British Columbia. I got a part time job working at a sports med clinic collecting data for the UBC research lab. I had only been in Vancouver a few months and becoming immersed in a science program was not my comfort-zone, however I was hellbent I would do whatever necessary to get into medicine at UBC. I managed to snag a spot training with the UBC swim team – I just wanted to keep in shape and the varsity coach, an old friend of my coach from U of T, permitted me to train 6 practices /week with the team. While studying late one Saturday night in the UBC library, I suddenly became mindful of someone slouched in a chair by the library window smiling at me. I instantly recognized him from the pool. He worked out with the swim team two mornings each week, usually on the opposite side of the pool from the lane I trained in. Although I was in a new city, wrapped up in academic studies and trying to get on with my life, I hadn't yet acknowledged to myself that I needed to get out and start 'playing' gay. I knew from my lost opportunity with Matt that I was gay and wanted to find someone to love. I was lonely and deep down wanted to be part of a couple. I smiled at him with a nod of my head, acknowledging that I had seen him – then blushed beat red and immediately lowered my eyes and pretended to read again. Ten minutes later, the library lights flashed, signaling that it was closing time. Jason introduced himself to me as we waited for the Number 10 UBC Bus to open its doors to the students waiting to ride back into the downtown core. He carried the conversation between us for about 10 minutes until the bus doors opened and 40 students piled on. We sat beside each other in the few available seats in the back row. Jason was funny, handsome as hell and I knew what he looked like in a speedo. We sat together on the bus and talked about the swim team, school, skiing – and then he quickly suggested we exchange phone numbers before I got off the bus at Granville St. and he continued downtown. An hour later my phone rang. It was Jason calling to ask if I wanted to join him dancing at the Gandy Dancer, a gay night club in the warehouse district of downtown Vancouver. Throwing caution to the wind, I hailed a cab, met Jason on the corner of Davie and Granville and instead of going to the club, he suggested we head to a Davie Street diner for a late-night snack. We talked long into the night delighting at the irony of him being an RM (in Mormon lingo that means a returned missionary) and both of us conflicted about being members of the Mormon Church. After Matt's death I was baptised into the Church of Jesus Christ of Latter Day Saints (Mormons). It was a church I was familiar with as some of my Dad's relatives had been Mormon since the 1930's and their approach to family and eternal life seemed to give me the answers I was looking for at that time. Regardless of the Mormon stance against homosexuality, I felt a strong connection to LDS teachings and embraced it whole-heartedly. I was still an active member of the Church when I arrived in Vancouver but denying my sexuality was becoming a burden and I knew the day of reckoning was coming.

It took about two weeks before I realized I'd fallen in love with Jason, a second-year medical student. While I fumbled for the words to tell Jason I was in love with him, he blurted out that he'd fallen in love with me that night in the library watching me pretend to read as he flirted from his chair. We shared a passion for being active, spiritual and athletic – swimming, skiing and long walks. Jason had an older model Toyota and we drove to Whistler almost every weekend, rented cheap student accommodation, skied hard and spent most Saturday nights falling asleep in one another's arms studying or me charting data for my part-time job, both of us dreaming of the day I'd be accepted into medicine. I had shared my story of fathering a son who had been given up for adoption and how I wanted desperately to adopt children. We shared a mutual longing to be fathers and to give our parents grand-children. We fantasized about settling in a small town in BC's Interior, where we would become part-time village doctors and spend the rest of our free-time skiing with our kids and hiking in the mountains. I got another part time job waitering at a burger joint on West 4th to make ends meet as neither of us had much money and it took us both having two part-time jobs to afford all that we did. Amazing that as students we did more skiing (we both had UBC ski club cheap passes) than people we knew who had full time good paying jobs. We packed lunches every day, rarely ate out, walked the seawall or took long walks out West Hastings toward the ship yards, occasionally stopping for a shared box of fries at The Only (Vancouver's best small fish and chips store) before walking back to our apt at 14th and Granville. We didn't have a tv and every day we talked for hours discovering something new about one another. Our inter-twined lives were the embodiment of what I wished I'd had the courage to experience with Matt.

But twelve months was all I would have with Jason. On a wickedly bad-weather Sunday afternoon his life ended on the highway home from a day of skiing at Whistler. I hadn't gone skiing that weekend, instead I worked a double shift that Sunday for the extra money we needed to buy our first tv and get cable installed. Mourning him was once-again like walking around in cement boots. It just wasn't fair, and I became numb to the notion of loving someone, only to bury them again. Jason's family took over the planning of his funeral and my involvement was zero and my presence barely tolerated on the day of the funeral. His brothers arrived to clean out our apartment of all 'his' things and I was left with only a few shared possessions, feeling hopeless and alone. I never heard from Jason's family again despite my many attempts to contact them. It was a devastating year after that. I'd swim for hours in the UBC pool – it became my refuge, my sanctuary, my imaginary world into which I could retreat and be alone with the two men I'd loved and lost. I ached over losing Jason and I grieved all over again for Matt.

Alone, I continued to explore adoption options, but no agencies would consider me. Social workers laughed at my presumption: "Why would you get an adoptable child when we have couples on our waiting list?", was the common response to my inquiries.

I worked my way through school, switched from the pursuit of medicine to business and while at UBC started up a muffin company and a West-End apartment cleaning service, even spent three summers working as the cruise director on an Alaskan cruise ship. Life slowly became vibrant, fun and carefree, but after working for Expo 86, it was time for me to return to Toronto and establish roots.

Cruise Director David

I was hired by CN Hotels to become one of 5 National Directors of Sales in their Toronto head office. Transitioning back into corporate life in busy Toronto in 1986 was easier than I'd anticipated – however it was also a city I'd left as a straight man and was now returning to 'my' city uncertain and anxious about being gay. No one in Toronto knew I was gay and my family certainly had no idea. It wouldn't be an issue in the hotel industry or for those in the CN Hotel sales office, but I was treading softly and remained guarded about my sexuality. I still mourned Jason and the dreams of parenthood we'd shared – day by day thoughts of my past life in Vancouver were quickly becoming distant memories.

Fourteen months later I left my job with CN Hotel to start up a head-hunting business. As my Dad said "Why not head-hunting? You always seem to land on your feet." It took a few years to gather steam and carve a niche market for myself placing mid-range sales and marketing people into the pharmaceutical industry and recently graduated environmental lawyers into corporations across Toronto. I had an office in Yorkville and finally felt a measure of career success. In 1988 my Dad died unexpectedly of lung cancer – it was difficult to imagine life without Dad at the other end of the phone when I'd call home in the middle of the day just to say hi.

It had been one of the busiest weeks of my headhunting career. I had just interviewed sales manager candidates for various assignments at Motorola. By Friday at 3 p.m., I'd had it with prima-donna's. Not one of my candidates had more than seven years' sales management experience yet each gave me the impression the industry would fall apart without them.

I went to the Y for a long swim. It was a warm autumn Friday afternoon and I decided to walk along Yonge Street for a while. Two hours later I found myself standing at Melrose and Yonge, only ten minutes from my house. The dogs were happy to see me after being outside all day in the yard chasing squirrels and digging for moles in the back garden. Many of the gay men I knew humanized their pets, but though my two corgis were beloved, I continued to focus on my goal to adopt children. As some parents with young children dream of the day they will bring home a puppy for the kids, I longed for the day I'd have kids with whom my dogs could play. The corgis anchored me to my dream of adoption becoming a reality.

Earlier that year I had founded the Fraternity, a group of gay men, mostly those in the professions of business, the arts, teaching, politics, healthcare and law, who got together several times each month for social and educational meetings. After five months our membership was already at a hundred sixty-five. Saturday, a new member, Nick DiCicco, telephoned at noon to firm up our late afternoon date. I'd met him the week before at a Fraternity brunch. Although he was a charming, handsome and popular fellow, I really didn't want to disrupt the relaxed solitude of my day off by going downtown. Feeling awkward about breaking this date at the last minute I reluctantly said I'd meet him as arranged. As I raced out the door I patted the heads of my two corgis and said, "I won't be long."

Nick

We met just inside the door of Alexander's Bar at the Sutton Place Hotel and found a quiet corner table. Listening to Nick's sexy baritone voice had me mellowing in no time. I was intrigued by the respectful way he talked about his parents and siblings, how he spoke of growing up in Guelph, entering the priesthood at seventeen, coming out as a gay priest within a large circle of like-minded elite Jesuits, being educated from coast to coast in North America and having studied in Rome and at Yale. Nick was at a crossroads in his vocation as a Jesuit. He had just started a year-long sabbatical from his doctoral studies at Yale to resolve whether he should return to full-time ministry. One hour became two, and finally after three hours of drinks and intensely satisfying conversation, Nick turned to me and said, "Well, I think I have complied with all your demands. You wanted to know about my financial and emotional status and I've told you I'm poor in money but rich in heart. You've made it clear you're not into a fly-by-night relationship. I'm eager and willing to adopt children and you told me to bring along a current health certificate. I didn't have enough time to get one from my doctor prior to our date." he said half joking.

Mesmerized by this man, I listened to him talk about his dream to find a lover with whom he'd grow old, confessing his desire to have children and his love of dogs. Nick talked of wanting to challenge conservative social conventions that would restrict his right to marry a man in the church. He spoke at length about the work of his Yale friend, Dr John Boswell, a scholar of same-sex unions in pre-modern European history. Boswell, he said, argued it was time for the gay community to make gay marriage a possibility before the turn of the new millennium. I was enchanted by Nick's feisty attitude as well as his compassion for those who sought to keep gay men locked in a "don't ask don't tell" dungeon. Our sometimes-intense conversation was interspersed with hearty laughter and lots of dreamy smiles and eye contact across the table. I could feel a tingling in my chest and my mind was telling me I had fallen in love after only a few hours of talk. I was profoundly attracted to this man. As if out of a daze, I awoke to ask him to repeat his last remark, embarrassed that I had become lost in the sparkle of his green eyes.

"I've told you everything there is to know about me except about my health status." Almost off-handily, I asked, "Are going to tell me you have diabetes? Don't worry. I'm not that superficial. Go ahead, what is wrong with you?"

Nick leaned forward and lowered his voice: "I became HIV-positive about a year ago. My doctor informed me I was positive on my first day at Yale, then said I might have a year to live. But I'm as healthy as can be.

I've been part of the cross-border drug study in Buffalo for the past ten months, testing a new drug called AZT, and it's working well." Without blinking he whispered across the table, "It is important for you to know this up-front, David."

The scourge of AIDS in the 1980s had every gay man running scared. People diagnosed with HIV became ill soon afterward and died—end of story. I knew of three classmates at UBC in the early 1980s who died within six weeks of being told they had acquired the "gay plague." Exposure to HIV was a death sentence. By the time I'd left Vancouver in 1986 I had attended 17 funerals.

For a moment I could feel my breath being taken away as Nick shared this grenade of sad information. I'd grabbed for his hand when asking jokingly if he was diabetic, but he had nervously pulled his hand away from my grip. In the next moment I reached for his withdrawn hand and took it back into my grasp. I knew I was in love with this man sitting across from me and I had to let him know it. We'd deal with his HIV+ status together.

"Nick, I am so sorry you tested positive, but you know new drugs are being discovered every month to fight AIDS and soon there will be a vaccine and then a cure. Don't worry," I continued, tightening my grasp on his hand. "You won't go through this alone. You now have me on your side. I'm not one for histrionics, alarm bells….and maybe I'm nuts not to play the diva and run for the hills. Four hours ago, I wasn't optimistic about coming downtown to have coffee with you. I know it sounds premature and probably sounds like I'm desperate for love but …. I've fallen in love with you."

I could hardly believe what I was saying. Part of me wanted to slap my face so I'd clue in to the reality of having just learned Nick was HIV+. The other half wanted to hug Nick, make love to him and tell him we'd beat this together. I'd been sitting with him for three hours, intrigued by his life adventures and hearing about his vocational conflict. I wasn't scared about catching the deadly HIV virus from him as much as I was feeling fearful about what lay ahead for Nick. My mind and heart were debating my motive for loving this man. Was knowing he was HIV positive intensifying my feelings because of some warped saviour complex? I wasn't into martyrdom, so it couldn't be that. I looked at his face to see tears welling up and I chuckled, "If you think tears will get you into my pants, you're nuts! The next time I make love I want it to be with my forever guy. There is so much more for us to learn about one another. Let's just take it a day at a time. Besides, I told you on the phone that it was my policy to date without any sex for at least six weeks."

This announcement brought a smile to his lips and he squeezed my hand. "Thank you, David, I feel the same about you. I have since talking to you at that Fraternity brunch a week ago."

We'd spoken about so many things in the hours since we first arrived at the bar that my head was spinning. I suggested we go for a walk along Wellesley Street to the University of Toronto grounds as it was a pleasant cool night. As we walked along dimly lit walkways throughout the historic campus, Nick asked if he could hold my hand. I was mortified by his suggestion of a public display of affection.

"It's dark, David. Who'll see us?"

"I'm no prude in private but in public," I said, "it is a definite no." Nick laughed, and I could feel my heart thumping as we walked around Hart House Circle before finally heading back to the subway station. He suggested driving me home, but I knew I had to proceed through the turnstile or I'd be with this wonderful new beau, racing in his car back to my place, about to break my 'no sex for six weeks' rule.

Surprisingly, I didn't dwell on Nick's HIV status during my ride home on the subway. I couldn't get the scent of his cologne out of my memory, nor his green eyes, deep, mellow voice or the glimpse he had given me into his character. I fell into bed exhausted at 10:30 p.m. with both dogs stretched out beside me. As I lay there, halfway between sleep and awake, my heart began to pound as I thought of Nick.

Within three months of our meeting each other, Nick moved into my house on Melrose Avenue. Soon afterward, he semi-retired from the Jesuit community, got his Bachelor of Education and was hired for a teaching job while my executive search business was mushrooming with sales doubling each month. We acquired two golden retrievers, and within two years they had produced nineteen puppies from two 'unplanned' litters; we kept three of the pups. Perhaps most importantly, we spent $40,000 U.S. registering and searching unsuccessfully for a surrogate who would carry a baby for us, then decided to have a home-study prepared, just in case adoption became an option for us within North America or internationally. It was also a time for saying goodbye to many friends; between 1987 and 1992 we attended the funerals of thirty-seven friends and acquaintances who died of AIDS-related complications, all under forty years of age.

Four years into our relationship we moved to the suburb of Richmond Hill with our five young Golden Retrievers and two aging Welsh Corgis. Living with someone HIV positive made me a pariah within a few of my heterosexual circles and I began the process of coming out of the closet, growing prouder and more militant as each month passed. Had the rebel within me finally awakened?

This was a period when we fought for recognition as a couple and tenaciously pursued any path that might lead us to children we could adopt. Then, by happenstance, we received a referral to a social worker who was prepared to work with us. It took months for her to find an adoption agency in California that would consider our application, a process that cost us another $25,000 U.S.

As we waited for our social worker to finish the rough draft of our home study, summer 1991 ended. Nick was excited to be joining a new school in Markham, Brother André Catholic High School, as head of chaplaincy and religion. We hosted one hundred and fifty Fraternity members on our 2-acre property for an end-of-summer regatta; teams of wanna-be athletes did human chariot races, swam relays in our pool, participated in Jell-O-eating contests and ran a mini-triathlon through an obstacle course mapped out around our 2-acre yard.

It seemed our lives were charmed, finally.

FINDING MY BIRTH PARENTS

RIFLING THROUGH SOME OLD FILE cabinets during the Labour Day weekend, I came across long-forgotten files on my own adoption. Nick saw me reading the notes I had made and suggested I either toss the material or once and for all search for my biological parents. When I told him that I didn't need to find them to fill any voids in my life, he quietly made the obvious point that subconsciously I was interested, if only to meet them and see what they looked like.

"Why else would you have kept the files this long if you didn't want to thank her for giving you up for adoption?"

"Good point," I admitted, and decided to make one final effort.

When I was eighteen and disenchanted with the idea of going off to university before seeing the world, I visited the office of the mother of a dear friend of mine who worked at the Peterborough Children's Aid Society. The reason was simple—she had access to my closed and forgotten adoption file and I wanted that information. Just in case I decided never to return to Canada from my travels, I wanted the medical history information locked in that file. To my amazement, Mrs. Kirk had my file on her desk when I entered the office. She knew of my impending departure and asked me why I wanted access to the information. She listened to me and then sat back in her chair and looked at me quietly for a few seconds before saying, "I must attend to a matter in the front office for a few minutes. Please do not look in this file while I'm gone as it contains all that personal information that is supposed to stay locked away. I'll be back in a few minutes." And with that she walked out with a kind grin on her face. I searched through that file for two minutes, copying down any information I could. But mostly I got the name of Clara Sampson, a reddish-blonde haired girl, who'd grown up in the south-end of Peterborough before finding out she was pregnant at age 18. Her married sister had wanted to adopt me, but the CAS convinced Clara that her sister adopting me wasn't a good idea. No background on the birth father. I noted my birth weight, that I was put into foster care because of hematomas on my scalp after being surrendered to the CAS in Peterborough. As Mrs. Kirk was steps away from opening her office door, I closed the file and stuffed my notepad into my pocket. Upon her return she looked at me and asked if there was anything else she could help me with. I said no and hastily hugged her. I told her I'd see her upon my return from my travels and left her office, satisfied I had whatever information I needed in the future if I wanted to seek out the people who'd been responsible for my birth. I'd had this in a file for almost two decades and had never done anything to explore the identities of the man and woman who'd given me life.

The next day I called a friend, Jennifer Parnell, about her dad's alumni connections with a local Peterborough high school. As the chair of the upcoming seventy-fifth anniversary reunion of Peterborough Collegiate Vocational School, he had access to the archives and every yearbook. I reached him and asked if he recalled a reddish-blonde student from the early 1950s at PCVS. He remembered her immediately and said he'd search through some old yearbooks to see if he could find her photo. I told him the reason for my inquiry and the sleuth in him was excited to be of any assistance in solving my mystery.

A few days later, Jennifer arrived in our laneway just after supper. Her parents had been visiting the night before and her dad had left behind an envelope for me. She was eager to help me search for my biological parents and drove up after work to deliver the envelope containing a photo of my birth mother. I ripped open the envelope and unfolded a photocopy of graduates from the 1953 yearbook. Smack in the middle of the back row was a black circle around the face of a woman I imme-diately recognized as having my features. Jennifer and Nick looked on, mouths agape, unable to believe how similar Clara looked to me. We scanned the names of other people in the photo and noticed one with the same last name as a high school friend of mine. Wondering whether this familiar surname, Gregson, was her aunt, I made a few calls. One name led to another and within the hour I had the phone number of Clara's youngest brother. Nick opened a bottle of white wine and poured three glasses and we nervously enjoyed several sips before I dialed the Peterborough number.

A man answered the phone. I pretended to be on the alumni com-mittee for the high school's upcoming reunion. "Clara can be reached at home or her office," he said. Quickly I copied down her address, phone numbers and other bits of information he shared with me. "She's married and has two adult kids, Annabelle and Iain. Clara and her husband live in a very nice neighbourhood on the Scarborough bluffs and her son Iain owns a cottage on Sandy Lake." I thanked him and said I hoped we'd see him at the reunion.

Could this be possible? That I had pieced together the puzzle of my birth mother in less than three days? What should I do now? I'd had enough excitement for one night but turned to my friends with a raised glass, face shining with happiness, and proposed a toast. We decided that I should give myself a few days to come up with a game plan to meet Clara.

Soon I was writing an initial letter introducing myself as the infant that Clara put up for adoption thirty-seven years earlier. In the cold light of day, it still sounded good to me and Nick concurred it was succinct and gave a good description of the person I had become and the life I had lived. Because I knew where she worked, I decided to pay a visit around lunch hour, hoping I'd see her going for lunch, strolling on the lawn or sitting under a tree. Maybe I'd ask the receptionist to point her out as she walked in from the parking lot. Regardless, I would drop off the letter. It ended saying that I had waited a lifetime to meet her and hear her voice. We had to meet at least once, my letter said, for me to look into her eyes and say thank you for having made the painful decision to carry me to a full-term birth and then place me for adoption.

I sat in the parking lot attached to the side of her office complex. It was 12:45 p.m. on Thursday and I was hell-bent that I was going to drop off the letter to the receptionist and ask her to deliver it to Clara. Just as I was unbuckling my seatbelt and reaching for my door handle, a grey sedan slowly manoeuvred past me and moved into a vacant spot. I sat mesmerized by the sight of my birth mother. She still looked much like the girl in the grad photo I'd seen a few days earlier. I got out of my car in a dream state and followed her, keeping my distance so as not to arouse suspicion.

She walked into the office building unaware I was behind her. I gave her a one-minute head start and then I opened the door to the lobby and walked over to the receptionist. I asked if I could leave an envelope for Clara, and she said Clara had just come back from lunch and I could catch up to her just beyond the closed door if I hurried. I told the receptionist that I too was in a hurry and just wanted to leave the information that Clara had requested. Without waiting for a reply, I turned around, my heart beating wildly, left the lobby and walked to my car. In my letter to Clara, I suggested that she call me at home later that night or the following day, so we could arrange a lunch to meet. I drove away wondering if this woman would be happy or angry that I had traced her identity and was about to unveil a secret from her past she had presumably been hiding for over three decades.

I returned to my office and finished an afternoon of interviews for two sales specialists. My usual thoroughness in such interviews abandoned me—my mind was miles away, my thoughts on Clara, wondering if she might just tell me to not bother contacting her again.

Just after 8 p.m. the phone rang, and a woman said, "May I speak to David McKinstry?" Nick knew by the look in my eye the caller must be my birth mother and he smiled and motioned for me to bring the portable phone over to the sofa, so he could listen in.

Clara was nervous, and it showed in her voice: there was a measure of caution in her tone. She said my letter had caught her off-guard and that upon reading it her body began to shake and she had had to leave work for the rest of the day. Her husband had known about me before they were married but they hadn't discussed her giving up a child for adoption since before their marriage thirty-five years earlier. Grant, her husband, had encouraged Clara to call me, supportively saying she owed me that much. Clara dialed to connect with her past.

I fired questions at her in rapid succession. Before long she asked if my adoptive dad had worked at Outboard Marine as Director of Purchasing. I said, "Yes, Eric was my Dad." Clara told me that she had worked briefly in his department at the time of her unplanned pregnancy. She had quit his secretarial pool and gone to Toronto to live until she gave birth to me. She asked if I was the McKinstry who had attempted a swim across Lake Ontario ten years ago. She said when she saw my photo in the paper as the Sunshine Boy she had an eerie feeling in the pit of her stomach but hadn't been able to pinpoint the cause. Now she knew she'd subconsciously recognized the features of my face bearing an eerily familial resemblance to that of my biological father and herself.

We talked for ninety minutes. My half-siblings—were they aware of having a half-brother out there? Clara had not told anyone about the pregnancy except the biological father, her best girlfriend and later, her husband. She was nervous about confessing to her children that she'd had a baby out of wedlock and said it wasn't a conversation she thought her son would understand but she felt her daughter might be okay with it.

I asked about my biological father, but she provided only non-identifying information. I could tell that her husband must be listening, in the same way Nick was. I suggested that we meet for lunch and Clara said she would call me Monday morning to set up a place and time for us to meet, adding that after speaking to me she was relieved she had telephoned.

I hung up the phone emotionally drained. Nick hugged me and smiled. Had we just opened a Pandora's box? I had the weekend to think about that and plan what I'd say to Clara over lunch, as well as worry I might not be what she expected her baby to be like as a grown man of thirty-seven years. I wasn't about to tell her about Nick, as I wanted her to get to know me better first. I then became confused about my reasons for contacting her, experiencing guilt for having connected with her while Mum was alive. Would this Clara revelation threaten Mum and make her think I was trading her in for a newer model? At the same time, I tried to imagine what it had been like for this woman to hear my voice for the first time since hearing my cries in the maternity ward of Mount Sinai Hospital.

Clara called me shortly after 9 a.m. on Monday suggesting we meet at the Silver Dragon, a Chinese restaurant only minutes from her office. Her lunch hour was flexible, and she could extend it to a couple of hours without any problem. She'd spent the weekend feeling less hesitant and was becoming more excited about meeting me with each passing hour. I, too, felt the same way. The timing was right, so unbelievably right.

I had a busy morning of phone calls and reference checking for an ace candidate. He would be meeting the regional director of sales later that afternoon, a fellow who had given me many job searches over the past few years. If he found my candidate suitable I would garner a $13,000 headhunting fee. Since we had to pay ongoing advertising expenses at the California adoption/law firm, any big money I could earn would significantly underwrite our costs. Our American lawyer had placed forty-five children into adoptive homes during her career. Her services were prominently advertised in magazines read by female university students, who might be pregnant and wishing to find a home for their babies. I budgeted $1,000 a month for her advertising costs, so this one fee could pay for an entire year's worth.

I arrived at the restaurant, found my way to a quiet table near the back, ordered a cup of coffee and told the waiter I was there to meet Clara Trueman. She obviously ate at this restaurant frequently, as the waiter said he would direct her to me. Five minutes later I watched her approach and my eyes drank in every second of her movement toward me. She was smiling, and I stood up to greet her as she closed the gap separating us. I started to hold out my hand to shake hands, thought better of it at the last second and let her walk into my waiting arms and we hugged briefly before sitting down.

"You look so much like your biological father it took my breath away as I walked toward you," she said." She ordered a glass of wine, squirmed briefly in her seat, then smiled as she became more comfortable. It was exhilarating to sit across the table from the woman who gave birth to me. Although I was happy seeing her face-to-face, there was also an abrupt sense of closure to my search. Here I was meeting her in person, being able to compare the reality of this woman's attractive features with the imaginary version of the birth parent I had conjured up in my fantasies for decades. In a surreal sort of way, our luncheon meeting seemed almost anticlimactic.

I'd brought photo albums of my childhood and family. I gave her copies of the *Toronto Star* articles about my attempts to swim Lake Ontario, as well as a photo of my ex-fiancée, Maggie, all to make a good first impression and to somehow validate her decision to give me up for adoption.

As more coffee and wine arrived, our comfort level with one another grew. I told Clara one of the pressing reasons for me searching for her was to tell her face-to-face how much I appreciated the anguish she must have gone through just to give me life. I wasn't prepared for was her quick response. "Don't make me out to be a saint. Unlike girls today, I didn't have any options back in 1953. Being a pregnant teenager meant I'd be a liability, and humiliation, to my family. The moment the Doctor confirmed I was pregnant, my life changed – if I stayed in Peterborough and pregnant, I'd be a social pariah. The 1950's in Peterborough was a wonderful era to grow up in but if teenage girls found themselves pregnant, you were branded a slut, whore, sleaze and you got on the first bus out of town, knowing you could never go back. People were so quick to judge those of us who got pregnant, but the teenage men got away penalty-free, usually getting a hearty congratulatory slap on the back from the good ole boys network."

I tried to mask my shock as she began a thirty-minute description of her experience as a pregnant teen during an era when only "bad girls" got caught having sex before marriage.

"Your biological father was well known in Peterborough as a

nationally-ranked lacrosse player in the 1950s. His name is Paul. He was fair-haired, handsome with broad, athletic shoulders, and a charming laugh. He was the gorgeous boy next door that every girl in town wanted for her boyfriend. I got him, and he gave me you," she said matter-of-factly. "I came from a broken home with alcoholic parents. My dad abandoned our family early on. He died a long time ago. My mother was a single parent of four children and she found it difficult to handle us. I was sent down the street to live with my grandparents when I was a youngster. It was really hard for my mother to work and be a parent to all four of us."

I was aware that Clara's sister Alice had wanted to adopt me, but the Children's Aid Society had talked her out of that option. I asked about her sister. Clara told me that Alice had married and lived only a few blocks from my house in Peterborough and that I probably had attended school with her son and daughter. Now that my memory was being jogged, I remembered how the south-end gossip mongers on our street had viciously derided the mother of a grade four classmate. The talk was all about how horrible it was of this unruly woman to abandon her children to the care of her husband and then leave town. This news was scandalous in the 1960s.

"Alice was a good mother, but her husband was an alcoholic and she just didn't know what to do. She had to escape to survive. She left the kids behind rather than uproot them from their home, school and neighbourhood. It wasn't fair of people to judge her as harshly as they did. She was a trailblazer for the many women who today leave their kids with the husband and no one says boo about it. She felt trapped and was desperate to get out of that marriage, move far away and at that time she felt leaving the kids behind was her best and only option. I know from personal experience how unfair judging others can be, so I was supportive of my sister and tried to keep in touch with her kids as best I could."

Wow, I thought. I could have been adopted into that family and that would have been my fate. Wasn't I lucky that the social worker finally convinced Clara that an intra-family adoption wouldn't be in the best interest of her baby.

Since Alice, and Clara's best girlfriend, were the only ones to know about her pregnancy besides Paul, Clara decided to leave town before her pregnancy showed. Paul and Clara had been in an eight-month relationship, but Paul's ex-girlfriend kept hounding him to go back with her. Clara and Paul had broken up just weeks before her pregnancy was confirmed. Clara, scared, went to the Children's Aid Society to see what she could do, and was counselled to speak to the biological father as soon as possible. The CAS told her that other than marrying the father, she had no option but to go to a Toronto halfway house to live until she gave birth to the baby. An adoption would be arranged in Peterborough and the file would be sealed and no one would ever know she'd had a baby out of wedlock.

Clara approached Paul eight weeks into her pregnancy and told him she was pregnant with his child and asked what they should do about it. It crushed her emotionally to hear he'd reconciled with his old girlfriend and, adding salt to the wound, was now engaged. Hurt to her core, Clara walked away from Paul feeling abandoned and all alone once again. The CAS brought Paul in for a meeting to discuss his financial responsibility for Clara's costs at the Toronto residence. As long as his fiancée didn't have to know about Clara's pregnancy, he was willing to pay any amount of hush money. Paul tried many times to talk to Clara, but she wouldn't have anything more to do with him. The mere very sight of him enraged her and all she could think about were the what-if's. He was the love of her life. She left town shortly afterward, telling everyone that she had a job working in a Toronto hospital training as a nurse.

I congratulated Clara on being so courageous. She sat back in her chair and took a sip of wine. I was surprised when she glared at me and said, "What choice did I have? Abortions weren't legal. I knew that once I left Peterborough that summer, I'd never be able to return. Girls who left town and returned ten months later were branded sluts because everyone assumed they'd been away to deliver a bastard baby." I was stunned by her monotone.

"I couldn't even come home that Christmas because it was obvious I was very pregnant. I was dreadfully homesick and lonely. Being pregnant had ruined my otherwise carefree life. I lied to my family and friends and told them I had to work at the hospital over Christmas." Some of that long-forgotten pain began to find its way to her eyes. She wiped the tears with her napkin, looked up with embarrassment and continued.

"You were born with sores on your scalp, nasty-looking open sores. It wasn't serious, but the CAS wouldn't take you into their care until the sores healed. I remember how cold and bleak that hospital room was. Being unwed, I was given a private room because my baby was going up for adoption and they wanted to sequester me from the happily married, decent mothers, almost like I was diseased. There had been no happy shouts from the nurses in the delivery room as they cut your cord and weighed you. No one happily shouted, 'It's a healthy boy!' No one said, 'Congratulations on the arrival of a healthy baby boy.' There was no counselling provided about what to expect in the coming days before I signed the final paperwork to give you over to the CAS. No postpartum information that young mothers get today—absolutely nothing."

Her tears were evidence of the upset reliving the events of my birth was causing.

"Paul was my first true love and without much sex education at school or from home, I believed him when he told me I couldn't get pregnant the first time," she mused as her hand gripped the stem of her nearly empty wineglass. I decided to give her a breather and tell her what I'd been told about being placed in my parents' arms.

"I was in foster care for three months before being placed with my parents—I suspect the hematomas took longer to heal than initially expected. I was handed over to my parents' family physician, who then telephoned them to say their baby boy had just arrived in town." Clara stared directly at me as I recounted how I came to be placed in the McKinstry home in April 1954.

"Did you whisper anything to me during those few hours you were allowed to hold me?" I inquired. It surprised me that I sounded just like a reporter.

"I was too numb and too ashamed to talk out loud to you. I just cradled you, so embarrassed to look into your eyes. I felt like the worst person on the planet giving my baby up for adoption." Tears fell down her cheeks.

"You must have been horrified at the prospect of giving me up," I said, and for the first time I reached over and took her hand in mine to give some comfort while she told me the rest of the story.

"I was a walking zombie. I will never forget that feeling, knowing I was about to be given a life-sentence without my baby. My heart was pounding, I wanted to be sick to my stomach, and part of me wanted to run away with you but the other part of me knew I couldn't do that to my baby. You had been taken to the nursery and then about 10 minutes later two women from CAS came into my room with papers for me to sign. It happened so fast, so coldly…like a nightmare in slow motion. They told me I would be ok and then turned and left my room." Clara's entire body seemed to heave and shudder as tears from her memories of that day rolled down her cheeks.

With that she excused herself from the table.

Ten minutes later she returned looking less defeated after reapplying her make-up. "You must have been devastated at not being able to say goodbye to your baby," I murmured, watching her emotion-strained face closely.

"I had been abandoned by my parents, abandoned by Paul, forfeited the life I'd known in Peterborough, and now I was losing my baby. I suppose I was just exhausted emotionally and physically because of these losses. After crying myself empty, I felt rudderless, like I wanted to die and disappear. A week later I returned to the unwed mothers house for four more weeks until I got a job and found an apartment to share with some girls I'd met during my six months at that house. And that was it… end of story. At nineteen years of age, having just handed over my baby to CAS, I was told to be stoic and just move on with my life."

Clara seemed almost rigid and stone-faced. Telling me the story of my birth and being put up for adoption had drained her of all emotion. I got up and walked around to her side of the table and threw my arms around the mother who had given birth to me. I tried to give her comfort by saying I'd had a good life, and that I would always love her for having mustered the courage to do what she did all alone.

Finally composed, I asked if she was ready for another glass of wine. Clara smiled and nodded her head and began to ask me a host of questions about my life. But I wasn't through with my own questions. I wanted to know about my biological father, as I didn't have much information about him and she hadn't really given me any details—I could tell she had purposely neglected to mention his last name and it was obvious she wanted to shift the focus over to me.

After talking for almost thirty minutes about my life, I came back to the question of my biological father. "When you first arrived, you said I resembled him. What was he like? Was he tall? What is he doing now? Have you ever seen him since you left Peterborough that summer?"

Clara was reticent to disclose any identifying information — she felt it wasn't her place. Paul had been promised confidentiality by the CAS back then and she didn't want to disrupt his family today. Her best friend Marj had kept tabs on Paul and knew he lived north of Toronto and that he became a police officer after a successful athletic career back in the early 1960s.

Clara told me she had been loving and hating him for so long that it was difficult to talk about him. She had felt chronically wounded by his rejection when he learned she was pregnant and other than paying some of her bills at the halfway house, his reputation was unscathed.

Our luncheon had been nearly three hours of non-stop talking; Clara told me she must return to the office. She gave me her work number and said I should call her there rather than at home. Her son was still at home and she didn't want her husband to be made uncomfortable by the sound of my voice on the phone. I smiled at the ease with which she gave me her office phone number and asked, "If you're giving me your work number, am I to assume this meeting was positive for you? Clara grabbed my hand and said this had been one of the best days of her life. She suggested we meet again for lunch on Friday at the Silver Dragon.

I got into my car and headed home to Richmond Hill. I couldn't wait to tell Nick about my lunch with Clara. I wanted to get home and record in my journal all that my birth mother had shared of her life without me.

During supper by the pool, Nick listened to the details of my luncheon with Clara intensely curiously. We discussed the ramifications of the meeting. Life would never be the same, as I now had the face of my birth mother locked in my mind. Would I tell Mum about meeting Clara? Would Mum feel threatened by Clara or sad that I had searched for my birth mother without consulting her? The warm September air was conducive to sitting and relaxing poolside with the dogs. The warm water was an invitation to skinny dip. As we hung onto the side of the pool Nick asked me how I had arrived in the arms of my parents. I told him that my folks, childless for the first fourteen years of marriage, recognized that their infertility wasn't going away. My mother endured numerous miscarriages and one spontaneous abortion at 5 months and finally her physician suggested they try adoption.

A few years after starting the adoption process, in late autumn, they were contacted by Miss Young of the CAS in Peterborough and told of a child who might be available early in the new year. They had been told not to get their hopes up just yet but that they would be assigned this child once born. Mum was thirty-nine and Dad had just turned forty-three. They owned their own home, had a large extended family. They were active members in their neighbourhood United Church, the Kawartha Golf and Country Club and the YMCA. They desperately wanted a family and Mum was so eager to nurture a child.

While anxiously awaiting news of my birth in January 1954, my mother's father became ill with a prostate infection. Antibiotics were still a developing medical phenomenon at that time, and within a few weeks of falling ill, my seventy-year-old, otherwise healthy sports-minded grandfather died. My parents were consumed with funeral details and adjusting to life without this beloved family patriarch when Miss Young called to inform them that they would soon have a son to raise. Elated, they readied the house for my arrival. Neighbours and family held several baby showers and they were well stocked with diapers and baby clothes by the time I finally came to them in early April.

"Out of the blue on a Wednesday afternoon, my parents' physician, Dr. Carlton, telephoned Mum at Outboard Marine with the news that I would be ready to go home with them within hours. She worked on the switchboard at that time. Within minutes of receiving that auspicious call, she handed in her notice and at 5 p.m. she and Dad drove to Dr. Carlton's office to bring me home."

My parents' experience was the sweet to Clara's bitter. Nick wondered aloud if our adoption experience would be anything like this and we spent many hours that week discussing different possible scenario's that could lead us to becoming a family.

Three weeks later, having had five lunches with Clara, I decided to invite her for supper one night. She seemed quite eager to see my home and meet the dogs. Nick was also very keen to meet her. Only four months earlier, Mum aged seventy-seven, had cornered Nick and me over supper and announced that she knew we were a gay couple and made a joke about Nick no longer having to move into the spare bedroom when she came to visit. Our new honest friendship with Mum deepened over that summer. It was so special being able to tell her about the love of my life and honestly share our dreams of having a family. I figured if my seventy-seven-year-old mother could handle the news, then Clara should be able to hear it without a great deal of disquiet. Besides, as Nick and I had discussed many times, we wanted our relationships with people to be honest and open, which meant that those people we felt close to had to be told about our romantic love for one another. If Clara couldn't handle this information, then better we tell her now than she finds out later through someone else, when her rejection for me being gay would be more painful.

Clara took the news like a trooper. She had wondered why I hadn't mentioned any women in our conversations and when I told her I was gay it was just like another piece of the puzzle dropping into place. She told me several male relatives in her family were suspected of being gay. I told her lots of research was being done on the genetic predisposition of families that produce generation after generation of homosexuals. She wasn't ready to buy into those studies just yet but nonetheless she was eager to meet Nick. I hauled him out of the office where he had been listening at the keyhole. Almost immediately Nick felt a solid connection to Clara. Over supper I asked her once more to consider tracking down Paul's phone number. She said she had been discussing it with her husband and they felt she should go ahead and let Paul know about me, though she was nervous to call him because they had parted on such bad terms thirty-eight years earlier. But after meeting me, Clara said she no longer hated him, though she resented having been a second choice, when to her he was number one. She agreed to call her friend Marj to track him down.

Within days, Clara called my office to say she had spoken with Paul, telling him, "Something we shared thirty-eight years ago has resurfaced and he would like to meet his biological father." Clara said Paul suggested they meet for dinner the next day as his wife would be home any moment and he'd never told her about Clara's pregnancy. I asked Clara to call me as soon as she got back home to tell me about her reunion.

Clara phoned just before Nick left for school the next morning. He grabbed the extension phone, so he too could listen to her account of the meal with Paul the previous evening. Paul had been a cop for thirty-one years and lived in Stouffville with his wife. They had three adult children, one named David, just eleven months my junior, who as luck would have it was a physical education teacher in Peterborough. Clara said she'd been nervous about seeing Paul after all those years and lied to her husband that some of the women from the office were going out for a ladies' night. Clara was like a schoolgirl telling me about her reunion date.

Paul did want to meet me. He told Clara he'd often wandered around malls and streets while doing neighbourhood walkabouts wondering if Clara had given birth to a boy or girl. Could he be seeing his child and not know?

"So, do I call him, or will he call me?" I asked. Clara said Paul would call me in the next few days to arrange a time when we could meet. Paul had told Clara he needed time to digest all that she had told him about me and to get up his nerve to meet me. Once again, I waited nightly by the phone. Three days later I got a call from a rather nervous Paul.

"Is David there?" I knew immediately who it was. "This is David," I replied, "and this must be Paul," praying my guess was correct. "Yes, this is Paul, I'm your…." He didn't seem to be able to say the words, so I said them for him, "You're my biological father."

Paul laughed and said he didn't know what he should call himself but that this was one of the happiest moments of his life. I could feel my throat thicken and eyes start to mist. We didn't talk long as he was on a work phone and couldn't tie up a line with a personal call. He asked if I knew a convenient Richmond Hill coffee shop where he could meet me. I suggested one in a plaza we both knew and agreed to meet there the following evening as he drove home from work.

Nick wanted to come along but sensed this was a trip I should do solo. Besides, Clara hadn't told him about me being in a relationship with Nick. Being a cop, I figured he might not take too kindly to his offspring being gay, so I felt I should meet him and feel him out for his views before introducing him to my husband.

From our house, it only took a few minutes to drive to the plaza. I wished I had suggested a restaurant or something different that would afford us some privacy for our first eye-to-eye contact. Paul had told me what type of car he would be driving. No beams came for several minutes but then in drove a car that fitted his description. A man about my height and build got out of the car and walked toward the coffee shop, peering in the window, obviously looking for someone who might be waiting for him.

Inside, Paul stopped and looked about. He saw me in the corner and smiled and we both knew this was it. By the time he had walked ten paces across the room he had tears in his eyes as he grabbed me and hugged me close.

"I can't believe this is happening. I'm so glad to meet you, David," he said, his emotions getting the better of him. "This should be a *20/20* program."

I gently pushed him away from me, so I could get a good look at my other blood relative, then peppered him with questions about himself, his kids and his sports career. Paul asked about my life, my parents, my siblings, dogs and which sports I liked. We told each other of our mutual love for animals. Paul said he and his wife were very involved in the Canadian Kennel Club, owning a small kennel with ten Canadian champion dogs. Paul asked if I was dating anyone.

"No one special at the moment," I lied.

I asked Paul what it was like getting Clara's telephone call and subsequently having supper with her. I could tell Paul was smitten with Clara. Over the next hour we kept buying cups of coffee while interrogating one another. Then Paul glanced at his watch and said he had to get going. He said his wife had no idea that her archrival had given birth to his son. Paul said sadly their marriage had been dead for many years; even so, he didn't want her knowing about this just yet. He suggested we call Clara and arrange a lunch for the three of us the following week. Paul said he wanted us to get to know one another and not to lose any more time.

Over the next ten weeks we met for lunch each week and had a supper to exchange our first "family" Christmas gifts. It was early December and I had several things I wanted to discuss with them. The first was to tell Paul I was gay and in a long-term relationship with someone who was HIV positive.

Paul listened and as I finished telling him about Nick, he reached over the table and said, "Your mother already told me, David. I've known for a few weeks that you are gay. Through dog breeding circles, my wife and I have been best friends to a gay couple affected by AIDS. In fact, I was a pallbearer for Jim who died of AIDS last spring. I'm not worried about AIDS or that you are gay." Then he whispered across the table, "When do I get to meet Nick?"

But I had a second thing on my mind.

"I want to meet my half-siblings," I announced. Neither of them looked away and I knew that they had discussed this matter already. Paul didn't want his kids to know about me until he told his wife, which he planned to do within a few days. Clara suggested that we drive to Belleville to meet her daughter first and then she would tell her son about me. Paul said his kids would be fine with the news of having a gay half-brother. Likewise, Clara said her son Iain might be a bit taken aback by her having borne a son before she met his dad, but me being gay would be a non-issue for him.

A few days later Paul told me he had been having lunch with Clara most days for the past six weeks. He said they had just been enjoying one another's company so much that they decided to spend as much time getting caught up on the lost years of their lives. He said he had told his wife about me the night before and the air at home was even more icy than usual. His wife had had a fierce rivalry with Clara and it was still a sore spot with her thirty-eight years later. She wasn't keen on him announcing this news of having sired a child with Clara, but Paul said she would have to get used to it as he intended to tell their children about me before Christmas.

Within a week he gathered his two sons and daughter for what he called an important meeting. With his wife purposefully absent from the room, he told them about the circumstances of my birth and how I had resurfaced recently. He was proud of me, he said, and told them he hoped they would want to meet their half-brother as much as I wanted to meet them. Telling his kids that I was a physical education graduate, had taught, was an athlete, and now lived in Richmond Hill with my gay lover who was HIV positive somehow heightened their curiosity and they wanted to arrange meeting me as soon as possible. They were also intrigued to know how their mother had reacted to this news. Paul said Kay's absence was an obvious indicator of her reaction.

I'd grown up in awe of friends with brothers. Now I had three half-brothers between their two families, and one who shared the same name as me, had studied physical education at Western while I was in physical education at the University of Toronto — we had many things in common. I was impatient to meet them as Christmas approached. Nick and I were hosting Mum and my sister Karen in Richmond Hill over Christmas and I decided it was time to tell Mum about my news. I wanted my family to know before I met my half-siblings.

Mum took the news well; she said she was glad I'd finally pieced together the puzzle and added that she didn't believe adoption information should be sealed. She appeared genuinely interested and asked many questions about my recent discovery. My sister worried that Mum might be threatened or hurt, but Mum said, "I *am* his mother. I'm the one who held my arms to him when he hoisted himself up and walked at eight months of age. Your father and I taught him character and morality and we devoted our lives to the two of you."

Paul told me a few days before Christmas that his son Dave had been pestering him to get my phone number. Paul gave it to him but told him not to call until he got the go-ahead from me. I said it would be great for Dave to make the first call.

Within an hour Dave telephoned. Our forty-minute conversation flowed easily, and I felt very comfortable with the sound of his voice. We agreed to meet at his house on December 27. Dave said his wife, Nancy, and their two young kids were eager to meet me, as were his brother and sister.

What a thrill it was to go into the festive season having just met my biological parents and finally being able to explore the faces that had created me. I could see how my hairline was the same as Paul's, how my hair colour was a combination of his light blonde and Clara's red hair.

On Christmas Eve, Karen and Mum arrived early for supper so we sat around the fireplace and chatted. Christmas morning, we enjoyed one of Nick's specialty breakfasts and opened our gifts. Nick left for Guelph to spend some time with his family. He wanted to accompany me to meet my biological half-siblings, but I told him I needed to do this solo. The day after Boxing Day I drove Mum back to Peterborough. She was excited for me to meet my half-siblings and wished she could there to watch my reactions. She encouraged me to enjoy each second of this process.

I called Dave from Mum's for last-minute directions to his house. He said the coffee was on and *our* siblings had just arrived and were anxiously awaiting me. Mum kissed me goodbye and in less than ten minutes I drove into my half-brother's laneway. As I sat in the car looking toward the house, I could see the front curtains fluttering, small hands parting them to reveal two young children peering out. I approached the house, and a tall, handsome man in a sweater came out the front door and waved.

"You must be David." I gave a nod and he walked over and said, "I'm Dave," then bear-hugged me—he was on the verge of being overcome by his emotions. He was taller than me by two inches, broader in the shoulders, but I was immediately struck by the familial resemblances such as square shoulders, face structure and a grin that was undeniably us. This is something biological kids take for granted, while I was in awe as my eyes scanned this biological brother standing in front of me.

Dave introduced me to his wife and children, then we walked into the living room where his brother and sister were waiting. What a surreal experience! I just wanted to observe every inch of them. I felt an immediate connection with Dave, whereas his sister and brother were much more reserved and cautious. Dave's wife, Nancy, ironically looked identical to the woman I had dated twenty years earlier in Grades 12 and 13. I looked at their children and imagined that they probably had the features of children I might have sired had we married. It was a moment of reckoning with the past, all the what-ifs, specifically in terms of the children I had always wanted. We talked and ate for three hours, exchanging information about our youth, our relationships with parents, our families, careers, political leanings, pet peeves and highlights of our lives. Politically, Dave and I were also in sync as the only NDP members in the room.

I told them I was gay and about Nick and his health status, making it clear that if my being gay or Nick's health was a problem for them, then I'd expect them to be honest and express any concerns to my face. My forthrightness and protectiveness of Nick and my relationship made them smile in unison. They said I must be one of their family because listening to me shield Nick was no different from the way they would defend their own spouses.

I left Dave's house three hours after arriving, then went back to Mum's house, where we sat and chatted about my experience. Mum was concerned I might have higher expectations about an enduring friendship with my half-siblings than they might want. She was also concerned about the emotional toll this could have on me if they weren't as inclined to return the desire for a strong sibling attachment. I told her that seeing

Dave was like seeing myself and that Dave's wife resembled the woman I loved in high school. Looking at his children, I said, gave me a deep sadness about the children I might have had with Nancy and how 'our' kids would have probably looked like my niece and nephew.

I still hadn't told Mum about the son I'd created with Becki almost twenty years earlier. Seeing Dave's kids reminded me of that loss of a son—a child I'd most likely never meet. The afternoon ended with me reminding Mum that she and Dad were my one and only parents and I had no desire to replace them and develop a new parental relationship with Clara and Paul. Although Mum appeared confident in her own space as my mother, I felt the need to reassure her I was born into this world to be David Ross Irlam McKinstry, son of Dorothy and Eric McKinstry, and they'd be the only ones I'd call my parents.

I left before it got dark for the drive back to Richmond Hill. Nick would be waiting anxiously for some word from me and I just wanted to hug him close and share the news of my meeting with my paternal half-siblings. I also sensed that Paul and Clara would be waiting for some word on my reaction. They had already started to refer to me as "son" in conversations and to say what a blessing it was that they had a love child, a child they had created and could now revel in as a product of their earlier relationship. It was like having a second chance at "their" family, they said.

It was a long drive back to Richmond Hill to Nick and the dogs. I found myself pondering what had just transpired and going back to the day I'd first connected with Clara by letter. Could reuniting with Clara and then meeting Paul and his children become a problem if everyone didn't gel or one or more became possessive of this developing relationship? Later that evening Nick listened to my account of the meeting with these biological half-siblings. He didn't speak for a long time. I knew his silence meant he was carefully processing the facts and emotions I'd shared about meeting my half-siblings and considering how the relationship could enhance or jeopardize my sense of family from this point onward. There was no going back to not knowing what I now knew. Nick snuggled up close and told me to let it unravel as it was meant, and if I didn't have a deepening spiritual connection to the participants then I'd know within a short time whether to pursue an ongoing relationship and most importantly, get an honest sense of my half-sibling's longer-term interest in me. "You may not have to make much of a choice, if they aren't into it as much as you are. For the moment, just sit with your thoughts after every meeting with them. You have an acute insight into others and you'll know if it's going to work long-term. You do that every day in the head-hunting business; just apply the same principals to this experience and you'll put the pieces of this puzzle together the way it is meant to be."

We had just poured another glass of wine when Henri Nouwen rang our doorbell. Henri, an internationally acclaimed author and theologian, and Nick had worked on several recent spiritual retreats together and he often dropped by our house for coffee. Being gay and constrained by the Catholic Church's stance on homosexuality, Henri enjoyed our home and small dinner parties with a few of our Jesuit friends where he could be himself. Henri sat down, and Nick gave him the abridged version of meeting my biological parents and having just returned from meeting my half-siblings for the first time just hours earlier. Animated after a glass of wine, Henri kept asking questions, mostly about how this affected my Mum. I was glad to have Henri's input and his curiosity was amusing at times, which helped to break the bewildered mood I'd been in since leaving Peterborough. Henri reiterated what Nick had counselled me to do: to process and meditate on the reasons behind my curiosity and assess my feelings accurately using a formula of fifty percent emotion and fifty percent intellect. They were both right, of course. I just had to be mindful of my, and everyone else's, emotions and give this experience a meditative, prayerful approach and adequate time, and in the end follow my gut.

CHAPTER EIGHT

OUR WEDDING

A FEW DAYS AFTER MEETING my paternal half-siblings, Nick decided to visit his parent's home in Guelph. They held an annual post-Christmas levee for many family, friends and business associates. Nick's Dad owned a well-known local real estate company and was highly respected in the Guelph business community. I was tired and wanted some down time with the dogs and to think about what had transpired during the past week of meeting my 'blood' siblings, so Nick ventured off alone.

I tried to reach Nick by phone at his parent's home a few times that night. It was 10 p.m. before I could get through to him. He told me one hundred people were milling around their home and no one heard the phone ringing earlier. By the sound of his voice, the party was going well. Lots of his high school classmates and neighbourhood friends were there. Nick had taken the portable phone into the attached garage, so he could talk privately. We laughed at the odds of us both having a brother named Dave and Nick said he'd return in 48 hours. In the privacy of the garage he murmured softly that his love for me just kept growing, and for the zillionth time he asked, "Will you please marry me?" I laughed and answered, "Maybe."

Two days later he arrived home around 2 p.m. looking exhausted. He hadn't been able to sleep much the past two nights, he said, because he had been on the upper bunk in a room shared with our two-year-old niece. She had chicken pox and had been awake numerous times during the nights crying and needing attention.

"Don't you realize that chicken pox is a virus and with your weakened immune system you could easily catch it?" Nick looked sheepish and said he hadn't known what to do when he discovered she was sick. If he had made a fuss, it could have compromised his secret: his family at this point were unaware of his HIV status.

I berated him up and down for half an hour. He wasn't only risking *his* health but *our* life together. I was trying my best to keep him alive. Finally, he lay down on our bed and fell into a deep sleep—or pretended to be asleep. He wasn't a fighter and hated arguments, especially when he knew I was right.

We had kept the HIV secret from his family for four years. Mum knew about Nick's status, but he was opposed to telling his family until his health began to worsen. But now I felt it was imperative to have at least one person in Guelph who could run interference for me, an ally who would alert me when one of our nieces or nephews was ill with a childhood disease, so I could keep Nick safely away from compromising situations. Since his return from Yale, Nick had been building a wonderful new adult relationship with his only brother, Dave, and it seemed logical that I share Nick's health status with him. I had become close friends with Nick's brother and his wife Karen over the past few years. I knew they'd be devastated to hear this news, but I could no longer chance Nick's health by staying silent.

I poured a tall glass of Glenfiddich and took the portable phone to the recreation room. After resurrecting a roaring fire in the hearth, I settled into the wingback chair, and dialed the number. By a stroke of luck Dave answered. I knew his life would change forever the moment I broached the subject of his brother's HIV status.

Dave listened for the twenty minutes it took me tell him the story of Nick becoming HIV positive, his medications and their side effects. I told him that Nick zealously guarded his privacy about being HIV positive primarily because he already felt personally vulnerable and violated, knowing his health history was no longer a private matter within the medical community. Just being HIV positive meant so many levels of the medical establishment and Government would have access to his records.

"I'm just reclaiming my brotherhood with Nick after so many years of him living far away from us and now I'm going to lose him." Dave lamented. He asked many questions about how long Nick had been HIV positive. Did he know who gave it to him or when he got it? Was I HIV positive? Did Nick's Guelph friends know about his health? Dave was so upset at one point that he excused himself and Karen took hold of the receiver. She had been listening beside Dave and was comforting him. Dumbfounded by the news, Karen asked if Nick knew I was calling them. I told her no, and that I didn't want Nick to know what I had told them. I explained that exposure to chicken pox could be lethal to someone with a compromised immune system. I needed to know I had someone in Guelph who wouldn't let another dangerous situation innocently occur. I made it clear that even the most seemingly insignificant communicable disease could be fatal for Nick.

Dave came back on the phone and said he wanted to digest this information overnight. He said he'd call tomorrow to continue this conversation and he wouldn't tell Nick what I had just disclosed. I had no sooner put the phone down than I heard Nick letting the dogs out into the yard through our bedroom door. My timing had been perfect, and I went upstairs content I had done what was necessary.

I made supper and we were sitting down to eat when the phone rang. I grabbed the portable phone from the bedroom. It was Dave DiCicco calling back to tell me that he had thought about our conversation, but he wanted to talk to his brother in person. Dave felt that he owed it to Nick to hug him and tell him he loved him. Dave wanted Nick to know he would be by his side every step of the way.

I half-heartedly tried to convince Dave not to discuss this matter with Nick, but I knew my words were falling on deaf ears. Dave said he had almost got in his car and driven down to see Nick without calling me first. He was determined to come ahead tonight to be with his brother. I acceded, knowing if I had been on the receiving end of such devastating news about a brother, I would probably have done the same. I told Dave I would tell Nick why he was coming to visit.

I wasn't sure how Nick would take hearing I had breached his confidence. Would he understand my motivation for telling Dave, especially considering the severity of the chicken pox scare? When I returned to the dining room I didn't know how else to tell him but to give it to him straight. Surprisingly, he wasn't upset; in fact, he said he was glad I had spoken to Dave. He hadn't figured out how to tell his brother, so my revelation took a heavy load from him. Exhausted emotionally, Nick cried on my shoulder. Then we moved over to the sofa to sit and wait for Dave to arrive.

It was very moving when Dave walked into our front hall and hugged his brother—the two were crying into each other's shoulders. Slowly they separated and, clutching each other's arm, they came into the dining room. I got them both a glass of wine and sat down across the room from them, looking with envy at the brotherly love that held them together. They needed time alone, so I took three of the dogs out for a long walk. An hour later I returned to find Nick packing an overnight bag on the dining room table. He and Dave were going to drive back to Guelph immediately so in the morning Nick could visit with his sisters to disclose his secret. With his siblings informed, he'd then tell their parents. Nick hugged me hard and then Dave joined in our hug. I didn't want to let go of Nick, but I knew he had to do this on his own.

Nick called from Guelph late the following afternoon to give me a report on how the disclosure had gone with his family. "I got Mom alone and told her while Dad was at the office. She was really mad," Nick said. "She asked how someone so smart could be so stupid and then she went into her bedroom and slammed the door."

I asked how his dad had taken the news. Nick said he just sat looking at him for several minutes before angrily asking, "Did David give you AIDS?" Nick told him I had not been the one. "I think Dad wanted to hear you'd given me the virus. After a few more minutes of digesting this revelation, he said you must be very special or totally crazy knowing about my health and still going into a relationship with me." I laughed, and Nick said his dad understandably had a heightened respect for me.

Nick's sisters knew AIDS killed, so his news was profoundly emotional for them: The eldest, Lori, had been married to a bisexual man who had died of AIDS in the mid-1980s. Nick said he was driving to London to reveal his health status to his sister Lori, in the morning and he would be back to Richmond Hill in time for our New Year's Eve supper.

An hour after Nick's call, his sister Teresa phoned. She talked about AIDS and how infectious it could be and wondered if she should be worried about her newborn baby around Nick. She had many questions and I felt honoured she called me for answers. Likewise, with his sister Diana, she called and talked to me for 45 minutes about her relationship with Nick and how they were really two peas in a pod. I felt as if I had crossed over into an elevated and more familial relationship with his siblings. In time, I sensed Nick's parents would be just as welcoming to me.

Nick carried on his usual frenetic pace during January. Having worked as Chaplain and a religion teacher in the Catholic school system for many years during his active Jesuit career, he loved being involved in all facets of school life. He often took on the responsibility for the school choir, glee club and directed many school drama and musical productions. We made several weekend trips to Guelph to visit his family and reassure them Nick was fine and quite able to function normally. Nick was developing his spiritual discernment lecture series for several Catholic parishes. During most of January he recorded these lectures on cassettes to be sold in Catholic bookstores. A bigger project presented itself after several people approached him about setting up his own little church community, as they enjoyed his brand of preaching. Nick didn't take much convincing.

We both felt that there was a place for a church in Richmond Hill for those who were gay or straight: we called it Agape, the Greek word for brotherly love. Mum arrived with her sewing machine and helped Nick create a banner for his new church. Nick began canvassing for potential members from his list of disconnected reformed Catholics. We rented the common room of the library across the street from us to use for Sunday morning services. The first service was overflowing with seventy-five friends and family arriving to see Nick in his priestly robes and hear his message of faith, charity and hope.

Agape had a faithful following of forty regulars every Sunday for the month of March but it dwindled to twenty regulars by the end of May. Occasionally, Nick would speak to a congregation of thirty, made up of teachers and school board friends who wanted to see Nick in action. We were trying to get the message out to the gay community north of Toronto, but we didn't seem to be drawing the audience and were steadfast in our belief that it would take time to build Agape into a strong congregation. But time was running out for Nick.

It had been an unusually bad winter in terms of his health. Colds, flu and aches and pains were constant nuisances. By May Nick had missed eleven school days due to several bouts of illness. He became obsessed with monitoring his weight and every few weeks he'd announce the latest loss stats. This was so upsetting for him that in mid-June I manipulated the correction knob at the back of the scales to show pounds being gained. Yet his size thirty-two pants always looked baggy. I bought several new size 32s and Mum adjusted the waistbands to size 29 without his knowledge.

In late June, the doctor reported that Nick's T-cell count had seriously dropped, from over four hundred to two hundred and eighty in the past two months. A follow-up visit in mid-July showed another dramatic decrease in his T-cells, now below two hundred, the line in the sand, so to speak, between being HIV positive and having full-blown AIDS. Thrush, a contagious disease of small white eruptions on the tongue, mouth and throat, was a constant irritant for Nick; it was painful for him to eat when his medication no longer kept this oral fungus at bay.

The first six months of 1993 had been exhausting for Nick with Agape, teaching, and putting together a lecture series on discernment for audiotape distribution. It had cost Nick thirty-seven hundred dollars to produce a six-cassette series of audiotapes and within two months he tripled his investment. Unfilled orders piled up on his desk. With his failing health a constant concern, the success of his tape series provided a welcome emotional boost. In August he repeated his original order of audiocassettes and sold three hundred sets within ten days. Knowing that people were clamouring to buy his taped series was good for his mental health.

I talked to my half-brother Dave several times each week. We seemed to share a sense of the brotherhood within our grasp and mutually agreed to actively nurture this young relationship. In Dave I saw the brother I had yearned for most of my life.

Meanwhile, I met Annabelle and Iain, Clara's two adult children that summer. Annabelle was married with two young children. She was cute, wise, insightful and doing a great job of raising her kids. I felt a connection with Annabelle because we were close in age and she readily shared her memories of growing up with Clara as a mother.

Iain seemed to be an unconventional twenty-six-year-old, in some ways a younger version of me. I immediately felt of all the half-siblings that this half-brother had a rebellious streak and preferred to walk roads less travelled. He wanted to be a career downhill ski enthusiast at Whistler or a water-skier in the Caribbean. He was very good at talking about his interests but seemed disinterested in my background. If we didn't talk about hockey, then we didn't talk about much. Iain had been a promising hockey goalie in his youth, while I couldn't find one redeeming thing to say about a game that valued thugs on the ice. Clara told me Iain was popular, incredibly kind and generous to his friends. We were brothers—I assumed there had to be a depth to his soul, but I wasn't very good at cracking his code. I had a feeling that we were more alike than dissimilar – maybe that rebel streak in us both? However, at that time there wasn't a lot of interest on his part to explore a fraternal bond with me as he packed and prepared to move west.

Iain notified his parents of his intention to sell the cottage he'd built on Sandy Lake. Clara, knowing we had been looking for a country place, suggested to me that I drive Nick up to see this property early in July. Sandy Lake has a limestone base and the water appeared turquoise blue. The cottage was perched high on a hill overlooking the waterfront and the look of peace on Nick's face told me he wanted to buy it. For two years we had toyed with the idea that when Nick's health declined, and he couldn't teach any longer, we would buy a country home and set up a small bed and breakfast operation. From July onward, we obsessed over finding a way to afford the hefty price tag.

Upon hearing Nick had fallen in love with the Sandy Lake property, Iain's kindness and generosity shone through. He lowered the price to make it affordable. My business was being hit by the recession and I hadn't had much commission come into our account for months. I had stashed some cash away and we would be fine for another six months even if business continued to spiral downward. Nick's audiocassette sales had put $16,200 into our savings account, but we needed another $20,000 for a down payment to qualify for a mortgage.

Nick started back to school in September and we spent two weekends at Sandy Lake trying to make up our minds about purchasing it. We were convinced it would be a good investment. My business had slowed significantly so I had relocated my business to our office at home with a part-time secretary.

It was a difficult start to autumn and we decided to go to Vermont for a weekend holiday. During our trip we debated and discussed the pros and cons of setting up a B 'n' B on Sandy Lake. We had to decide if it was feasible for us to purchase this property, especially because Nick's health could continue to decline. Nick also wanted us to get married. We'd had this discussion so many times in the past and I just didn't feel it was necessary for two men to get married to signpost their commitment to one another. However, Nick spoke persuasively about the need to publicly make our vows to one another. He felt marriage was necessary to help family and friends understand the depth of our commitment. That seemed to make sense. I was agonizingly aware of Nick's decreasing strength and stamina. Our physician had explained to us that Nick could qualify for long-term disability and that he should give it some serious thought. That doctor said it made no sense to spend his last years working like a dog. Nick had lost a further twenty pounds and I finally acknowledged that full-blown AIDS was going to be far more debilitating than just being HIV positive. If Nick wanted us married, then I would do it to make him happy. We laughed several times en route to Vermont about how Nick wanted this wedding for spiritual reasons and I wanted to have it as an excuse to invite every heterosexual to whom I'd ever given a wedding gift — it was payback time!

During our trip I admitted to Nick I'd spoken to his doctor about what to expect from the AIDS stage of this disease. Nick just squeezed my hand and put his head on my shoulder as we drove and admired the Vermont landscape exploding with vibrant autumn colours. He knew what lay ahead but was stoically focused on us in the moment.

Sunday night when we returned and finished unpacking, I dropped the calendar down on the dining room table, turned to Nick and said, "So when do you want to get married? Pick a date—we'll need at least five weeks to organize it, design an invitation and determine who to invite." After checking both of our busy day-timers, we agreed on Saturday, December 11. We also decided that we should go full-speed ahead with the purchase of Iain's property on Sandy Lake.

With the help of a mortgage broker and a 60-day $20,000 loan from our good friend, Philip Lowry, we were on our way to owning the Sandy Lake cottage. Philip knew we'd repay him, but his generosity permitted Nick to edge his way comfortably into full-time retirement. Most of the latter part of October and early November was spent preparing for our relocation to Sandy Lake. I was winding down the job-search business and only had to collect for a $23,000 upper-management placement I'd made weeks earlier. By October 31st I'd closed the door on McKinstry and Company and put all my energies into organizing our wedding. Tom Harpur, a well-known religious personality, author and *Toronto Star* columnist, agreed to officiate and Philip's cousin, a music teacher at Crescent School, would be the soloist. One-hundred-and-twenty-five wedding invitations were mailed out and we were flooded with RSVPs by early November. Most of the people we hoped would be there to support us didn't let us down. Mum wasn't sure she should come to the wedding as it could unbalance her relationship with my sister, Karen, who had become a born-again Christian and who rented the basement apartment in her home. Nick's dad sent us a cheque to cover Philip's $20,000. loan, the wedding expenses and another to pay six months of mortgage payments. However, Nick's parents didn't think they were ready to handle a gay wedding ceremony but would support us in every other way as a couple.

Nick's siblings were going to be there, and both of our Dave brothers agreed to give toasts to us. We stopped the Sunday morning services for Agape in October when we decided to move north, but we wanted the charming library pavilion where the services had been held to be the spot for our ceremony. It was convenient to our home and had parking for one hundred cars. We couldn't have alcohol in the building, so we went with non-alcoholic apple wine. Nick felt this was best regardless so that guests wouldn't leave inebriated from our wedding.

Nick's health continued to be precarious at best. One day he would be fine and two days later he would spike a fever and be out of sorts. Our wedding day arrived amidst the first snowy blizzard of the season. Nick's sister in London called to say the highway was closed and she wouldn't be able to come. Thankfully the snowstorm didn't deter his other siblings from driving from Guelph, but several older family members left messages that they wouldn't be attending because of the weather. I spent the afternoon at the library decorating, cleaning, and setting up the music system while Nick rested in bed. Philip and a few other friends joined me at the library to set up one-hundred-and-twenty-five champagne glasses filled with strawberries. Nick had been ill most of that week and by Thursday he just fizzled. I was busy trying to make sure our wedding was going to come off without any hitches. Nick's health was very concerning me, and I was more than edgy.

Friends and family had been dropping off or sending gifts all week and I had them out on display in our dining room. As sick as Nick was, he would get out of bed and come to the door to greet another gift messenger. He delighted in opening the gifts and arranging them on the dining room table for display. A few days before the wedding, a dear friend of ours dropped by with a wedding gift for us and to tell us he couldn't attend our wedding. Father Henri Nouwen was world-renowned in Catholic and theological circles for his books. He was the spiritual director at L'Arche in Richmond Hill and his being gay was known only to us and a select few other friends. Henri felt coming to a gay wedding with Tom Harpur officiating could result in too many questions if the word ever got out he'd been there. We understood and agreed it was a sad commentary on life in 1993 for gay men. He gave us his blessing, we shared a prayer and he bid us good luck and said he'd come to check out Woodhaven once we got settled in.

Saturday's snowstorm had been predicted since Thursday night and we were prepared for numerous cancellations. Nick got out of bed around 4 p.m. and slowly began to shave, shower and dress. We had gone shopping weeks earlier to find coordinating outfits to wear: green wool blazers and turtlenecks that would be fashionable but casual enough to meet our needs.

The musicians got stuck in the snowstorm and arrived late. We were still setting up the musicians when the first guests started to enter the library's glass-sided foyer at 7 p.m. Nick arrived twenty minutes later; I was relieved to see him able to stand upright for our wedding. Whatever else he did beyond saying 'I do' would be a bonus for me. The flow of guests into the chapel area revived and invigorated Nick and he became the consummate host, seemingly impervious to the lethal virus attacking his immune system.

With ninety-seven guests in attendance, our ceremony started at 8 p.m. and vows were completed by 8:25 p.m.—the first gay wedding most of our family and friends had witnessed. Gratifyingly, we received wonderful comments from guests about our officiant Tom and many commented they felt they'd shared in something spiritually enriching and socially significant. By 9:30 p.m. our guests were leaving and at 10 p.m. we headed home. Nick undressed and went to bed. Several of my new in-laws were staying the night so we cracked open champagne and unpacked the boxes of wedding gifts and envelopes left behind by well-wishers. We had registered at the newly opened Home Depot and had received over $5,000.00 in Gift Certificates which would come in handy for our B 'n' B renovations. The next morning, Nick arose and made a hearty breakfast for his siblings before they headed back to Guelph. We sat for a while in front of the roaring flames in our fireplace awe-struck by the wealth of well-thought-out and personalized items we'd received.

On Monday morning Nick returned to school, now a 'married man' and feeling much better. I picked him up after school to drive to the

TD bank to sign mortgage documents. Nick was steady on his feet that afternoon, but he looked pale, so I walked with him into the bank to witness his signature and feel part of the process. Because I had declared bankruptcy in 1987, our mortgage broker felt Nick would qualify easily with his salary for this cottage property and my bankruptcy should be kept out of the qualification equation. Nick could put me on the mortgage later, but for now he would be the sole mortgagee. We waited a few minutes for the branch mortgage officer to usher us into her office. She didn't question my tagging along—I joked I was there to be his witness. She produced the forms from a file folder and proceeded to tell Nick where to sign. A few minutes later, she got up and shook Nick's hand and congratulated him on his new home purchase. As we were turning to walk out the door, as if in an afterthought, the bank officer said, "Oh, do you want life insurance on the mortgage, Nick?"

Having been in the insurance business right out of university, I'd told Nick he'd need a medical to qualify for mortgage insurance and that he wouldn't get it with his HIV status. Nick responded questioningly, "Does anyone qualify for mortgage insurance? What if I had a terminal illness?"

"Don't worry," she said pointing to a line at the bottom of a page. "The medical is just a formality and just about everyone gets mortgage insurance through the bank—just sign here. If there are any concerns from the underwriters, you'll be called."

Nick looked at me and I just shrugged and said, "Go ahead if you want."

Nick signed, and we left the office. As we walked to the car, Nick said, "Do you think I'll get mortgage insurance?"

I offhandedly told him that the bank would contact us and ask for the name of his physician. "When they hear you have AIDS you won't get mortgage insurance. Trust me, you won't get it, Nick," I said as we drove out of the parking lot bound for home.

A few days later we received notification from the bank about our mortgage approval. As we read over the document, we noticed the mortgage had been insured. "I thought you said I wouldn't get the insurance," Nick said and playfully gave me an elbow in the ribs. I suggested to him that with so many people getting mortgages, perhaps it was a new policy of banks to give anyone mortgage insurance without a medical. Busy with the move, we put the documents away in our file drawer and kept on packing for our new home, which Nick named Woodhaven Bed and Breakfast.

For six week's we'd been moving boxes and smaller pieces of furniture to the Sandy Lake property, but just before Christmas Day we started to pack up our house in earnest. We were making daily trips to Loblaws to get packing boxes. On December 27 our second Welsh Corgi, Meaghan, died of kidney failure at fourteen years of age. Nick was so traumatized by this pet's death he barely got out of bed for 24 hours.

We left Richmond Hill with three moving vans full of furniture and belongings and headed north in a horrific snow squall to our new home on Sandy Lake. Nick commuted to school or stayed overnight with friends who offered him a basement bedroom whenever he needed it during those first few weeks of January. But on a Friday in late January, Nick called in sick, knowing the following week he'd initiate his long-term disability claim. We were off to a new stress-free life. Little did we know that our first few months of full-time living on the lake would be busy with of adventures, like our dogs running off in pursuit of deer or fox, with Nick or me in hot pursuit, often wearing just galoshes and ski jackets over our housecoats.

Renovations began immediately, which kept me busy day and night. Friends and my new in-laws arrived most weekends for the first few months after we transitioned to Sandy Lake to assist us building bathrooms, erecting new walls and converting the huge double car garage into a chapel for Nick. He was so excited watching his spiritual sanctuary become a reality.

My half-brother Dave gave us a hot tub he had been storing in his basement. He had no room for it, and happily donated it to Woodhaven. Nightly Nick would relax in the hot tub while looking at the silent, crisp wintery sky full of stars. We often sat staring out the living room windows, watching snowstorms whirl up from the lake. What sights we'd see from our perch behind the floor-to-ceiling windows of our living room; rabbits, deer, and coyotes traversed the frozen lake's shoreline in front of Woodhaven. We put up bird feeders to attract cardinals, blue jays and yellow finches. Five golden retrievers, a new B and B business, lots of hope and love in our hearts, and a ton of carpentry projects to keep me occupied. We would frequently comment to one another, "What more could we ask for?" And in unison we'd say, "Children to adopt."

CHAPTER NINE

GOODBYE, NICK

I LIKED MY NEW LUMBERJACK role, which helped make the multiple treks to the woodpile pleasant, regardless of the bone-chilling winds. January 1994 was the coldest on record in more than fifty years; the day we moved the last of our possessions from storage into Woodhaven it was -26 Celsius, and extremely low temperatures were the norm until the end of February. I had to chop and split wood twice a day to feed the fireplaces. But we loved being so removed from the city and its urban noises and hyper-stresses. Nick sat and read by the floor-to-ceiling windows that provided us with a panoramic view of the frozen lake, forests of green coniferous trees and abundant wildlife and birds.

Early in March Clara and Paul confessed they had been having a torrid love affair for the past year. We suggested they sustain a veil of secrecy, as it would make their lives hell if the word got out. Nick took it upon himself to speak to Paul by phone about the implications it could have on my relationship with his son Dave. Nick foresaw Dave wanting nothing further to do with me if he discovered I had been privy to his father's infidelity with Clara. Paul said he was aware how their affair could negatively affect or even destroy any future relationship with my half-siblings, maternal and paternal. But both felt, and we agreed, that their last chance for true romantic love had to take precedence over the feelings of their adult children.

Paul and Clara were very supportive of us and we promised to maintain their secret. Clara percolated with excitement as she told us about checking into a hotel under the name of Mr. and Mrs. Camden. She had become a teenager again, reliving her first love. Paul, equally at home in Clara's arms, was in a dead-end marriage and he ached to be with Clara full-time—he just couldn't think of a way to gently break the news to his wife about her arch-rival resurfacing forty years later and stealing his heart.

Clara, much more resolute than Paul, separated from her spouse and moved into an apartment. To maintain her dignity, Clara knew she had to end her marriage, regardless of what became of her rekindled love with Paul.

Over supper they asked Nick how he felt about divorce. Nick said staying in a dead marriage wasn't God's plan for anyone. Contrary to the view of his church, Nick said that they were very lucky to have found passion for a second time in a world where most people have difficulty finding it even once. I agreed—at age sixty, having raised their families well, neither Paul nor Clara should live life by other people's rules. At some point we all must take stock—sometimes that means facing difficult decisions, such as leaving a marriage that has run its course. They were thrilled to have reunited with a son they could call their own. This created an instant new family, and they said convincingly that their relationship with Nick and I had given them a familial connectedness that deepened their resolve to be together. It was becoming easy to have an adult relationship with them and share in their happiness.

By late April 1994 our kilometre-long driveway was losing its snow cover. The two neighbouring rental cottages had prospective tenants regularly driving up the road to check them out. Naturally, anytime a car ventured close to our house, the canine burglar patrol would let out a cacophony of barking and wailing. One morning they caused me to race outside to check a Jeep Cherokee preparing to venture down the still-treacherous hillside road to the cottages below us.

Our dogs were standing directly in front of the vehicle and neither Nick nor I could scatter them to let it through. Finally, these sentinels saw a squirrel in the distance and ran off with Nick in pursuit. I saw the reason for the dogs' interest: a young grey female standard poodle was cowering in the backseat, terrorized by our pets.

I introduced myself to the driver, who was checking out one of the cottages for rent. Brendan, standing six feet five inches tall and striking a Marlboro Man pose, said his wife wanted to find a dog- and child-friendly place to rent for the summer. Casey, his wife, had given birth to their first daughter four weeks before and they'd gone off to Florida for a week of R and R while he scouted out various properties. As usual I was forthright about defining Nick as my husband during the introductions. Brendan was unfazed and in turn asked us all sorts of questions about our choosing to live in the country.

After seeing the rental cottage, he returned to his jeep. Nick was outside raking a few leaves when Brendan rolled down his window and said he had liked the look of the cottage and hoped he would be first to call the owner about renting it. Nick suggested he use our phone to call immediately. Twenty minutes later, Brendan said, "Looks like we'll be neighbours for the summer." He bid us goodbye and said he would introduce his family when he brought them to see the cottage in a few weeks.

Later that same day, another car ventured up our laneway. Two women, off to find a summer cottage for their families to share, parked their car in our lot and proceeded down the hill to check out the remaining rental cottage. Lynn and Lindalee loved it and once again we suggested that they use our phone to call the cottage landlord. We found these women engaging and full of energy. After sharing some herbal tea and fresh pie, our newest neighbours headed back to Toronto. We felt relaxed and happy about the two sets of non-rowdy neighbours with whom we'd spend our first summer on the lake.

We seemed to have become a haven for local gay priests and nuns over that first winter. Wednesdays were common 'days off' for them and it became almost a ritual on Wednesday nights that we would have eight-ten religious around our dining room table. Our local Bishop had been supportive of his diocesan priests who were in same-sex relationships, often with other priests within the parish. Woodhaven provided refuge for them; a place they could relax, enjoy the company of other like-minded religious and just be carefree while outside of the parish walls. It wasn't a secret within religious circles, but it was always a matter requiring the utmost of discretion outside of the parish. I found it quite interesting that I'd never met a 'straight' Jesuit since meeting Nick and being introduced to this side of religious orders. So many scholars sat around our table and conversations often centered on celibacy in the church and how it was a rule of men, not of God. Making religious celibate was the only way the Church could insure that all parish funds came under Rome's control, rather than being passed down from priest to son in typical patriarchal fashion during the early centuries of the church and prior to Pope Constantine's celibacy decree in the 6th Century.

Each week, the completed renovation projects were ticked off a long list we'd drawn up. Ross Kennedy, an old family friend, master builder and carpenter and the father of three girls who had grown up with me on Orpington Road, was our source of carpentry expertise. He guided me every step of the way, frequently reminding me to use four screws where two would suffice. It took three weeks for us to renovate the huge attached garage into two rooms, a chapel for Nick and a library for his two thousand books. Nick, too tired and sick to heave sheets of drywall, would stand on the sidelines being our gopher. The rooms took shape and Nick was beyond thrilled the day I returned from town with a huge carpet remnant for his chapel. He was in his glory having a library and a chapel in his home. He spent hours every day there praying and meditating. Then, following a rest, he would catalogue books to organize the shelves of his new library.

For most of the winter I had been trying to find a physician in Peterborough who would take Nick on as a patient. The local AIDS physician's practice was full—he already had 200 patients. The provincial Tory government under Mike Harris had slashed health care budgets and the physician shortage in Ontario during the 1990s was worrisome and daunting. I decided to contact a local community AIDS advocacy group for help in finding a local doctor; the regular medical trips to Toronto had become exhausting for Nick.

Dr. Tony Jeffery graciously accepted Nick as a patient. Besides providing extraordinary medical care, we found Tony to be a delightfully intuitive person. During house calls to check on Nick he would marvel at the contents of our library. Tony, a budding writer, and Nick struck up a special doctor-patient relationship as Tony became the key player on our health management team.

Nick's bouts with fatigue and a sore back had been worrisome. Tony assured us it was probably the pain from the disease taking root in different parts of his body. He told us he wasn't going to soft pedal Nick's test results. From our first appointment, Tony was gentle but blunt when discussing Nick's prognosis. Never keen to hear that his health was steadily declining, Nick told Tony that he'd gladly die when God called him home rather than when his doctor announced it was time to go.

During those first long winter months in the quietude of Sandy Lake, Nick became obsessed with native folklore and mythology. On several occasions we ventured into the Whetung Ojibwa art gallery, at the Curve Lake Reserve, only twenty-five minutes from Sandy Lake, to purchase books on local Ojibwa legends, folk heroes and the shamans who were mediums between the visible world and the invisible spirit realm. Nick sensed we were living on sacred ground. Many times, he would awaken from a deep sleep and tell me that he had been sitting across from an elderly native on our lawn, being told the history of this area. Nick believed that an eighteenth-century shaman would be his guide to the afterlife. Some days I just wasn't into hearing all this talk of impending death and shamans swooping down to wrench Nick from my life. I'd laugh and say, "Don't talk nonsense. You're hallucinating again. It must be time for your meds."

My mother visited for a few days each week. She said it was heaven on earth having us close enough for her to see regularly. Mum and Nick's relationship was genuine, warm and frank. She had no intention of letting him die before his time and regularly filled our freezer with home-cooked, nutritious meals. Mum was deeply concerned about Nick's loss of weight and fading energy levels—she knew, though, there was nothing to prevent the downward spiral that presumably lay ahead of him.

Dr. Tony patiently listened to my inquiries about new research and drugs to reverse Nick's worsening health. He told me not to expect miracles as Nick was certainly heading into the AIDS home stretch. When I pushed Tony for a time estimate, he was reluctant to be specific. "It could be a year, or it could be as soon as six months. Nick's body has been pummeled by eight years of this disease and extremely toxic drug therapies. His body is tired, and this is the main reason for his steadily worsening health. Don't fight to keep him alive at this point. The inevitable will come soon and you both need to concentrate on living out his remaining days with dignity. Don't expect miracles at this stage of his disease." I never shared Tony's words with Nick, hiding those journal entries from him.

With winter and spring renovation projects completed, I finally found a place for some of our belongings. The remaining boxes were destined for a big yard sale at the end of June. I put up posters at the general store and on trees lining local roads. I felt it would be a good way for us to meet other neighbours on the lake.

At our yard sale I introduced Nick and said we had moved here to set up a bed and breakfast. No one blinked an eye upon hearing we were married. Sandy Lake was the fulfillment of a dream for us. Karen and Mike Sullivan dropped by and bought a spare mattress for their cottage. We learned that Mike was an elementary school principal with the York Catholic School system and, ironically, before going into teaching, he had worked for London Life as a sales agent just down the street from the London Life office where I had worked after graduating from U of T.

Each time we met new people on the lake, I'd inquire about upcoming summer events. Was there a cottagers' association? Wasn't there a mile swim or regatta for the families on the lake? By early July we began organizing a regatta for the upcoming Civic Holiday weekend. I made flyers and delivered them around the lake to everyone hundred and twenty-three cottages. Our steep-hilled waterfront wasn't ideal, so I inquired about using the Sullivan's beachfront. They had young kids and were thrilled to host the first regatta.

I modeled the roster of canoe and swim events after the Stoney Lake regatta I had known in my youth; we even added a Woodhaven Mile Swim to mirror the Lech Mile Swim in which I had participated annually when my family spent summers on the island we owned on Stoney Lake. I sensed that someday I'd have children who would likewise have fond memories of summer regatta's.

On the morning of the 1994 Sandy Lake regatta, Nick wasn't feeling well. Mum was up for the weekend and she stayed with him while I led a flotilla of neighbours, all in canoes, down the shoreline to the Sullivan's. The regatta was a hit, with thirty families from around the lake joining in. When Nick arrived with Mum in tow later in the afternoon, I made a point of introducing him as my spouse and without hesitating everyone applauded and thanked him for his contribution to the regatta—we'd bought trophies and ribbons and medals for the winners. Nick's smile spread over the crowd like a sunrise over the lake. We felt so welcomed—it appeared these cottagers genuinely wanted us to feel part of this lake community. We'd been introduced to so many families—expat Sri Lankans, Indians, Swiss, Jamaicans, Italians, Asians, and Christians, Muslims, Jews and Hindus… this United Nations Sandy Lake community just felt like home for us. Our immediate neighbours, Barbara and Herbert Ho Ping Kong, had introduced themselves shortly after we'd moved to the lake. Being physicians and Catholic, originally from Jamaica, they were intrigued to meet the Jesuit who had moved in next door. They became friends, always ready to lend their medical expertise when Nick's health floundered during our first season on the lake.

We hosted several spontaneous cocktail parties that summer, the numbers of people growing each time. Nick was in his element hosting these get-togethers and loved chatting with our neighbours. Cocktail discussions spanned a myriad of topics, including that gay people should be given the right to adopt. Every few days one or both of us would spend time on the computer exploring adoption options and surrogacy programs and keeping ourselves abreast of changes in foreign and domestic government policies that would open the door for us to adopt.

A week after the regatta, I drove Nick to Sunnybrook Hospital for his bi-monthly round of blood tests. I let him off in front of the doctor's office and we agreed to meet an hour later. I ran a few errands and returned to our rendezvous spot, waited ten minutes for him, then decided to park the car and head inside. I assumed he had run into some acquaintance and had lost track of time.

The office was full of gaunt-looking men and women. I asked the receptionist about Nick and she said I should use the side office and the doctor would see me shortly. Within minutes Dr. Moira Richards, Nick's doctor, stormed in berating me for not having brought Nick in sooner, implying I should have known his health had suddenly and seriously become compromised. She said that he had been admitted and was on the infectious disease floor.

"He may not recover this time," she said. "We're doing a series of tests, but you can see him now," and left the room as quickly as she had entered. My anger over her totally unexpected confrontational attitude jolted me upright. If I hadn't been staggered by this news about Nick's health, I would have sparred with her over her tactless manner regarding my husband's declining health.

I found Nick in bed hooked up to an IV cart. He looked at me with eyes full of disbelief. I knew he too was feeling blindsided and anxious upon hearing how grave his condition was. He had been poked and prodded by every neophyte on-call physician and all he wanted was to go home. Though he knew he wouldn't be leaving that day, his deep green eyes told me he just wanted the two of us to return to Woodhaven and distance ourselves from this nightmare.

I sought out the attending physician, informed him who I was and asked him to tell me what was happening with Nick. He brushed me aside, saying he couldn't discuss Nick's health with anyone but Nick's family without Nick's permission. Enraged, I told him he was totally out of touch with the reality of his patients. "Who the fuck do you think I am? I'm his husband!" Apparently, my words, heard by everyone else from one end of the corridor to the other, didn't even cause this fellow to pause. He just turned and escaped into an elevator.

Was Sunnybrook all about impersonal nastiness, arrogant ice-cold physicians with the people skills of crocodiles? I marched angrily back to Nick's room and gave him an account of my meeting with his attending physician. I grabbed a piece of paper and scribbled the following: "Let it be known that my same-sex spouse, David McKinstry, is also my power of attorney and all my health concerns must be shared with David upon his request of such information." I handed the note to Nick and without glancing up at me he signed it, winked at me and said, "Give him shit, honey!"

With this note in my grasp, I stomped back to the nurses' station and loudly proclaimed so all could hear from Toronto to Sudbury that I wanted to speak to Nick DiCicco's attending physician. My patience was never above average and at that moment it registered below zero.

The young physician who had declined to share Nick's chart with me was paged and within ten minutes stood before me. I handed him the scribbled authorization. He escorted me into a side office and apologized for not sharing the information with me in the first place, stating he himself was gay, and added that he had been working twenty-four hours straight and his own patience had dropped off the map hours ago. I appreciated his contrition. We sat down, and he told me that Nick had pneumonia and their team wanted to do an ultrasound and x-rays to determine if there were any pockets of cancerous cells floating around Nick's organs, especially in his lungs and gastrointestinal tract. An hour later Nick was on a gurney being wheeled away for further tests.

It took 36 hrs of testing before the doctor scheduled a closed-door visit with us. Nick's AIDS specialist, Moira, joined us in Nick's room and in her familiar blunt manner informed Nick his tests showed pockets of cancerous shadows in his brain and liver. Their suggestion was a biopsy to determine the extent and type of cancer. The only good news was that Nick's pneumonia was under control. As his breathing improved, he got antsy about going home. Two days after the biopsy and a battery of further tests, the doctor informed us that Nick's immune system had been caught off guard by the cancer cells that had taken root in his brain. The prognosis wasn't great, but they were going to keep him here for another few weeks of tests.

Nick seemed keenly aware of their unspoken message: no hope.

"Why would I stay on here if you have already identified terminal cancer? What do you expect to find with more tests? Could you possibly find out that I am not as bad as you thought?" he asked point blank. The doctor shook his head and said that further tests wouldn't change the prognosis, which was that Nick had, at most, four to six months to live.

I could feel the blood drain from my legs and I felt woozy as I stood beside Nick's bed. With my hands placed squarely on Nick's shoulder I questioned the need to keep him in hospital if the prognosis was so poor. Dr. Richards appeared to dance around the issue of Nick being a guinea pig for some upcoming studies about AIDS patients.

Nick told the doctor he was checking himself out within the hour. "There isn't anything else you can do for me and I want to be at home at the lake." Our young doctor smiled sympathetically, almost as if he too felt Nick should just go home and enjoy what time he had left.

Nick's face looked ashen and my legs still felt wobbly. One part of me was strangely energized by the feel of Nick's shoulders beneath my hands and the other part was coming to grips with the fact that Nick wasn't going to be the first person to beat AIDS. I lay beside him on the bed and for a few minutes the reality set in and I became inconsolable. Tears burned my cheeks and Nick became my comforter. He didn't say a word; he hugged me tightly and whispered, "Let's go home."

January 1st,1995 Nick's health began its final descent. The cancer and other AIDS related issues were quickly strangling the life out of him. Nick was put on a morphine drip and the dose incrementally increased, as per the doctor's orders, every few days. I was told this would keep Nick pain-free, but it would also cause his respiration to slow and ease him out of this life and into the next. Family arrived to help with his care most weekends. The morphine drip was keeping him mostly comatose, but he did have lucid moments filled with conversation, laughter and tears. Since November we had wanted to see the new Tom Hanks movie Philadelphia, but Nick hadn't been well enough for us to travel to a Toronto theater to see it. A friend brought us a VHS copy of the film just before Christmas in case we wanted to watch it. One bright afternoon, during one of Nick's lucid days, we watched Philadelphia curled up beside one another. Nick lucidity only lasted for 75 minutes before he lapsed into a deep morphine sleep. I continued to watch the film and when it ended, I was overwhelmed with terror, knowing the weeks ahead might resemble this film's final death scene, and Nick actually dying of AIDS. It was a profoundly emotional wake-up call for me. My bubble had suddenly burst.

Nick had been resolute in his instructions to Dr. Tony and me that he didn't want pain at the end of his life. Tony arranged for the at-home morphine drip to keep the ever-intensifying pain at bay. Nick spent much of January in a stupor, mellow and pain-free.

It was just after 11 a.m., on Friday, February 2, 1995, when I heard the phone. Mum had obviously grabbed it in the kitchen after the second ring. Nick's health had rapidly deteriorated in the past forty-eight hours. Although we'd made adoption inquiries a major focus during our life together, Nick knew he wouldn't live to see a child placed in his arms. Exactly six months after leaving the hospital, Nick lay in a haze from morphine, surrounded by love; intellectually we all knew death was close at hand but emotionally none of us was ready for the *grim reaper* to arrive.

Mum walked in with the portable phone, saying it was a woman calling from the California law firm. I hadn't heard from our adoption specialist for several weeks and expected this to be just another update on our file.

Diane asked, "How is Nick today?" There was excitement in her voice. She knew his health status was precarious. I told her he was comatose because of the high doses of morphine. She was silent for a moment. She'd lost several good friends, including her brother and his companion, to AIDS over the last decade. Then, in a vibrant tone, she proceeded to tell me that she had received confirmation just an hour before about a possible baby for us. Without taking a breath between sentences, she continued to say that a twenty-two-year-old student, five-and-a-half months' pregnant, had chosen our profile for her baby. I told her to wait just a moment, so I could put the phone up to Nick's ear. My hand was shaking I was so excited.

I positioned the portable beside his ear and grabbed the bedside phone, so I could continue to listen as well. "Hi, Nick, it's Diane. I have good news and I hope you can hear me." She gave a quick synopsis of what she had just said to me, then continued, "This young woman is a grad student at a midwestern college and is five-and-a-half months' pregnant. The tests have shown the fetus is developing normally and we can expect this baby to be healthy. She read your profile and decided, regardless of Nick's worsening health, that she wants the two of you to have this baby. Her brother was gay, and a Jesuit, and he died of AIDS a few years ago. "She told us her brother's greatest regret was not having had children. Choosing you to have this baby is her way of fulfilling her dead brother's wish to be a parent." Then there was a pause on the other end of the line. "David, do you think Nick understood what I just said?"

I was thrilled and feeling more emotionally anchored to Nick than I had for months. We were going to have a child. "Yes, Diane," I responded from the periphery of my dreamy state. "I am sure he understood."

I told Diane he was unresponsive, so we were keeping a bedside vigil. Her legal veneer shattered, and I could hear her crying on the other end of the phone. "Let me know when Nick dies, David. Give him a hug goodbye from me and please keep telling him about his baby."

I hung up the phone not knowing whether to laugh, cry or put a birth announcement in every Toronto paper! Excitedly I shared this information with Mum and we reconvened by Nick's bedside, outwardly willing him to follow God's voice and go home to Heaven when the time was right.

The afternoon passed uneventfully. Mary, Nick's mom, called from Guelph several times, each time relieved to hear her son was still alive. The DiCicco family was congregating at Mary and Jim's home for supper and to wait by the phone together. I had given them hourly updates and spoke to Mary several times about staying close to the phone as Nick's vital signs were decreasing by the hour. By 8 p.m., Mum was tired and left Nick's bedside to rest her back. I continued to sit quietly; a nurse was staying with us for a few days to help with Nick's care. She looked concerned and frequently took Nick's blood pressure and monitored his pulse. She told me his vitals were slowing down, but while I heard her words I still thought a miracle would happen. For most of the day she had suggested I give Nick permission to let go and move on. I paid lip service to this advice, saying, "Let go Nick. Go into the light when you're ready. I'll be okay." But I never believed that he would die soon. I imagined that by 11 p.m. everyone would be off to bed and I'd crawl in beside Nick and we'd see another sunrise together. It was blissful and spiritual lying beside him. I repeated over and over that he shouldn't stay behind for me if it was his appointed time to meet God, to just let go whenever he was ready. I felt like a fraud telling him to let go of this world while I prayed silently for the Angel of Death to pass us by for at least one more night.

At 8:28 p.m., I got off the bed and told the nurse I was going to get a cup of coffee from the kitchen. I hadn't moved in two hours and my back was sore. I patted Nick's knee and jokingly said, "I'll be back in a few minutes, honey. Don't go anywhere while I'm gone."

I walked to the kitchen, past Mum reading in a living room chair, and poured myself a mug of coffee, then looked across the lake as I walked slowly past the living room windows. Swirls of snow were eerily dancing across the ice because of high winds. As I walked back into our bedroom, the nurse was holding Nick's wrist. She looked up at me through tears and quietly said, "Nick is getting ready to go."

My coffee mug fell to the floor and I leapt onto the bed and nestled down beside Nick. I could hear air being exhaled from his lips, but I couldn't feel his wrist pulse. Oblivious to anything but him, I held Nick close and whispered in his ear, "Breathe, Nick, breathe. I lied. I'm not ready to let go. Please don't go, Nick."

Being an experienced palliative-care nurse, she touched my shoulder with her hand and softly murmured in my ear, "He's already in that tunnel of light and he wants to go home, David. Just hug him and tell him you love him. Remember, hearing is the last sense to go, so keep talking to him." With that she walked out into the living room and closed the door.

For every second of those frantic first few minutes I lay beside Nick I wondered if I should begin CPR. I couldn't grasp that he was going or was gone. Why did he wait until I left his bedside to take me seriously about letting go? I didn't want him to go. His body continued to gasp and exhale for 20 minutes before his body finally lay still, and his eyes were like lights that had been turned out suddenly signalling that he had moved on. Thirty minutes or so must have passed before Mum entered the room. We cried in unison, each touching Nick's hand and silently saying goodbye. Jenny, our oldest golden retriever, had been lying across the end of our bed most of the night, keeping Nick's feet warm. As if perfectly timed and choreographed for a movie, she lifted her head and uttered a pitiful, low-pitched, funereal howl to tell the world her master had gone to his final rest.

As per Nick's instructions, after being embalmed he was waked in his chapel at Woodhaven for two days before being moved to Toronto to have his Jesuit brothers conduct the funeral service. The two-day wake at Woodhaven made us all feel better able to cope with Nick's funeral. I just couldn't have imagined leaving Nick behind each night in a sterile funeral home. We had been able to toast his memory, sit in our house-coats sipping coffee by the coffin, have private moments of prayer in the chapel and talk to him anytime day or night as we slowly adjusted to the reality of his death.

I called Diane at the California law firm to inform her Nick had died only hours after she told us the good news of the baby. Diane said she would tell the young woman about Nick's death and relay his excitement upon hearing she had chosen us to have her baby. Although I was still in shock over Nick, I was overjoyed at the thought of a little Nicholas or Nicole being born four months from now.

Nick's funeral was held at Our Lady of Lourdes Catholic Church in Toronto, which held six hundred people; besides family and friends, the pews and aisles were packed full of his students, associates, Jesuits from across the country. It was a magnificent tribute and very moving for Nick's parents and siblings to see the impact he'd had on so many over his short 39 years on earth.

During that first week after his death I kept myself busy answering well-wishers, returning unused medical supplies, sending out death notices to insurance companies, banks and government registry offices. I walked through our house talking to Nick as if he were standing beside me. It was comforting to think of him still at Woodhaven. I talked about missing him and shared just about every thought that came into my head. The reality of the baby news had my head spinning. I spoke three times that week with Diane and told her this baby would carry Nick's name. I put together a list of necessary renovations required to make the house baby-welcoming. Which room would be converted into a nursery? What colour should I paint the walls? I immediately hired two local carpenters to convert two bedrooms into one bigger nursery beside our Master bedroom. Somehow, walking around the house chattering on like an idiot about baby preparations, asking Nick what he thought about this or that helped me get through that first fifteen days after the funeral.

Three weeks later, Diane called me just after 3 p.m. She had terrible news. The young pregnant woman had been in a car accident, which had brought on labour. At twenty-six weeks old, a baby girl had been delivered alive at the accident scene, but she had died eight hours later in hospital. Losing Nick had ripped my guts to shreds and now, only weeks after his funeral, I was losing our baby. She was baptized Nicole thirty minutes before she slipped away peacefully into the night and hopefully into Nick's waiting arms. The hope and love I had for a future baby were dashed. Thoughts of this child had become my life preserver in the days and weeks following Nick's death. Was God listening to my prayers? What had I done to make God turn away from me?

CHAPTER TEN
MICHAEL

IN APRIL 1995 THE TORONTO-DOMINION Bank sent me a letter stating they believed Nick had lied about his HIV status on the mortgage insurance application. It only took a few weeks for handwriting analysis to prove the bank wrong. Nick was a southpaw and the analysis established that the person who filled in the insurance application had been right-handed. Yet my claim was still being refused by the bank and I had to shame TD publicly to get some action on the matter. I hired a lawyer who was media-savvy and he arranged for me to be interviewed by the *Toronto Star* and the *Globe and Mail* about this case. Before those stories went to print, I appeared on *Canada AM* and came out as a gay man on national TV. I wasn't embarrassed about being gay however a small circle of friends and family knowing about my life was in stark contrast to having everyone in Canada now being privy to my sexuality and my fight against the bank over its refusal to honour my late husband's mortgage insurance. The bank initially made the issue that Nick was gay, but the backlash from vocal gay organizations was immediate, so they changed course, maintaining the problem was that Nick hadn't disclosed he was HIV positive in his application. This case made for some juicy, attention-getting national news headlines in the early summer of 1995.

Lindalee Tracey, Peter Raymont, Lynn Cunningham and numerous other Sandy Lake friends joined me in protesting this injustice, spending a long lunch hour marching outside the TD office on Toronto's Bay

Street. We had signs and yelled through bullhorns, asking how it was possible in 1995 that a major Canadian bank could use the gay card to justify not paying out on a mortgage claim by the same-sex spouse of a TD mortgage holder. The TD Bank security guards finally attempted to curtail us and force us off the sidewalk just in time for the news cameras to begin recording; we made the six o'clock news. Ten months later I dropped the case—the bank had more lawyers and money than I did, and I had to preserve what little financial integrity I had left.

Meanwhile, for eighteen months after Nick's death, Woodhaven was in a constant state of renovation. It grew from a three-bedroom operation into a five-suite country lodge. Money was coming in sufficiently to pay the bills and keep me in the black. I loved being the proprietor and spent most of my nights on the computer devising marketing and advertising schemes to reach a wider range of clients. Woodhaven radio advertisements played on CFMX 96.3, airing many times each day using the jingle, 'David and his five Golden Retrievers look forward to welcoming new guests and their pets to Woodhaven on Sandy Lake.' By the end of the summer of 1996, getting me back into the dating scene became an obsession of several good friends. I'd had some interested men telephone me, but I didn't take their offers for a date in downtown Toronto serious– most of those first phone conversations ended soon after I stated that if they didn't want to pursue parenthood with me, there was no point in having a first date. No one seemed too interested in joining my rebellious quest to shift society's outlook about gay men and women becoming parents via the adoption option. I kept focused on building Woodhaven into a sustainable business operation and my quest to adopt children, lots of children!

Telephone calls to American adoption firms became a daily routine for me in October. Nick had been dead for twenty months and I was no further ahead in my mission to be a parent. Every day I would phone Toronto to speak with, or leave explicit long messages for, various officials within all branches of the CAS.

I cleaned out closets in preparation for winter and found old scarves of Nick's in a drawer. I sniffed them in hopes of smelling his scent. Then a thunderbolt: I realized I couldn't *remember* his scent. Was I sniffing musty old scarf smells or was it the aging aroma of Nick lingering on his clothes? I panicked and rushed to pull some of his sweaters from my cupboard—there was no noticeable smell. I knew I was losing touch with Nick's physical presence. The time had come to let go.

A few weeks into November 1996, I received a supper invitation in the mail from a Fraternity friend in Toronto. I'd known Frank for years and I telephoned to find out more about his dinner party.

Supper, he explained, was only a ruse to get me to meet some of his single friends. A month earlier I would have been insulted by this invitation but now I sensed the time was right for me to get away from Woodhaven and my self-imposed hermit existence. I asked about the fellows I would be meeting. Frank refused to provide much information other than the fact that both men were outdoor types, and each was interested in meeting me. Frank had told them about the 'Woodhaven Widower' before sending me the invitation. I told him I would be pleased to meet his friends. Since Frank and I would both be attending a mutual friend's eightieth birthday party in a few days, I suggested we sit at the same table.

Our mutual friend, Bob Grimson, eighty years old, with mischief in his eyes and the soul of a teenager, was an icon in the Fraternity movement. A retired businessman living in Rosedale, Bob was a collector of well-known Canadian artwork and a generous supporter of the gay business community. Since our first meeting ten years earlier, I'd always known him to have younger gay men around him, acting as their mentor. Bob had been an astute businessman in Toronto between the late 1940s and the end of the 1970s. Gay bars were a big business in the 1970s and one of Bob's many claims to fame had been his ownership of the Quest, the first gay-owned/operated bar in Toronto. Bob's entrepreneurial success, his kind heart and his generous benevolence made him an icon within many circles of Toronto's gay community.

Bob captivated his audiences of younger Fraternity members with stories of police raids on bars and private homes in the late 1940s to break up alleged gay parties. In the 1950s Rosedale's closeted gay and lesbian socialites would invite gay men and women to closed-door parties in mansions north of Bloor Street. Men and women would arrive in cabs together but once inside, the men stayed on the main floor while the women would head upstairs for their private party. If the police arrived, then everyone would find their assigned opposite-sex partners and pretend that the party was straight. Bob told me stories of entertaining Hollywood stars who would come to Toronto regularly to enjoy the gay house-party circuit of the 1960s. At age eighty, he continued to play tennis four times each week and could whip most younger opponents. Nick and I had thoroughly enjoyed Bob's friendship and I had remained in close contact with him since Nick's death. Bob was very encouraging of my efforts to adopt, saying often that if he was only forty years younger he would be leading the charge for legalizing adoption by gay men and women.

Bob's birthday party was spectacular and a virtual who's who of the Canadian theatre and gay community were in attendance. It was a momentous evening with many well-wishers and friends, and I felt honoured and grateful to have been invited. I'd had a great time and received a few calls early the next week from fellows to whom I'd been introduced during the event. None really grabbed my attention. I was looking forward to the singles supper at Frank's condo. I had been spending loads of time on my NordicTrack exercise equipment since Nick's death. I was a svelte 170 lbs again and went on a spending spree to buy new clothes to dazzle my two blind dates.

I had been at Frank's for only a short while when the first of the two men rang the buzzer. It didn't take long for me to realize that there was no spark between Robert and me. "This could be a long evening," I murmured to myself. Surely Frank must have had some inkling of my tastes in men. But he had gone overboard with preparations, with attention to every dramatic detail; I wasn't about to tell him I was disappointed with Bachelor Number One. Small talk filled the room and I began to unwind with my second glass of wine. I certainly wasn't interested in this self-centered urban accountant/gym bunny and hoped the next guest would be more my type. Although I wasn't desperate to meet someone, I was ready to move forward and ease into dating opportunities. Becoming a parent remained a dream that never left my consciousness. I was ready to do it alone but having a companion with whom to share that adventure would be ideal.

More than anything, I missed being part of a couple, although I was happy with myself and who I had become and certainly wasn't looking for someone to make me complete. Still, I missed having that right someone to wake up next to and hoped I could have something like the love I'd had with Nick. I really did enjoy my privacy and would never lose myself in someone else's identity. But I could feel parenthood nearing, and as discouraging as the adoption quest had been so far, I clung to the hope that I'd meet someone who would share my vision of a future with children, dogs and country living.

Just as Frank made the rounds with a cheese tray, there was a second knock at the door. "That must be Michael," said Frank as he flew past me to open the door and greet Bachelor Number Two.

Michael walked in with a big grin, handed Frank a bottle of red wine and removed his coat. I was out of view as he entered the room and without missing a beat, Bachelor Number One said, "Hello, Mike, nice to see you again."

Frank looked at the two of them, chortled and asked, "And how, pray tell, do the two of you know one another?"

Both men laughed about having dated a few weeks ago. Frank turned his attention to me and pulled Michael around the corner, so he could introduce us. Immediately I thought he looked like the movie star Tom Selleck. He put out his hand to shake mine, smiled politely, turned back to face Robert and began talking about the coincidence of meeting at Frank's. Red flags immediately began waving in my mind. These guys like one another, so why am I here?

As if Frank had read my mind, he asked if I would help him in the kitchen. I followed him, and he opened the oven door and began making low-level noises, so his whispers wouldn't be heard in the living room.

"So, what do you think so far? Anyone stand out?" He peered eagerly into my face to see which one I'd state was the fairest in the land. "Did you know they knew each other when you invited them to meet me?" I replied in a whisper.

"Who would have thought that they had dated!" Frank said in mock disgust. "Anyway, that aside, who do you think is more your type —tell me quick so the hors d'oeuvres don't get cold."

I whispered that Michael was more my sort and that his full moustache gave him a handsome, roguish air. That was enough for Frank. He smiled and said, "My yenta instincts are working. I had a feeling you'd choose Michael the moment you met him."

Returning to the living room, Frank announced that supper would be in half an hour, so we had lots of time to sit and chat. I felt a tad awkward sitting between Michael and Robert, thanks to Frank. But the moment silence fell on the room Frank would pipe up with another quip about something or other and conversation would resume for another few minutes. Michael began to warm to me as he asked about Woodhaven, quizzing me about the workings of my lodge, its size, was it gay-only, how far from Peterborough was Sandy Lake, and much more. I asked if he knew the area and Michael responded that Peterborough was his hometown. Astonished, I said I too had grown up there and asked which high school he had attended.

We discovered that we had gone to the same high school, Kenner Collegiate, albeit four years apart. Now, conversation flowed easily between Michael and me, with lots of questions about people and places we both knew. Had he gone to the YMCA? Had I been a competitive swimmer? Had he been involved in musical productions at Kenner? Did I like being back in the Peterborough area?

It was Robert's turn to help Frank in the kitchen and I found myself staring into Michael's deep green eyes, observing his extraordinarily long eyelashes and the perfectly manicured moustache that covered his upper lip. His cologne was appealing also.

Frank and Robert returned to the room with plates laden with food. Robert set one plate on the table and said, "Here you are, Michael," then immediately sat down beside Michael. Like an ever-watchful grandmother, Frank took note of Robert's positioning. He winked at me as he placed my plate beside him on the opposite side of the table, so I was facing Michael.

The meal, conversation and wine were superb. Robert travelled a lot and spoke about the exotic places he'd visited. A teacher, Michael talked about his many March-break vacations to Mexico, Cuba and Aruba. I asked if anyone in the room liked winter and only Michael showed an interest in the snow season and cross-country skiing. In fact, he had been looking to buy lakefront property up in the Kawartha's for several years, hoping someday to build a cottage he could access year-round.

Frank inquired about my dogs, as I had often joked with him when he'd call that I had been out scouring the woods for my runaways.

"Who is looking after the goldens tonight?" he asked, trying to keep Michael's attention on me.

Before I could reply, Michael asked, "Are your dogs golden retrievers?"

I said I had five auburn-coloured American goldens and he sat back in his chair, folded his arms, looked directly into my eyes and said, "I grew up with American goldens. They're wonderful dogs."

"There aren't many around who know about the reddish-coloured variety. Do you own a dog now?" Michael said his ex-lover had a sheltie named Kip and since he continued to share an apartment with him, it was almost like having a dog.

Frank, changed the course of conversation again to the bed and breakfast business, asking how Woodhaven was shaping up. I presented an overview of my marketing strategy and described how I hoped radio advertising would give me a greater market share of dog-friendly people who wanted to enjoy a country retreat.

"I'm sure you'd get many people who live in city apartments and can't have pets, who would enjoy coming to that type of lodge as well," said Michael.

I had been observing Michael for almost two hours but still hadn't been able to figure out how he and Robert were connected. Every time I spoke, Robert had to one-up me with a story about himself. I wasn't going to play that game so after dessert I excused myself and said I had to get back on the road to Woodhaven.

As Frank saw me to the door I thanked him for the wonderful evening and in turn shook hands with Robert and Michael. I had no indication from Michael whether he was more interested in Robert or me, but I figured since they both lived in Toronto they'd continue to date. I felt like an odd man out at this singles' supper and just wanted to get back to the comfort of my slippers, the dogs and the lake.

Michael called on a Sunday night two week's after Frank's dinner party. Skeptically, I asked if he had tired of Bachelor Number One and was now calling the consolation prize. He laughed nervously and said he'd had one date with Robert two weeks prior to supper at Frank's and wasn't interested in having a second. Being very shy, Michael said it had taken him all this time to get up the nerve to call me. Hmm, good response, I thought.

Upon hearing he was interested in me rather than Robert, I decided to try to break the ice with humour: "So you think you want to date me. Are you sure you're up to the challenge, Michael? I'm not some easy, sleazy Toronto ghetto tart who puts out on the first date." We laughed in unison and I was glad he'd found it amusing, too.

Michael said he would like to drive up and go for a long walk with me and the dogs around Sandy Lake. We spent thirty minutes on the phone discussing country life versus city life and he asked lots of questions about being a bed and breakfast owner. He was engaging and sincere and I felt eager to have a face-to-face date.

Michael telephoned me Tuesday evening, just minutes after I'd spent an hour on the phone with my favorite cousin Maribeth who felt it was good for me to have reached a point of wanting to date.

"The next man of your dreams isn't going to drive up your mile-long laneway some Sunday afternoon," she'd said. "You've got to get out there and let people know you're ready to meet someone special again." I had yet to tell her about Michael's call, so I took hold of that moment to mention that the man of my future dreams might indeed be driving up my laneway within five days. I promised I'd call her after my date with Michael and give her the full scoop.

A few days later, Michael called to firm up a time when he should arrive on Sunday afternoon. I joked that he was calling because the sound of my voice was such a turn-on. He laughed and confessed that he was eager to spend some quiet country time with me in my Woodhaven world. He asked if we could take the dogs for a walk around the property at some point, as he really enjoyed being outdoors and watching dogs run through the bush.

My weekend guests departed Sunday around noon and I'd just finished cleaning the guest rooms when the dogs started barking. A quick glance in the mirror, a finger brush of my hair, a quick gargle of mouthwash and I was as ready as I could be to welcome Michael.

I let the dogs out and they bounded excitedly to his car. Michael wasn't fazed in the least by five very boisterous large dogs, each whimpering and jostling the others out of the way to be first to jump up and give him a wet lick. It had rained the night before, leaving puddles on the gravel driveway, but there was a hint of winter in the air. I didn't want to get my Birkenstocks wet so I just waited in the open doorway for him to walk to the house. Holding a covered plate high above his head in one hand, he finally reached the door smiling, his food and himself having managed to survive the gauntlet of excited canines. In a country setting Michael looked even more ruggedly handsome than he had over supper in Toronto. I began to fantasize about a sudden snowstorm forcing him to stay over tonight. It felt almost too good to be in his company.

He said the drive up was refreshing, just being out of the city and into the country made him relax and come alive. I was impressed with the homemade apple cake he'd brought along. "After a weekend of looking after guests I thought you might appreciate someone else's cooking."

I gave him the grand tour and told him I had just finished cleaning guest rooms minutes before his car pulled into the parking lot. Nick's Suite, I explained, had been built as a chapel but was now a much-preferred guest room, adding that I was bored with the arrangement of its furniture and was interested in spiffing it up. So, we spent the first hour of our date rearranging furniture and attaching a patchwork quilt to the wall behind the bed. I found myself frequently looking at him and checking out his physique.

The dogs were anxious for a walk by the time we finished. We visited the entire property as I blabbed on about my Sandy Lake neighbours and what a great community I had landed in. I asked Michael many questions about himself, and he asked me many more. The sky became quite dark, the air chilled noticeably and we retreated to the house. As we neared Woodhaven, large flakes of snow began to blow around us. I had been waiting for snow since November 1, traditionally the day I usually start decorating for Christmas.

With a snowstorm outside, the dogs nestled in a circle by the fireplace, some twitching in their dreams, others fast asleep. Michael wandered around the house, investigating various rooms, while I made a batch of hot apple cider. Two hours after he arrived, we joined each other on the sofa. What a busy afternoon it had been of impromptu decorating, walking and talking. The next few hours flew by as we continued to learn about family members, career and personal goals. Michael asked about Nick and his family, and life post-Nick, the Fraternity and about adoption roadblocks I was encountering.

"It isn't in my nature to give a quick overview of anything. Are you sure you want to hear about my adoption struggles?" I asked. Michael nodded and said he was very interested in hearing it all.

We had two pieces of his apple cake each and three more cups of cider before I finally stopped talking. It was 6:30 p.m. before I realized Michael had been trapped on the sofa listening to me for hours. After a bathroom break, Michael returned to the sofa and sat closer to me than he had previously. A bit unnerved yet very excited by his closeness, I smiled and nervously nudged him saying, "Sniff some catnip while you were in the bathroom?"

Michael smiled, and with the mounting sexual tension of the moment broken, he suddenly launched into a very serious topic.

"I would love to be a parent. I went into education because I enjoy teaching children new concepts and ways of looking at the world. I couldn't begin to imagine how great fatherhood must be. I also can't imagine being a single parent in today's world but I'm sure the rewards are worth the time and effort."

I sensed some yet-unspoken conflicts about his own sexuality, his family, and about the direction of his life. He explained that his parents had divorced when he was seventeen and that his mother's departure from the house was much more of a relief for him than an upset. Michael said his childhood years had been confusing and frustrating, always knowing he was different. In his earliest recollections he knew he was gay. His mother had constantly pushed him into being more sociable, but Michael had resisted for fear of people discovering his sexual orientation. His relationship with his dad got better once his mother left the family home. Michael described his mother as not being particularly warm and their relationship was quite arm's length and formal. However, the relationship with his father was much more open and friendly. He said both parents had remarried and that family get-togethers, infrequent as they were, always involved both parents and their new spouses.

I was immediately struck by how emotionally vague his remarks about his family seemed to be. He'd found it easier to remove himself psychologically than confront them with the news that he was gay. There was a palpable suffering, a loneliness in his eyes, as I listened to him talk about his family. His distress seemed to stem from the absence of deep friendships in and out of his family unit; there was no mention of good friends, couples or singles, gay or straight. As open as he was, Michael probably wasn't aware of how lonely and alone he sounded. I wanted to take him in my arms to protect him and explain how he was missing so much of the world. I could sense a soul ready for an awakening.

Michael asked me about my relationship with my family. I told him how my mother, almost eighty-two, was an integral part of my life as both a parent and a friend, supportive of anything I desired to do with my life. I said she was excited about the prospect of becoming a grandmother; however, her enthusiasm had suffered somewhat over the years as more and more adoption roadblocks cropped up. I admitted that I felt she had resigned herself to be the mother of two childless adult children and that being a grandparent probably wasn't in the cards for her.

My sister, Karen, was a different limb on the family tree, I explained. She had become involved with a 22-yr-old man when she was just eighteen. He was a leftover hippie from the 1970s who just never seemed to fit in. He had turned away from his Baha'i roots to become a born-again United Pentecostal Christian. After my sister embraced Pentecostalism, she'd distanced herself from me because of her conservatism and my lack of being born-again. When I finally told her I was gay, she ranted on that the devil himself had wrapped his arms around me and swallowed my soul. She married Dale, much to my disappointment at the time, but over the years I came to love him like a brother. He had grown in his view of the world and life, while Karen hadn't budged from her narrow church doctrine.

Feeling strangled and suppressed, Dale eventually walked away from his Pentecostal ways and my sister six months after our dad died in 1988. He had been the provider and Karen the homemaker. With few skills, she moved in with my mother and went to Trent University to become a teacher. She was bitter, which had a lot to do with her feelings of abandonment by her birth mother, her husband and me, due to my being gay, plus our father's death. I told Michael that my sister had provided no support to me when Nick was dying of AIDS. Nonetheless I had great respect for the way she had picked up the pieces of her life, returned to university at age thirty and was embracing her new career as an elementary school teacher.

There was a wonderfully warm look of understanding that crossed Michael's face, reflecting how saddened I was by the loss of Karen in my life, especially considering how close we had been growing up. "That must be an agonizing juggling act for your mother," Michael noted wisely.

"Mum's been a wonderfully insightful and non-judgmental supporter of us both, and she's fiercely loyal to our family. I'm sure it would be painful for any mother to have her only two adult children at such odds with one another."

There was a silence as he digested what I'd been saying. The sound of the wind hurling wet snowflakes at the picture window indicated the early evening storm was worsening. I suggested Michael consider getting back to Toronto before the storm forced him to call in sick tomorrow. Despite having my wish of a snowstorm come true, I now was concerned for his safety.

Two and a half hours later Michael called to say he had arrived safely in Toronto. We agreed that there was a strong mutual attraction and he asked if he could visit the following weekend, but I told him I was hosting women and their children from a shelter who'd be arriving for Christmas on the next Saturday, December 23. I explained in detail that after Nick died I didn't want to spend Christmas surrounded by family and felt instead if I opened my place up to people in need, I wouldn't feel as bad over the holidays. It worked that first year after Nick's death and I was continuing with this new tradition. Only men having had a recent police check could enter my place while the shelter residents were visiting. We could see one another the following Friday, but by noon on Saturday he would have to be out of the lodge until after Boxing Day. Twice that week he called. Each time we spoke I could feel myself wanting to know him better. I could tell he was a kind-hearted, loyal man, and his charm and good looks were very appealing.

He arrived for a late supper on Friday night and I knew in my heart that he was about to become a permanent fixture in my life. He'd brought along a present. I was a bit embarrassed that I hadn't spent any time buying a gift for him and explained that all my Christmas budget was going toward providing gifts and food for the moms and their children. I had told Michael that I usually drank eight to nine cups of coffee per day and that the seat of my jeep had coffee stains from me driving with flimsy paper cups. My first gift from Michael was an Eddie Bauer deluxe travel coffee mug.

I said to myself, this guy's a keeper.

CHAPTER ELEVEN

MAGGIE AND CATHERINE

I WANTED TO SHARE SO much with Michael. He was always asking me about the special guests who had come to Woodhaven in the past and what type of people could he expect to meet if he became a regular fixture. We sat in the living room and looked out at the snow blanketing the trees on the horizon as I told him about one pair of guests and their Pembroke Welsh Corgi named Chubby.

June 1994 had been a magnificent month for business at our new bed and breakfast. Singles, couples, gay and straight, were making reservations at Woodhaven, seventy percent of them dog-owning families looking for a place that welcomed pets. Nick had been feeling quite good for the past month, with few recurring bouts of AIDS-related illness.

We decided to offer free holidays to the exhausted staff of Casey House, Toronto's AIDS hospice, and to volunteers with many other charities. This benevolence fed Nick's desire to live his faith. I, too, enjoyed the feeling when we provided a much-needed holiday for people who gave so much to others through their professional and volunteer work. Also, providing holidays to Casey House staff allowed me to pick the brains of the front-line workers in the fight against AIDS to learn how best to fight the battle to keep Nick alive.

A frequent guest that month was Jane, a redheaded Scot, who had been a nurse at Casey House since its inception. Jane was a tall woman who walked with a mission in her stride. Even on holiday, she moved at the speed of lightning, always sure and determined of her destination, whether walking down the hill to get in a canoe and paddle around the lake or marching down the hall to the hot-tub room for a thirty-minute soak. Jane had inquired if she could invite friends, a Barrie-area couple, to visit her for the afternoon and we said we didn't mind at all. Any time that guests invited friends to visit them at Woodhaven meant free advertising for us.

Jane's friends arrived just after lunch. They were a quiet, older couple, apparently in their early sixties, introduced to us simply as Maggie and Catherine. Our dogs wouldn't leave them alone, even when I tried to shoo them away. Maggie said they loved dogs and had a six-month-old Welsh Corgi at home. I told them that we had had two Welsh Corgi's for seventeen years and suggested that they bring their pup up to visit us any time they were in the area.

A few days later, I received a call from Maggie curious about availability for them and their dog to come for three days over the July long weekend.

Our first July holiday weekend as owners of a country bed and breakfast was full of fun and exciting people. We had a gay couple with a black lab, a heterosexual couple with an infant daughter, and Maggie and Catherine with their pup named Chubby. Rick and Dylan arrived late Friday night with their dog, Piper. The remaining two couples turned up an hour after lunch on Saturday, within fifteen minutes of one another. After human and dog introductions were completed, everyone headed down to the waterfront in pursuit of hot sun and cool water. Soon everyone was swimming or sunning themselves on the deck. Chubby was splashing around on the shallow beach, challenging crawfish that came across his path and keeping us in stitches. It was late afternoon before anyone stirred from the waterfront.

Supper was going to be barbecued shish kebabs. Nick oversaw putting a salad together using his mother's secret herb dressing recipe. By 8:30 p.m., the guests were crammed into the small, screened-in deck. Sandi and Peter put their infant daughter in a portable pram and rocked her to sleep as the sun began setting over the horizon. Within ninety minutes, we were all yawning. Nick had excused himself thirty minutes earlier and I was now ready for bed, too.

Maggie and Catherine were the only guests staying for Sunday-night supper. Sandi, Peter and their baby were heading into Peterborough to have a meal with relatives, while Rick and Dylan, celebrating their eleventh anniversary, were off for a quiet romantic supper at a nearby steakhouse. All seven dogs were totally exhausted and lay in clusters around the dining-room table as Nick prepared an Italian meal for Catherine and Maggie. As we sat around the table after supper, Nick asked Maggie how they came to know Jane, the nurse from Casey House.

Maggie told us that Jane was the membership coordinator of a lesbian social group they had joined twelve months ago, and a great friendship had arisen quickly among the three of them. I realized we knew very little about Maggie or Catherine. The entire weekend had gone by without much discussion about what each of the guests did for a living. I asked Catherine how she'd met Maggie, how long they had been together and what they worked at during the week.

Catherine smiled at us, poured herself another glass of wine and then began to tell us about the life she shared with Maggie. They had both emigrated from England in the late 1950s, Maggie coming from Lancashire in 1956 and Catherine from Bournemouth in 1957. Both landed jobs as teachers in the Catholic school system. Catherine laughed as she reminisced about meeting Maggie for the first time at a Catholic primary teachers' meeting in June of 1958. Several new schools were being opened in Port Credit and Oakville, and Toronto-area teachers were being recruited for available positions in these towns. Maggie and Catherine were both hired for the same school in Port Credit: Maggie teaching Grade Six and Catherine, Grade Two. During the summer of 1958, they ran into one another at school meetings and by the first day of classes in September, each knew that there was something special about the other. Catherine said that being lesbian, Catholic and a teacher wasn't an acceptable combination in those days, so they were very discreet. By early autumn, they had secretly dated enough to know that they were in love.

They found two apartments in the same building where several other teachers lived, not far from the school. The single teachers at their school did a lot of socializing and for a few years, they had an active social life, going to movies as a group, belonging to bowling leagues and, of course, going to mass on Sunday. Eventually, all the single teachers got married or left the school and Maggie and Catherine became the last two unmarried teachers on the staff. Maggie got an offer in 1963 to change to a new school just a few miles away. They agreed that a change of school for one of them meant that they wouldn't always be known as the "last two single women" on staff.

Maggie moved to a new apartment building when she changed schools, making sure that there was no room for idle gossip within teacher circles about their "best friendship." They still spent every night together and were apart only during Christmas vacations when both flew home to England to visit family. To ward off suspicion or malicious gossip, they wouldn't even travel on the same flight.

In 1965, a retiring teacher at her school suggested that Catherine buy the duplex that she was about to sell. Catherine and Maggie discussed the idea for weeks and finally decided to pool their resources and purchase the duplex together. In the summer of 1965, they moved in a week apart, furnished two households but used Maggie's side of the duplex as their "matrimonial" home. The dilemma for them was how to arrange easy yet discreet access between the two sides of the building. In late August 1958 they had a steel fire door installed in the common wall of the basement. Maggie and Catherine's social circles had diminished considerably but they both maintained a few friends of their own, mostly other teachers. They made sure that none of them were mutual friends. And so it continued for almost three decades. Each woman would drive her own car to work every day. They shopped for groceries separately but shared all the food in their cupboards. Maggie told us that she couldn't count the number of times she would be making supper for the two of them, run out of ingredients and run down to the basement's secret door in order to rummage around in Catherine's kitchen to find more butter, spices or eggs.

Nick spoke up finally and said that he, too, had been a Catholic schoolteacher during his many years as a Jesuit priest and he understood their need for total discretion and secrecy.

Considering the Catholic church's stance on homosexuality, had their love affair been discovered they would have been fired and publicly humiliated. Maggie said that they both had a deep faith and didn't want to lose their church community or routines. And so, they continued until 1991, when they retired with full pensions.

"So," I said, "have you broken down the wall between the apartments of your duplex to make it into one big home for the two of you and Chubby?"

Maggie said that the day that they retired they put the duplex up for sale. And when it sold they relocated to a small hamlet outside of Barrie, where they built a three-bedroom bungalow, complete with a large master bedroom and en suite bathroom with a huge in-the-floor whirlpool. Catherine told us that two weeks after moving into their new home as wife and wife, they went out and bought Chubby from a breeder in Orillia. They quickly discovered the dog breeder had just lost her partner of forty-one years to breast cancer. Their new friend was introducing them to all sorts of couples like themselves who had recently moved to the country to enjoy privacy and retirement.

Maggie asked about us: our life together as a couple, how had we met, what we had studied at university, what professional roads we had traveled. "Nurse Jane" apparently hadn't said anything to them about Nick having AIDS, and he was very forthright in telling them that part of our story. Tears began to stream down Maggie's cheeks and Catherine reached over and took her hand. Within a short while, she excused herself and left the porch to regain her composure. Nick looked at Catherine and said that he was sorry he had upset Maggie. Catherine said that neither of them had known anyone with AIDS. She also said that Maggie was very emotional and that hearing the news about AIDS being part of the Woodhaven team was probably too much for her to handle. Catherine assured us that she would be fine in the morning. Shortly afterward, Catherine excused herself and took Chubby out for a break before bedtime. She said that they would see us at breakfast. I cuddled closer to Nick and we sat silently, enjoying the breezes wafting through the screened porch until our other guests arrived safely back.

The next morning Maggie entered the screened porch where I was sitting with a cup of coffee and the paper. She sat down with a heavy sigh in the wicker chair next to me. She apologized for her behaviour the previous night. I told her it was difficult for some people to hear the news and we probably should have been more careful about telling them Nick had AIDS. Maggie said that she thought the world of us and was so happy to have found a holiday spot like Woodhaven.

"Your library, the two of you, the fact that we can bring Chubby with us to your place—it's a dream come true for us. But hearing that Nick had AIDS really devastated me last night. I don't know much about it except that it is likely he will die from it, right?" She asked this in a way that almost begged me to lie. I told her that there was a very good chance that he would die of the disease, but not for many years. In fact, I told her, a vaccine might only be a few years away. I said that Nick had lost a lot of weight prior to moving to our new country life on Sandy Lake but that he had gained about five pounds in the past six weeks, which was a very good sign.

"Don't worry," I said consolingly, "I'm not letting him die just yet. I expect he'll be around to celebrate your 90th birthday!" Just then, Nick came out to the porch. He smiled warmly at Maggie and she got up and put her arms around him and hugged him close. She told him that she thought he was a wonderful man and she was sorry if her reaction to the AIDS news had upset him at all. I left the porch to give them a while to sit together and talk about AIDS and Nick's general health. I sensed that Maggie was feeling much less anxious when she came into the kitchen thirty minutes later for her second cup of coffee.

After breakfast—waffles smothered in fresh strawberries and whipped cream, porridge with cinnamon, toast and homemade preserves—our guests began to pack up for the trek back to their homes. A warm bond of fellowship followed each car out of the laneway that day. All three couples visited Woodhaven at least once more that summer.

In September, Nick's health began to decline rapidly and his medical team at Sunnybrook prepared me for the worst. They felt he would only live until Thanksgiving. Maggie and Catherine visited us every few weeks during Nick's last months of life. They participated in the mass in his bedroom with our local priest presiding, just three weeks before he died. Maggie's soft sobbing could be heard through the church during the funeral service. They continued to visit me every few weeks, often only staying for twenty or thirty minutes, just long enough for Chubby to run around and pee, before starting the ninety-minute trip back to their home.

They were an integral part of what became the annual Woodhaven Christmas. Not having family of their own, they used the event to shower the moms and kids with thousands of dollars' worth of gifts, borrowing a pick-up truck to deliver them. Maggie and Catherine always arrived a few days in advance of the first group of guests, never staying long enough to meet the moms and tots. They said that this was their way of giving back to the world and that "no one other than God and us needed to know who bought the gifts for these battered souls from the shelter." On the last morning of each group's stay, I would ask the moms to get the children to write or draw thank you notes to Maggie and Catherine.

Tragically, these two angels of mercy, along with six-year-old Chubby, died in a head-on car crash with a drunk driver in September 1999. I know they were visiting angels from God, sent to help me adjust to Nick's death and to show the moms and children from our program the true message most often left out of the season we call Christmas. What a blessing it was to have known them.

CHAPTER TWELVE
A COMMITMENT

IT HAD BEEN AN EMOTIONALLY charged week preparing to host six mothers and seventeen children from a Toronto-area women's shelter. The decision to hold Christmas for strangers again this year provided a philanthropic focus and enabled me to tell friends this effort was part of Nick's legacy. Twenty-three months after his death and I still wasn't entirely ready to let go of him.

I became oddly energized each time I over-extended my gift budget, knowing it meant wider smiles on the faces of the mothers and kids on Christmas morning—I'd spent much of the weeks preceding Christmas buying up age and gender-specific presents for the families who'd be sharing the holiday at Woodhaven.

Friends helped make this project a huge success. Neighbours introduced me to someone who worked with Disney Canada. He sent seven huge boxes crammed full of Disney gift items, ranging from new and classic children's videos to clothing and books. The goods must have been worth $2,000. A group of women from Mum's church put together an envelope of cash to be used to cover food expenses for the families. Another neighbour showed up one afternoon with $200 to be split among the women. She knew from her own experience of leaving an abusive husband, twenty years earlier, just how destitute an abused woman with kids could feel in that moment. Maggie and Catherine bought size-specific clothing for all the families, Barbie dolls, train sets and lots of other high-end toys for every child, plus $50 Hudson Bay gift certificates for each of the mothers as well as an assortment of smaller gift items to put in the mothers' stockings.

The women and children were to arrive at the bus terminal in Peterborough on December 23 and stay for four days. A member of Mum's church in the travel and tourism business, arranged with a tour bus company for a complementary deluxe coach, complete with TVs, to meet the families at the station and drive them to Woodhaven. What a sight to see a huge tour bus rumbling up my laneway. Twelve inches of fresh snow lay on the ground, offering a magical first impression for these special guests.

Each family was given a bedroom of their own; I had cots set up to accommodate everyone. The children were excited about playing in the hot tub. The mothers loved having their own bathroom. Friends and family had arrived the previous week to help bake gingerbread cookies and wrap gifts. There were so many presents they didn't all fit underneath the two eight-foot high Christmas trees.

Getting the children fed and supper on the table for the women took a concerted effort. A few friends had agreed to help at meal times. The children were out of the hot tub only long enough to eat supper and then rushed back into the warm water. After an hour of hot tubbing, I told the children to leave their mothers alone for two hours and put on a video upstairs on the big-screen TV. The kids could go wild up there, I said, but couldn't come down to the dining room while their mothers were eating.

There was a gourmet meal for the moms, compliments of several neighbours. But the women had been cooped up in cramped living quarters in the shelter—they were so happy to be on this country holiday that a meal of hot dogs would have been fine with them.

A bit of wine and the women began to talk openly about their abusive husbands. One woman's husband, a high school principal, had been beating her for years. For two months she had planned her escape with their three children. Four weeks before she had landed at the shelter with her kids. She hoped to be out and into temporary housing soon. Her

husband wasn't cooperating with her in terms of his financial responsi-
bilities and she had never seen a dime of her own money in fifteen years
as a homemaker.

Another woman had emigrated from Hungary with her son a year
ago to wed a wealthy businessman. After they were married, he treated
her like a slave in and out of the bedroom. He told her she would be
deported if he divorced her. As long as he didn't hurt her eleven-year-old
son, she stayed. One night her husband flew into a rage and broke her
nose while driving in the car. At the hospital, the attending doctor discreetly asked if her husband had hit her and she broke down and admitted the abuse. The police were called, and she was escorted home to get
her son and some clothes before being taken to a shelter. She had no
money, worried about deportation constantly, and never left the shelter
for fear of meeting her husband on the street.

Jenny, twenty-nine, mother of three small children, made us all gasp
with her story of abuse and survival. Although she had now moved out
of the shelter and had a good job, Jenny was still getting counselling for
her children and herself. One of the shelter staff had invited her to come
along on this country weekend as a gesture of support for all that she
had overcome.

Jenny had married her high school sweetheart at age nineteen. She'd
come from a home with a sexually and physically abusive father and
a frightened, subservient mother. Jenny's father had forced her to give
him oral sex from the time she was eleven until she was seventeen.
Unfortunately, her husband ended up being bipolar and was institution-
alized several times in the first few years of their marriage. Meanwhile,
Jenny gave birth to three children, all one year apart. Her husband
couldn't keep a job, drank too much and became verbally abusive with
her. The abuse quickly turned physical and by year seven of their marriage he was degrading her sexually. One afternoon in front of the kids,
he threw a tantrum over something and they scuffled in the kitchen.
When she fell to the floor, he dragged her into the bathroom. She
thought he would just rape her but instead he tried to jam her head into
the toilet bowl. Her eldest, a boy, had come to her rescue, hitting his

dad on the head with a broom. He let go of her and began to throttle his son. Shortly afterward the police arrived, having been called by a concerned neighbour.

Escorted by police, Jenny went to a shelter that night with the kids. After fourteen weeks there she was set up in a townhouse and enrolled in a skills program through the government. On welfare, Jenny was getting $1,250 per month, which was just enough for her to drive her car to classes, pay the rent and buy food. There were no extras and her husband had long since disappeared and wasn't paying support. Then the Mike Harris Tories began slashing Ontario welfare payments—Jenny's monthly income dropped to $1,050. She often drank tea while the children shared her portion of supper.

Somehow the Children's Aid Society was notified, perhaps because Jenny's daughter said to her kindergarten teacher, "Mommy doesn't have any food for supper." A social worker suggested the children be placed into foster care until her finances improved. Jenny pleaded with this caseworker to give her a week to borrow the extra money she required so she keep the kids and pay her bills.

From the moment she got married, Jenny stopped having anything to do with her abusive father. Her mother had separated from her father a few years after the birth of Jenny's first child—but unfortunately, her mother had died eighteen months earlier of breast cancer. Jenny hadn't seen her father since her mom's funeral, but through a cousin discovered his whereabouts. Jenny paid him a visit. She explained what had happened in the last six months and she asked him for a short-term loan. He refused. She increased the offer by saying she'd give him fifteen percent interest on the loan. Again, he flatly refused. Jenny sweetened the offer. She'd give him oral sex twice weekly if he'd extend her a loan. He agreed. She left with a letter from him to the social worker stating he would cover the discrepancy in her monthly expenses. Jenny was able to stay in her rented townhouse and keep her kids. She graduated four months later, and a local hospital hired her for a $32,000 IT position through the school's placement program. Jenny never set foot again in her father's house once she got her first pay cheque.

Glued to their seats, everyone was shell-shocked by what they'd heard.

I asked, "Why wouldn't he just give you the money, considering he had already abused you during your teenage years. You'd think he would feel he owed you this money with no strings attached?"

Jenny said her father had been a bastard all his life and he'd die a bastard. Later that night I wrote Mike Harris a letter about the heartache his welfare cuts had caused Jenny, how she had exchanged sex for a loan from her father to make up the welfare shortfall, so her kids wouldn't be thrust into foster care. Four weeks later I got a response from one of the Harris government lieutenants telling me about all the wonderful programs they had initiated to get people off welfare. No one had read my letter.

After four days of gourmet coffee, wine and eggnog by the fire, watching their carefree kids eat hearty meals, cross-country ski, sit in the hot tub and watch videos, the women were sad to leave. All too soon volunteers arrived to ferry the families back to the Peterborough bus terminal. It was time for them to return to their sparse apartments or to the crowded shelter. I had never felt so good about anything as I did about having provided, with the help of so many others, a special memory for these sweet souls.

Michael had volunteered to be one of the drivers to take a family to the bus station. I was glad to see him pull up to the house. I had so much I wished to share with him about this Christmas experience and wanted a few days of downtime alone with him in front of the fireplace. My six-week rule went out the window.

Waking up and seeing Michael sleeping beside me brought back a flood of memories about Nick. I wondered if my deepening feelings for Michael were happening too soon? I knew I was falling in love, yet the word caution kept flashing in front of my eyes. I didn't want to commit yet. I tried to reason with myself that falling in love couldn't happen this fast. Then suddenly it hit me. Why did I think it was impossible to be in love with Michael after knowing him for only four weeks? I'd fallen madly in love with Jason two weeks after he smiled at me in the library at UBC, and a few years later I fell in love with Nick after only three hours of conversation. Did I have a sixth-sense about love?

I wondered how Nick's side of the family would react to me dating, let alone telling them I was in love again. I wouldn't let them disappear from my life.

We spent a wonderful day together enjoying the outdoors. Alone over supper, I shared more about my vision for Woodhaven in the future. I told him I wanted to increase the number of moms' and kids' visits during the year as helping them had affected me immensely. Michael just sat and listened to me, occasionally adding a few suggestions of his own about helping various charities.

While we were cleaning up the kitchen, Michael said he was already in love and wanted to spend every weekend with me. I, too, was feeling good about letting myself love Michael. He was as handsome on the inside as he was on the outside, kind, and he wanted to share my life and be part of the adoption equation. Having dogs on the bed at night didn't bother him either. Who wouldn't love Michael?

Mum was thrilled to hear I'd met someone new. She liked Michael from the moment they met. Michael introduced me to his father and it was easy to see he loved Michael unconditionally and wanted his son to be happy.

By the end of February 1997, Michael and I were considering what we could do to upgrade Woodhaven. I didn't have much cash and told him we would have to pare down his big ideas to fit my meagre budget. Michael said he had been saving to buy a country home like Woodhaven and he'd waited a lifetime to have a lover like me. Michael said if we were going to be together, which we both admitted was right for us, then he would buy into my property, so we would be equal partners, allowing us to do a major renovation over the March break.

Michael felt that what was most necessary was a larger kitchen and a large separate dining room overlooking the lake. It would be the best use of our combined monies. Five days later we had created rough drawings of what a new addition to Woodhaven would look like and what features should be included.

I called in a local contractor to examine these sketches and within two days we agreed on his $120,000 price tag. With the stroke of a pen, the renovations were set to begin the first week of March, when Michael started his spring break. So much, so fast. We had only known one another for three months and he was about to commit his savings for this Woodhaven renovation project.

We decided to gut the master bedroom and the two adjacent smaller bedrooms to create a master with a large en suite bathroom. Our new design included a two-bedroom nursery with a Jack and Jill bathroom in between the children's bedrooms. An antique solid pine door would separate the nursery from the master bedroom. It would allow us quick and easy entry from our bedroom to comfort our kids if they had a nightmare or became sick in the night. Including children's bedrooms into our renovation plan was a testament of Michael's desire to co-adopt children. We were about to get the nursery—it was time to put children in it and become a family.

CHAPTER THIRTEEN

THE OTHER IN-LAWS

I CANCELLED BOOKINGS AT WOODHAVEN from the March break through to the last week in April, the estimated time it would take to complete the renovation work.

The first weekend of the construction was hectic. We dismantled shelves, moved furniture and pulled up carpeting to make way for the builders. Other than Michael's father and brother, Dave—imagine the luck of me having two partners, each with a brother named Dave—I hadn't met anyone else from Michael's family, and encouraged him to invite his mother and step-father to visit the following weekend.

Louise, Michael's mother, and her husband, Bill, operated a business in Whitby. Michael's sister, Peggy, lived in Kingston, where she worked as a therapist. Coincidentally, Peggy was visiting her mother when Michael called to invite them for a visit. I laughed and told Michael that meeting the three of them at one time could be fatal. Laughing himself, he responded, "Fatal for whom?"

We cleaned the lodge thoroughly. When their car appeared in the laneway, Michael dashed to help his mother walk across the ninety feet of slippery parking lot leading to the main entrance, while his sister and stepfather followed cautiously behind them. As they walked into the foyer I heard Michael explaining why the paths weren't salted: "The lodge is pet-friendly, and we don't spread salt as it burns their feet. The snow plow hasn't been by yet to spread sand on those icy patches."

As Michael began a house tour, I walked around the corner and introduced myself. They were strikingly reserved, and I wondered if they would warm up over the afternoon. With the tour over, it didn't take long for an interrogation to begin. But I felt they had the right to ask questions about my background, my business, Nick's death from AIDS and my love for Michael. From the pained expressions on their faces, I wondered if I was being too open with my answers.

Peggy squirmed in her chair and said she had a question for me. "Are you aware how much you talk about Nick, you and Nick, how Nick's family visits you regularly up here? I wonder if you're over him yet? And more to the point, are you emotionally ready for a new relationship with my brother?"

I thought this question reasonable—I did talk about Nick a lot, but they were the ones asking questions about him and there was something in her voice that irked me. "I was with Nick for almost a decade. We grew into mature adults more during our years together than in the years before we met. We became one another's best friend, lover and confidant. Even our two families intertwined and became support networks for one another throughout his life and now after his death. Nick had a dream to own a place like this, and together we built Woodhaven into a thriving business. I probably do talk about him too much for those who didn't know him." I was feeling awkward and wondered if she had a nasty streak in her. After pausing to take a sip of my coffee, I decided to hit back.

"Michael told me that you're single. Maybe you've never experienced the depth of love I shared with Nick, which would make it difficult for you to understand what we meant to one another. Let me assure you that your brother and I are steadfast in our commitment and love for one another. After all, we're going to adopt children together and become a family."

I sensed I had just delivered a well-aimed barb. Confident in my position on this matter, I smiled and looked directly into the icy, indignant faces of Michael's sister, mother and stepdad, feeling myself becoming testy as I emphasized the importance of Nick's proud legacy at Woodhaven.

"I'm slowly adjusting to Nick's absence, but I'll never be over him. He and his family will remain significant in my life, and Michael is aware of the role the DiCicco family will continue to have in our lives. Your inability to comprehend the value of Nick's contribution to Woodhaven, its name and philosophy, is becoming a red flag for me. It isn't an issue for Michael. In fact, Michael is as excited to meet Nick's family as they are to welcome him into their family. The DiCicco's are eager to put a face to the name they've been hearing for the past few months. Michael will be warmly welcomed into my large extended family, not as a replacement for Nick but as the man with whom I'll share my future." Somehow, I doubted they would appreciate how unusual and affirming it was for a gay man to have his deceased lover's family ready to embrace their son-in-law's new spouse. I paused and stared back at them with an equally icy glare. "Is that really so difficult to understand?"

Peggy and Louise spoke of their need to explore my readiness to be in a new relationship so soon after Nick's death. I told them I was not going to spend my future mourning the past and avoiding life. "My eighty-two-year mother frequently reminds me that her secret to a long life is to live in today, because you can't change yesterday, and you have no control over tomorrow. I am not about to forget what I had with Nick. He helped me become the man your son fell in love with. Likewise, I have fallen in love with Michael. Michael is my today and hopefully our tomorrows will involve adopting children."

I told them my marriage to Nick had shown me just how much I loved being part of a pair, sharing all the highs and lows, making plans for a future family.

Peggy said, "Our concern has been about Michael getting involved with someone who could be on the rebound. You've known each other only four months and already you have him financing renovations. We wish you would both just slow down and give your new relationship time to develop before spending his money on your renovations." So, this was the crux of their concern! They thought I was bilking Michael of his life savings.

I was seconds away from a terse serrated response when Michael beat me to it. "You could have addressed those concerns with me privately," he said, looking around the room. "My financial involvement is none of your business. If I am insulted by that comment, Peggy, I'm sure David is, too. He owns this place and he has already signed over half-ownership to me. I'm putting in $100,000 of savings and becoming half-owner of a $400,000 business. I offered to make this investment—David didn't ask for money." The smile spreading across my face caused Michael to blush when he glanced toward me. I beamed with pride.

"My relationship with David is about more than just him and me. I have baggage from my childhood and teenage years plus all those missed years between twenty and thirty when I lived in the closet, afraid to let anyone see me as a gay man. All those years when my family suspected I was gay yet refused to offer encouragement or give me any hint of their suspicions that would have triggered that conversation. We all have baggage. Yes, it has only been a short time since I first met David, but I know what I want. I know all about his baggage and Nick's legacy in this building. My involvement financially with David is a private matter and I don't feel it is your place to question me about that. I've always wanted a country place like this to call home. Just be happy for me."

Michael's mother, stepfather and sister all began to backpedal about their concern over him getting involved too quickly. It was as if they were clumsily climbing out of a mine shaft they had just dug themselves into. They neither looked at nor talked to me. I was an invisible observer.

Thankfully, Michael's family to left shortly afterward. I let Michael say goodbye on his own in the foyer while I let the dogs out at the front of the house. Joining me outside to watch the dogs chase the snowballs I tossed, Michael apologized for his family's conduct and restated that he had no reservations about my loyalty and love for him. I knew we'd be a good team.

Over supper that evening I updated him on my recent efforts to get the necessary paperwork and visas to adopt a child internationally. We'd already spent many long hours discussing my failed attempts to adopt, the changing political and social climates that were opening doors to desperate gays and lesbians hoping to adopt children, domestic adoption versus international, costs and our mutual desire to see this quest culminate with us becoming parents. So many hours of those initial months of getting to know one another were spent talking about parenthood and how our parenting skills complimented one another. We'd laugh and look lovingly into each other's eyes and agree that life couldn't get much better than this for us. I was sure God steering Michael toward me. Likewise, I knew I would be his best choice for a mate, someone who would accentuate his wonderful attributes. Most of all, I knew he would be a devoted co-parent for our children.

As the renovations continued, I busied myself with trips to an Oshawa clinic to get the inoculations required for most international travel destinations. Calls back and forth to various officials at Citizenship and Immigration Canada—the CIC—had my head spinning. Every time I felt I was about to enter the home stretch, a new set of affidavits or forms, each needing notarization, would arrive by mail. I became increasingly dismayed and anxious because of the poor quality of federal and provincial intra-departmental communication, constant delays and screw-ups, mismanaged files, as well as the inability of highly paid federal employees to return messages within twenty-one days. Dealing with the Children's Aid Society in Toronto, the federal immigration department's Case Processing Centre in Mississauga, and Ottawa made me feel like one unholy pest. Even Barbara, my CAS social worker, was stymied by the run-around I received from the various arms of this adoption process. Privately, I was going through a checklist of possible countries from which a single man could adopt children—a long list that was shrinking each time I delved into specifics. There was something about India that kept drawing me in that direction.

Weeks behind schedule, the renovations were finally completed, and it was time to reopen for business. Still, we were thrilled with the look of our dining room and its panoramic view across the lake. The new kitchen was mammoth compared to the cramped old one. Guests who had been regulars were booked in for the reopening weekend and said how thrilled they were with the changes. Woodhaven had grown by two thousand square feet, to sixty-eight hundred.

Michael was so proud of his kitchen. He had a penchant for cooking and I gladly let him take over that department. I had been buying Master Choice frozen meals and serving them to guests in my own crockery. Michael cringed at the thought of serving frozen dinners, so he lovingly prepared Thai, Italian and French gourmet meals.

Our pack of dogs was happy with the additional indoor space in which they could chase after tennis balls, tea towels or shoes. But Jenny was a bit out of sorts and limped frequently. After discovering a small sore on the pad of her left front paw I took her to the local veterinarian to be examined. I thought this visit would be routine, expecting Jenny might have a stone or small piece of wood imbedded in her foot and once it was removed she'd be back to her old self. But her life was never to return to normal.

The veterinarian was concerned immediately upon examining Jenny. Ten days and numerous X-rays and blood samples later, she announced that Jenny had blastomycosis, a rare but deadly fungal infection affecting only a handful of dogs in Ontario each year. She explained that Jenny had probably breathed in fungal spores, which had settled in her lungs. and said there was a million-to-one chance of the spores shooting out of the fungus at the exact moment Jenny had bent down to sniff the ground. Poor Jenny.

The prognosis wasn't good: blastomycosis was fatal, and Jenny's chances of surviving a few months were less than one in a hundred. But seeing the frantic look in my eyes after she announced the results of Jenny's tests, our veterinarian said there had to be some sort of new research being done. I wasn't about to let Jenny go without exhausting every avenue. I had lost Nick only two years before, a prospective daughter weeks later, and I couldn't face the death of another loved one just yet.

After many calls to experts around Ontario, the veterinarian explained that we should treat Jenny like AIDS patients, with fluconazole, an antifungal. I knew about this drug as Nick had used it for years.

Jenny's health took many turns over the course of the next few weeks. It was a daily struggle trying to find the right balance of medication to give her at mealtimes, so she wouldn't be sick or become uninterested in food and lose weight. I hated to force feed her and push pills down her throat but after a few weeks her body responded, and the pads of her foot began to heal. Jenny's brown eyes had some life back in them and she regained enough strength to take daily two-kilometre walks up and down the lane with me.

CHAPTER FOURTEEN

CANADA'S GAY ADOPTION TEST CASE

DURING THE LATTER PART OF that first summer with Michael at Woodhaven I received an unexpected call from Immigration Canada. The Government of Canada was aware of my activist stance on the extension of adoption rights to gay men and women. Would I consider becoming Canada's first openly gay man approved for an international adoption? I told the caller that in a perfect world there shouldn't be any connection between being gay and my parenting skills; he awkwardly suggested my adoption home study would be expedited if I agreed to become Canada's test case.

Official documents from Immigration Canada arrived by mid-September and, as I'd been told, my home-study stated clearly, I was gay. This document in my hands meant I could now pursue adoption in any country from which Canadians could adopt. The Immigration officials assisted me by sending this paperwork to thirteen countries. Not one responded positively—each rejection succinctly indicating that homosexual applicants, domestic or international, were barred from adopting their children. Fortunately, my adoption request hadn't been forwarded to India.

I was on the phone immediately to Immigration Canada to tell them none of their selected countries allowed gays to adopt. In the back of my mind was the nagging question, "Why would they change my home-study to indicate I was gay without first investigating whether it was possible for a gay man to adopt from any of the countries on their list?" Was my government just being superficial about appearing to be pro-gay anything?

It didn't take long for me realize that the federal officials really had no great desire to enable gay adoptions domestically or internationally. So why were they posturing to look progressive? Couldn't they see how cruel it was to prevent adoptable children from having a wonderful home with a parent who just happened to be gay? Considering the United Nations estimate for children in orphanages and foster care world-wide topped 5-6 million children, why would any government prevent ANYONE from rescuing one of those children and giving them a better life? Particularly given that more and more Canadians favoured changing laws to extend adoption rights to homosexuals. To me, it seemed as if the feds were merely paying lip service to be seen reflecting growing public sentiment in Canada in 1997 in support of gay people being allowed to adopt.

I decided to drive to Ottawa and confront some of these federal officials. I was seething mad, like a horse chomping at the bit, as I barreled down hallways of the various departments that had interfered with my adoption plans. No one would answer the simple question: Why hadn't Canadian Immigration officials done their homework before suggesting I become their guinea pig? Every so-called savvy political mouthpiece I cornered for an answer, skirted the issue and made every effort to tell me what their party had done for the betterment of human rights for homosexuals. If I'd carried a barf bag for bullshit, it would have been overflowing by the time I left Ottawa!

Week after week, my constant barrage of daily telephone calls to adoption and Immigration offices got me the same answer: "We had no idea gays couldn't adopt internationally—oh well, sorry, but there really isn't much we can do about it now." I was furious, and not about to be jerked around. I threatened to call the media across North America about this debacle. I even had friends pose as reporters and pepper Immigration officials about my case. None of my actions were taken seriously until I called MPP Susan Pupatello, a backbencher in the Ontario Liberal Party, and asked if she would help me. She agreed and called in some favours in Ottawa from her Liberal MP counterparts and within days I was informed that my old home-study would be deleted from the system, therefore negating any chance of India receiving documents identifying me as a homosexual. The new paperwork would offer the fiction of Nicci, my supposed late common-law spouse, whose dying wish was that I would pursue the adoption we had planned. No pronouns would be used in the home-study, just my name and Nicci's name with the implied inference to anyone reading this document that Nicci was female name. Unfortunately, as Pupatello told me, these changes could take many months to complete. Worst of all was the feeling of being lost somewhere in the bureaucracy, without any identifiable person accountable for the status of my paperwork.

Devastated, I put booking a flight to India on hold, expecting to wait for new paperwork until spring 1998. I would go to bed thinking about children in India that I might be able to adopt, children who could die of malnutrition before I'd ever have an opportunity to show them a better life. I began to shut down emotionally and could feel myself slipping into a depressed state, depending on Michael more with each passing month. Yet there lingered a nagging doubt in my mind whether he was as optimistic as I was that we *would* adopt a child. As much as I wanted to whole-heartedly lean on him I could feel myself building an emotional wall to keep the negativity I imagined at bay. On our first date Michael had said he'd easily buy into my vision for becoming a parent, but it was becoming evident he had never truly thought it would go this far. Not that he wasn't up for the challenges of parenthood; he just hadn't embraced the real possibility of our having children in our future.

In the face of one setback after another and me spending money on hopes of surrogacy or adoption in California; the years of fighting the provincial authorities, whose protocols to assess social suitability to be an adoptive parent seemed designed to exclude gay applicants—somehow, I had maintained my optimism. I had been telling people for years that I would have children under the Christmas tree this year, then next year, then the year after that; it was such an old storyline that I imagined no one gave my pursuit much chance of success. I began to have suspicions that friends were doubting the likelihood of my succeeding, and I'd emotionally banish them from my dwindling inner circle.

Meanwhile, Woodhaven continued to attract newer and more frequent guests. Radio advertising became the focus of our advertising budget. "David and his five golden retrievers welcome you to Woodhaven" became our trademark message. In early November 1997 I received a call from a woman who wanted to visit Woodhaven with her husband. They were retired, lived in Whitby and had lost their beloved flat-coated retriever a year earlier. They were delighted to know a lodge existed where they could visit and be swarmed by friendly goldens. Barbara and Ralph decided they would come during the week when the lodge wouldn't be too crowded. They arrived for their first visit a few days after calling me. Ralph, a retired dentist, had a delightfully warm smile and an engaging manner. He reminded me of my dad in many ways. His skin tone was like the dark olive of my 'black-Irish' father.

Barbara was a beautiful woman, short in stature, with an infectious giggle. They loved our dogs and Ralph would encourage them to sit on the sofa beside him. During supper I watched him out of the corner of my eye slipping food to waiting canine mouths resting in his lap. They had been at Woodhaven almost forty-eight hours when they told me Ralph was black. This led us into protracted conversations about race relations in the 1960s, and public and family reaction to their mixed-race marriage during an era when some U.S. states still outlawed interracial marriage. Ralph, born and raised in Windsor, Ontario, had served in the Second World War. Upon his return home from Europe, he applied to the Faculty of Dentistry at the University of Toronto in 1946. Ralph's having a Scottish-sounding last meant the dean's office had no idea about his background—students didn't have face-to-face interviews to get into the program. It wasn't until he started classes that his faculty advisors realized Ralph Stewart was black.

The only black student in the faculty, he was summoned to the dean's office a few weeks after classes began. The dean implied Ralph probably wasn't going to enjoy the course and that he might want to look for a different program of study. Ralph said he knew by then he was the first black man in the dentistry program and imagined the dean was trying to get rid of him. He told the dean he was a war vet and that he hoped to get his dentistry degree and return to Africa to help "his people" in remote villages. The dean, according to Ralph, bought this line and never did question him again about leaving the program. Ralph was the first black dentist to graduate from U of T and established his dentistry practice at the corner of Spadina and College, where he stayed for the first twenty-five years of his career. Barbara had been a special education teacher during her working life and they were an awesome couple with immense charm and caustic humour.

Ralph and Barbara understood my bitterness over adoption road-blocks and the Immigration department's apparent prejudice against a gay man wanting to adopt. If Ralph could be U of T's first black dental graduate, then I could become the first gay man to adopt internationally!

The following weekend, a military man, his wife and three children arrived at Woodhaven in need of some R and R. As it turned out, Blair and his family had been stationed in New Delhi with the Canadian consulate staff. During his three-year posting, he and his wife had adopted a young Indian girl. They were excited to give us some useful advice about adopting in Delhi.

I told Blair I was ready to go to India once my paperwork was finished. He suggested I stop making the completed paperwork my benchmark. "Just go and do your own looking and listening," he advised. He felt that I would score big points with Indian officials and consular staff at the Canadian High Commission in Delhi if I just showed up and said I was there to check out the various orphanages, even if my paperwork wasn't 100 percent completed. Blair's enthusiasm infected Michael that weekend and we finally seemed in concert regarding what had to be done to realize our goal to become parents.

I booked a flight for early January 1998. Confident in my blind acceptance of Blair's maverick suggestions, I knew that I'd be in Delhi for my forty-fourth birthday.

Two days later the board members of the organization Egale—Equality for Gays and Lesbians Everywhere—arrived for a three-day, mid-week retreat. Twelve representatives from across Canada came for a meeting with John Fisher, the national executive director. Egale had been in the news regularly since its inception, fighting for equality for gays and lesbians, especially in relation to recognition of same-sex marriage, pension and health benefits for partners in same-sex relationships, gay adoption rights and federal government pension rights for gays and lesbians.

The retreat brought an interesting mix of same-sex marriage advocates, gay left- and right-wing activists and strategists from every corner of the country. During one of their sessions, I told them about my upcoming trip to India and my eighteen-year fight for the right to adopt children. Most of the members had heard of my attempt to recover Nick's mortgage insurance from the bank, but few had any idea just how arduous this adoption journey had been. It left us all wondering aloud how many other gays and lesbians across Canada had had similar experiences with provincial adoption agencies? I was encouraged by the genuine concern of Egale and they promised to work harder on changing adoption laws.

The DiCicco clan arrived for our fourth annual Woodhaven pre-Christmas weekend. I excitedly shared with everyone that I was booked on a flight to India in early January. Although Michael was already a familiar new member of the DiCicco-McKinstry-Woodhaven clan, this was Michael's first Christmas celebration with Mum, Nick's parents, siblings and spouses and all the children. Michael had been preparing food for days prior to their arrival, hoping to please his new extended family by cooking up all sorts of seasonal treats and dishes. I longed for the day Michael and I would have kids of our own around the Christmas tree. I wanted our children to be part of the DiCicco extended family; besides being in-laws, they were friends I could count on.

Christmas was only a few weeks away. I hadn't taken any guest reservations after the DiCicco weekend, so I could get caught up on all the preparations for the three groups of women and children from shelters who would start arriving for three-day holidays December 20. I had had to increase the number of allotted days for the Christmas program because the demand had doubled since the previous year. Many organizations were involved in providing food, treats and presents for the children and families. The *Toronto Star* and *The Globe and Mail* had written stories on our Woodhaven Christmas program. The response from citizens across Ontario had been incredible: seniors knitting scarves and mittens; retirees sending me $5 from meagre pensions to help with the program; church groups donating money for the moms; and Joyce, a local hairstylist, putting together hundreds of dollars' worth of hair products in beautiful gift bags for the teenage girls and the moms. I was absolutely stunned by the outpouring of generosity.

We hosted seventeen moms and thirty-four children that year. Once again, late-night gab sessions around the fireplace added stories to my growing list of men's abuses of women. The last group of families left Woodhaven on the morning of December 29 and we sighed with relief. We had just started to strip beds when I received a phone call from a staff member at the Ontario CAS office in Toronto, to say my paperwork had just arrived. Still, what was missing was the important Letter of No Objection from the federal Immigration department, which, as the name suggests, indicates an adoption won't be opposed by the Government of Canada. However, she said I had enough documentation stamped "Approved" to be credible with orphanages in Delhi. She wished me luck on my trip and suggested I find myself an immigration lawyer." You have fought a tough fight with so many departments in both levels of government and if anyone is going to adopt a child it will be you. You had to be a rebel and step on toes to get this far. Find yourself a good immigration lawyer because I get a sense you'll need one to complete an adoption when you get back from India." I thanked her and bolted downstairs to share this news with Michael. She was right, I told myself – I wouldn't come home from India empty-handed!

CHAPTER FIFTEEN

STRANDED IN BANGKOK

IT WAS EARLY JANUARY AND all the necessary adoption documents were stuffed into my money belt. I'd purchased a ticket from a travel agency specializing in Southeast Asian tours. When I picked up my airline tickets, the agent asked to see my passport and medical documentation. I asked her if I needed any other documents and she said no. Finally, I had my ticket in hand and my departure date was only a few days away. The Indian Consulate office was close to the Ontario CAS office at 2 Bloor St. W. in Toronto. I dropped into the office of Laura Wen, my case worker's boss, to show her my ticket and to thank her for all her good will and help over the past year. She hugged me and said she hoped I'd keep her current on the outcome of my trip to Indian orphanages. It felt like I finally had someone on my side at this office.

Would I have sufficient cash to find a child, pay the bribes I'd been told would be expected by some Indian officials and cover my travel, food and lodgings? I had been saving for this trip. Every week I'd take my envelope of tips and buy American travellers cheques at the bank. I had been doing this for six months and combined tip dollars and money from guests who paid cash, I had almost $17,000 U.S. in traveller's cheques in my money belt. This had become my dark little secret. I knew Michael would flip out if he discovered that I hadn't been paying certain bills on time, so I could pad our adoption account. He was already deeply concerned over bills that seemed to be piling up, but I assured him we had a slush fund stashed in my steel box under the bed just for emergency repairs in the event he had to pay some bills while I was away. I was determined to have enough money to do a competent exploratory search to find us children to adopt.

I was now closer to my goal of adopting than ever before, fixated on a positive outcome: a family. Becoming a parent had been a driving force in my life forever and I had blinders on. I knew how upsetting it would be for Michael if he had to handle overdue accounts while I was in India, but I was looking at the broader picture of us becoming a family and justified my behaviour by repeating "Short-term pain for long-term gain" like a mantra. It was selfish of me—I confess I was obsessed.

In the weeks leading up to my departure I became acutely aware of the varying degrees of support of friends and family. Some felt I should give up on this quest, some said very little, others were elated I was on my way. I put people into two categories: bridges or walls. I had Mormon family members and several swim team friends who were LDS growing up and somehow the large happy family aspect of the Church had become a magnate for me. I thought about my life and how the ideals of the Church seemed a fit for me – although I knew the Church didn't accept homosexuality I deluded myself into believing I could overcome those desires. I was baptized into the LDS clan in my early twenties. I spent time at BYU in Provo, Utah. On numerous ski trips to Utah, I'd stay with family friends in Salt Lake over the course of a few years – always in search of a wife but always being courted by one of the 'only other LDS single, eligible, attractive young men' who were fighting our natural inclinations – that we were gay. Each time I'd get introduced to a nice young woman of marrying age, somehow her brother, cousin or someone I'd run into at the pool or in a restaurant whose gay scent was over-powering, and I'd be momentarily distracted from my pursuit of finding a wife. As I'd prepare to fly out of Salt Lake City bound for home I'd leave wondering how many Mormon guys my age, similarly stricken with secret homo desires, were living in Utah and masquerading as Republican, straight and married. While in Vancouver I'd been excommunicated for confessing my homosexuality. Finally, the lies and deception, especially when being constantly introduced to such lovely, eligible women through Church members who were unaware of my true sexual preference, wore thin and I confessed to my Bishop and was quickly and ceremoniously ex'd from the Church I believed in. What was the chance I'd have fallen in love with Jason, an ex-Mormon who had returned from his two-year Mission in Japan and then had decided it was time to confront his sexuality and likewise be excommunicated. We couldn't attend Church services or be around Church members who'd scowl at the ridiculous suggestion that anyone LDS could be gay. I still held on to the belief that my Heavenly 'parent' had already picked out children for us to call our own. I firmly believed we were all children with God before we came down to earth to live a life, and that we were connected one to the other. I also believed if I was up to the challenge, I'd meet the children my Heavenly Parents intended for us to adopt. Even though they were not of my bloodline, it wouldn't matter since they were my children whom fate meant for me to parent. This steadfast belief that *my* children were out there somewhere waiting to reconnect with me is what spurred me on. I'd experienced too many childless years, and annually sending out Christmas notes stating I'd be a father someday *soon*.

At the airport Michael handed me a big surprise as we unloaded my bags from the trunk of the car: an additional $7,000.00. He said he'd recently sold a diamond he'd bought years earlier as an investment. I looked at him and knew he was with me 100% in this quest. Regardless of his constant worry about our finances not being as solid as his mathematical mind thought they should be, he would be my right arm in good times and bad. A few years prior, Michael had had several hundred thousand dollars in savings, but now his financial safety net, was much diminished and he was always anxious about money. In that moment I broke my rule of no public displays of affection and embraced him tightly, an action that drew zero attention from the travellers milling around us.

My Vancouver friends, Mike Rickaby and his wife Chris, were at the airport to greet me. The next morning, they took me on a tour to show me how the city had grown and changed since my departure twelve years earlier. I told them I wanted to be alone for a few hours, just to walk around and collect my thoughts before boarding my flight to Hong Kong. I walked the old haunts from my younger days in that city, through the west end and down toward Stanley Park. The urge to visit the waterfront was overwhelming. I sat on the beach looking out at Point Grey and UBC in the distance, reflecting on the years I'd spent here. Ironic that it was in Vancouver that I really began my initial inquiries into adopting children as a single man—and I was about to fly from Vancouver to Delhi to adopt children.

I took a shuttle bus to the Vancouver Airport about 8 p.m. At the Cathay Pacific Airline check-in counter, I was informed my departure would be delayed until 3 a.m. The lounge was full of passengers, old Chinese couples, young Chinese couples with children, Caucasian businessmen and women eager to get into their comfortable business class and first-class seats. For those of us in economy, the flight was painfully long and uncomfortable. Halfway there I vowed I'd never travel to the Orient again except in first class.

Hong Kong was shrouded in fog and rain as we descended from the clouds. I had slept very little, but excitement pulsed in my veins as I deplaned and headed to find my connecting flight to Thailand. I had five hours to wait until I checked in for my connecting flight to Bangkok. I walked around the airport, had coffee and eggs, read my book and chatted with several travelers likewise waiting for connecting flights.

Finally, I was back in the air, heading to Bangkok. Immediately upon landing I headed to the Air India counter to check my bags for the flight that was to leave in three hours. I placed my bags on the weigh station and handed my ticket, inoculation certificate and passport to the ticket agent. She looked at my documents and stamped my ticket, then asked for my visitor's visa. Puzzled by her request, I said I only had my passport and ticket.

"You must have a Visitor's Visa to enter India. You can't get into the country without it. Where did you come from?" She said glancing down at my ticket to see my origin. "The Canadians should have told you to get that visa before leaving."

In disbelief I exclaimed, "No one told me about needing a Visitor's Visa," My face flushed with embarrassment.

"Well, you won't be going on this flight today so just move to the side, please." The agent motioned me away, so she could process the next passenger.

"Wait, I have to get to India. I am adopting a child. I have to be on this flight," I said cementing myself to the spot in front of the agent. "How do I get a Visitor's Visa in time to make this flight?" I tried to control the increasing edge to my voice.

"Sir, you will have to go to your embassy in Bangkok and apply for a visa. Call them at the pay phones and make an appointment." I grabbed my bags and walked away from the counter. I was tired from lack of sleep, the humid air of Bangkok had me in a lather of sweat, and emotionally I was distraught by this abrupt change in my plans.

Finding a phone, I searched in the telephone directory for the number of the Canadian High Commission. I explained to the receptionist that I needed to talk to someone who could get me a Visitor's visa to India as quickly as possible. I told her I was en route to India to adopt a child and that I just had to get on a flight today. In a soft voice she asked if it were possible for me to take a return flight to Vancouver, as it might be faster to go back and get the visa there than applying for it in Bangkok. When in a very sharp tone I replied that it wasn't possible, she directed my call to a woman named Denise, who urged me to come to their office and we'd would work together to facilitate a speedy resolution. However, she stressed that it was not possible to get a same-day Visitor's Visa to India. She gave me the address and suggested I change some money into Thai currency before leaving the airport.

At the baggage lockers on the main level I threw in my two bigger bags. A few steps away was a currency exchange kiosk. With Thai money in hand, I stepped outside and experienced the full brunt of the hot, steamy midday. Installed in an air-conditioned cab, I directed the driver to the High Commission. It took twenty-five minutes to get into the downtown core from the airport and double that to go the last fifteen blocks.

I was jubilant to see a Canadian flag as I walked over to the receptionist and said I was the one stranded without a Visitor's Visa to India. This didn't twig with her, so I said that I had an appointment with Denise.

"Denise is out at lunch, but she will be back in thirty minutes."

When she finally returned Denise told me I would have to go to the Indian High Commission and apply for a visa and that the Indians didn't take kindly to foreigners asking favours, such as faster processing of a Visitor's Visa. "It could actually work against you if our office asked their staff for a favour," she said.

Denise gave me directions and suggested I be as calm and polite as possible. I asked her how long processing would take and if I'd be out of Bangkok by tomorrow. She told me that it being Wednesday, it would probably be Friday before I was en route to India. I then asked her for a recommendation of a downtown hotel. We were standing by the receptionist and a young Canadian couple piped up that they were staying at the Tawana Hotel, just five minutes from the High Commission's office. It was safe and luxurious for $30 per night, breakfast included. I thanked them, and they hurried into the elevator beside me as I bid Denise goodbye.

On the way to the lobby I told them of my misfortunes. They had already been to India and said if I wanted to get my visa faster I should discreetly pass some American money through the wicket at the High Commission: "Better to spend $200 than $500 staying in Bangkok for two weeks."

I walked into the foyer of the Indian High Commission and was amazed at the number of backpackers standing or sitting around the walls. Finally, my number was called, and I approached the wicket. The expressionless official who greeted me was a bit intimidating, leaving me unsure how to start. Should I just pass him money, then ask how long it would take to get a Visitor's Visa, or what? I decided to take it slow and quietly explain my predicament. The man didn't smile, hold out his hand or give me any indication that he understood me. I repeated my story and he motioned for me to pass my documents through to him. I had put two $100 bills in the crease of my passport and handed it to him. He looked up at me and smiled. I immediately thought 'now we are speaking the same language.' Then he said something to his colleague in the back part of the office and grabbed some papers and began to write. Ten seconds later he handed me a slip of paper and told me to come back in one week to get my visa.

I was stunned. I had waited so long for this trip and every day I had visions of sad children in orphanages waiting for me to swoop down and adopt them. I felt like I had bloody knuckles from rapping on the door of parenthood. A rush of sadness overcame me, then remembering what people had told me about bribes, I leaned closer to the wicket dividing us and said quietly, "What would it cost me to get it done by Thursday?"

He looked at me and in perfect English said, "Come back in a week and we will have your Visitor's Visa ready. This is as fast as I will process your application." He pulled down the shutter and put up a sign that read "Closed." I stood there unsure of what my next move should be, but biting my tongue so I wouldn't yell, "You prick, give me my money back!"

I headed back to the Canadian High Commission, desperately hoping they could intervene on my behalf. Waiting a week for a Visitor's Visa would cost me time and money I didn't have.

Denise was off-site when I returned. I decided to take the advice of the couple I'd met earlier and check out the Tawana. The walk to the hotel took only a few minutes. It was as nice as any four-star hotel I'd ever seen. Was there a room for seven nights, possibly longer? I was in luck. A convention had just finished at the hotel that morning and a room overlooking the pool would be available within the hour. And where could I get an air-conditioned cab back to the airport to retrieve my luggage? A woman at the front desk said for less money than a cab I could hire the hotel's private driver and his air-conditioned Benz. Three hours later I returned to the hotel with my luggage and checked into a room overlooking the almond-shaped pool in the hotel's private court-yard. Looking in the bathroom mirror, I appeared as exhausted as I felt and smelled like diesel fumes, so I jumped into the shower to scrub off the grime.

Later I had a relaxed meal. I wanted to call Michael but thought it would be less expensive for me to send an email. The front desk clerk,

Nun Ning, told me I could use the hotel's back-office computer to send a message after 10 p.m.

The next morning, on my way to breakfast, I passed the front desk. It was 7 a.m. and Ning was still on duty. She smiled and hailed me over to her. "Khun David, you have email waiting for you in our office," she said.

CHAPTER SIXTEEN
WAITING

THE REASSURING EMAIL FROM MICHAEL told me I had his full support and that he looked forward to a successful outcome of my search in Delhi. Michael wouldn't dare to write words of love in a message that hotel employees could read before handing on to me. Instead, we had agreed to use of code words to indicate our love for one another in our emails. One was "bedtime," which meant "wish I could be there to hold you." I had only been gone a few days, but I desperately wanted to speak with him; however, long distance calls weren't in our budget.

The wrench in my travel plans had, in the quietude of my hotel room, led me to reflect on events of the past years that had found me on this journey to Thailand. I'd been blessed to have had almost nine wonderful years with Nick, experiencing his high energy and deep spirituality, and then his death from AIDS. I had come out publicly as a gay man in Toronto's press over the mortgage issue. Now, I was committed to Michael—I loved him 100 percent. He had bought into my dream of raising children and he was sacrificing in a major way to make my dream of *us* becoming parents a reality. My percolating yearning to be a parent was stronger than ever.

The next morning, even though the drapes were drawn to keep the sun out of my bedroom, I awoke and knew it was hot and muggy outside on the streets of Bangkok. It was January 16, my forty-fourth birthday. As I walked to the bathroom I saw a note under my door. It was from

Nun Ning informing me that two faxes awaited me in the office. She was smiling as I walked in. "Happy birthday, Khun David. Me wishing you much happiness today." It was obvious at least one of my faxes was a birthday wish.

In the dining room I opened the fax envelope and read a large, boldface birthday greeting from my Vancouver friends. But the second message immediately grabbed my attention. With guts twisting and elevated blood pressure I read and reread Michael's words admonishing me for my deceptive financial records. He wrote that he thought Woodhaven was on the brink of bankruptcy because I'd used money from our bill-paying account to fund this trip to India. In capital letters he had typed at the bottom, "I'm not used to dealing with this kind of pressure. I've never been irresponsible with money. My stomach is upset all the time and I'm feeling negative about you and our relationship."

No Happy Birthday greeting from my beloved partner, just a three-page dissertation on my financial mismanagement and how I had saddled him with a mountain of personal debt and doubts about our future together.

Michael was justified in feeling that I'd lead him to assume our accounts held sufficient funds to honour our bills. My full-on commitment to our having children and his need for financial stability were miles apart, and it was my fault Michael had sunk to such a low. I had to apologize and ask his forgiveness. The forces driving me to do whatever I believed I had to do were causing Michael so much grief. I needed to let him know to check the steel box under our bed and he'd have sufficient emergency funds to deal with any crisis while I was away.

I poured out my heart to Michael in a two-page fax. I had only sent my apology by fax minutes before receiving another fax message stating he had overreacted. We weren't broke, and he had already found the shoebox full of cash for emergencies. He hadn't remembered this secret stash until after sending his earlier angry fax. Michael expressed how sorry he was for calling me duplicitous on my birthday. Although we were in precarious shape financially, he said, one good summer season could remedy that, and he charmingly wrote of his unbridled support.

He wanted me to go on to India and get us a child to bring home.

Early in the morning of my fourth day, Michael faxed a letter and suggested I give myself a belated birthday gift from him. He had been talking to some fellow staff at Crescent School about my being stuck in Bangkok and they suggested I book a flight to Chiang Mai, in northern Thailand. Nun Ning at the hotel told me the flight and day-long tour was $68. Sitting around in Bangkok was boring and it made sense to take advantage of this opportunity to see more of Thailand than just the diesel-fumed-polluted downtown core. I booked a flight for the following day, then I spent the remainder of that morning making telephone calls to Thai adoption groups. By noon I had also arranged three appointments to meet with local orphanage directors. I wasn't sure what to expect when I arrived at an old Church of England orphanage. The woman at the reception desk was British and she appeared interested in my plans to adopt children from India. I told her I was waiting for a visa, so I could continue my journey, but felt I should explore a few Thai orphanages before leaving on Wednesday. I could see a schoolyard full of children through a window immediately behind her desk and she turned to see what I was watching.

"It's playtime for the children. We just received a new set of swings donated by a family in America who adopted a child last year," she said.

After several minutes of interesting chitchat, the orphanage director entered the lobby and greeted me. A matronly woman, perhaps sixty years old, who constantly fanned her face, she told me she had been in Bangkok for fourteen years and still wasn't accustomed to the humidity. We walked through the schoolyard behind the church to reach her office.

Once inside, she said that this orphanage was the first in Thailand to run an AIDS health program for its children, since seventy percent of the ninety children were HIV positive and were therefore unacceptable candidates for international adoption. She explained that most of her children wouldn't live long enough to graduate from public school. This wonderful woman spoke with such affection, I admired her ability to love, knowing she was going to lose these children, and reflected on the faith it took to keep herself motivated day to day. After a quick tour of the hospice unit attached to the school she walked me to the gates of the churchyard and bid me good luck in India. I told her I was meeting with two more Thai adoption facilities and she smiled at me in a very kind way. She knew that I'd run into the same scenario at the next orphanages: children who weren't one hundred percent healthy would never be considered adoptable by Immigration Canada.

By the time I returned to the hotel at 4 p.m. the heat had become unbearable. My visits to the orphanages left my emotions raw. The local English newspaper said the temperature for tomorrow would top forty-two degrees. I went for a swim in the hotel pool to cool off and digest what I'd seen at the orphanages.

I really thought Bangkok was hell on earth. The weather and pollution, especially the sub-standard air quality, would be dangerous for anyone with a respiratory ailment. I wondered how asthmatics coped here. I had good lungs, yet the pollution stung my air passages and made me nauseated if I walked around the Bangkok streets for more than fifteen minutes. Most people I passed on the streets carried handkerchiefs pressed close to their mouths and noses. The sex trade in Bangkok was apparently oblivious to AIDS. Everywhere I went taxi drivers would nudge me and ask if I wanted to have a fun time in Bangkok? They would brazenly flash photo albums containing pictures of nude men, women, boys and girls and then ask what my pleasure was. When I'd rebuff their solicitations, they would switch gears smoothly and ask where I wanted to go.

Chiang Mai was heaven compared to Bangkok. The flight was ninety minutes aboard Thai Air and I met dozens of Australian and Canadian tourists on the tour. The morning visit to a remote mountainside village was like a step back in time, with its shrines, elephant sanctuaries, temples and lush, colourful vegetation.

After numerous side trips to some of fine jewelry stores, I purchased a strand of pearls for $100.00 American—to give to our future daughter on her wedding day—my tour group returned to the airport and the short flight back to Bangkok. I'd only been out of city eleven hours, yet I felt revived spiritually.

The next two days passed uneventfully. I sent several faxes to Janice McCann at the Canadian High Commission in Delhi explaining why I'd been delayed in Bangkok and saying that I would be arriving in Delhi by week's end. Could she could spare some time to meet with me and review my list of Canadian-approved orphanages over coffee? Janice faxed me back and told me to call on her private line or at home when I arrived in India. She also wished me luck in my dealings with the Indian High Commission in Bangkok and emphasized that she wished she could help me out but was powerless to expedite the Visitor's visa process.

Wednesday morning arrived, and I headed off to the High Commission. The line-up for visas was long and the foyer of the reception area was packed with foreign business people, Indian nationals and international backpackers from everywhere. Within an hour I was back at the hotel and on the phone about available flights that day. Air India couldn't get me on a flight for five days, but Aeroflot had a 10 p.m. flight with one available economy seat.

I asked the hotel receptionist if I could pay for a half-day rate, so I could stay in the hotel until I left for the airport after supper. The front desk staff smiled and told me I could stay for free all day and they wished me best of luck getting a child in India. I had become quite chummy with these hotel employees during my eight days in Bangkok. I'd shown them photos of Woodhaven and told them I was a widower hoping to adopt children in India. My widower story always touched people's heartstrings—this story was documented in my home study and I had to maintain the fiction outside of Canada.

Aeroflot's check-in desk should have been an indication of what lay ahead of me. The staff were smoking in no smoking areas, and the throng of passengers looked like they had just arrived from filming a 1932 version of Ali Baba and his band of forty thieves. The plane was a 727 packed to capacity. Men dressed like Arab sheikhs were on either side of me and bent across me chain-smoking and talking as if I wasn't sitting between them. Soon after sitting, I asked them if they would like to trade seats, so they could sit beside one another to talk but they didn't seem interested in giving up their window or aisle seats. I had seven hours of flying time from Bangkok to Delhi and the ever-present foul stench on this plane was a result of travelers with poor hygiene and men who chain-smoked Russian cigarettes. I thought I'd left hell back in Bangkok, but this plane ride was a close second!

Hours later, my lungs ached from the second-hand cigarette smoke I'd been inhaling for most of the trip. The approach to Delhi was bumpy because of air turbulence and each time the plane swayed, so did my seatmates, who always seemed to fall into me. They hadn't shut up the entire trip except to eat when food trays were dropped in front of them. I had lost my appetite and the only thing I wanted was fresh air.

It was midnight Delhi time when the jet touched down. There was nothing friendly about this airport. No one smiled. Maybe it was because of the late hour. I waited at the baggage claim area with other passengers for almost an hour before bags started to tumble down the carousel. Another hour passed and still my luggage hadn't banged down the chute. I went to the baggage office to inquire about my suitcases and was told that my Aeroflot plane had already departed and that if my suitcases weren't on the carousel then they were en route to Moscow.

"Call tomorrow to Aeroflot office in Delhi," the baggage officer told me as he waved me off. "Aeroflot will send your bags back on next flight to Delhi."

I had my carry-on bag with a fresh shirt, change of underwear, books, glasses and all my documents. I wanted to get to a hotel and just get myself clean, to wash off the smoke that clung to me. The Canadian High Commission in Bangkok had given me suggestions of places to stay in Delhi and I called the first hotel on my list and asked if they had an available room. It was forty minutes from the airport and the rate was $160 U.S. for the night. I was incensed at this, yet too exhausted to fight and felt that after a good night's sleep I could scout out a lower-priced hotel. I needed to exchange some money into rupees, so I could pay the taxi driver. The only exchange wicket open at 3:45 a.m. in the entire airport had a mile-long line up of people waiting to do the same thing. It took another hour for me to get to the wicket—I was practically asleep on my feet. The man behind the counter was curt and asked me something in broken English. I didn't understand him, so I asked him to repeat what he'd said. He practically jumped through the wicket window. I glared back at him and just as curtly retorted, "Give me some fucking rupees." Quickly remembering the bribe advice from the couple in Thailand, I handed this fellow a $20 U.S. bill. He immediately smiled and asked how many rupees I wanted. I told him to give me whatever $300 U.S. would buy. Ten minutes later I was in an air-conditioned taxi heading to the hotel. The driver pulled up in front just as I was nodding off and said the fare was 1,000 rupees. That sounded fine to me. I had 25,000 rupees in my wallet, so I didn't challenge the amount, figuring it was probably a good rate. (Later I'd learn it was ten times the going flat rate from the airport.) I exited the taxi feeling sick from exhaustion. The reception area wasn't very fancy: in fact, it looked like a two-star hotel. It was 4:40 a.m.

My room was muggy and hot when I opened the door. I found the air-conditioning button and immediately switched it on to the high position before I jumped into the shower. By the time I'd toweled off, the room had cooled considerably, and I could feel myself fading on my feet. I crawled into the bed and within seconds left the conscious world behind. Little did I know I'd experience many more real-life nightmares during my first visit to this city, many highs and lows, before I'd finally connect with Mohini Raghunath, an orphanage director who believed in me and would make my adoption dreams a reality.

CHAPTER SEVENTEEN

ELLEN 'COMES OUT' AND MOHINI OFFERS ME A SON

I HAD BEEN HOME FROM India for several months, but I still hadn't fully recovered and had bouts of strange fatigue, stomach upset and shortness of breath for most of the late winter and early spring. Jenny, our sick golden retriever, was also struggling. Cool winter weather was good for her lungs and the blastomycosis was kept at bay. As it got warmer, her health began to deteriorate, and her pulmonary function rapidly became compromised. We didn't have a lot of available cash for vet bills—every cent we spent at the vet was on our line of credit. It was pre-season and guests were few.

Michael was worried night and day about our finances and kept raising the issue of selling Woodhaven. The very thought of this would put me into a fierce mood. I wanted to live here the rest of my life, I wanted us to raise our children at Woodhaven, and owning and operating this small hospitality business was what I wanted to do with my life. From the outset, I had offered unused bedrooms free of charge to people who needed a lakeside holiday. Michael was onside in spirit, but, this benevolence kept us on the brink of bankruptcy and we had daily discussions about Jenny's worsening health—we knew vet expenses could easily double. In a weak moment, I relented and agreed to list Woodhaven for sale. I called a local real estate agent and days later it was on the market. I was sick at heart showing the agent my home and signing the realtor's agreement of sale. I told her I wanted it priced high and she agreed. Meanwhile, I hoped once our summer season began and money started to come in that Michael would see we were sitting on a gold mine.

On April 27th, 1997 the world watched as comedienne Ellen DeGeneres, came out as a lesbian on TV in front of hundreds of millions of viewers around the world. Mum was visiting for a few days and watched this event with me. She smiled and said it was long overdue for someone like Ellen to come out on TV. Mum said, "Ellen is a trailblazer for gay people who work in TV just like you and Michael will be trailblazers for gay couples being allowed to adopt children so people like me can finally be called Grandma!" I was never surprised by anything Mum would say, after all she had been the first one to tell me a year after Nick died that life was for the living and I needed to get out and find love again.

A few days later, Wednesday, April 29th, I awoke around 5 a.m. and lay in bed wondering how long I'd have to wait for Mrs. Raghunath to call me about a son to bring home. Nick was everywhere that morning—in my dreams and in my half-awake state of mind. I must have stayed in bed semi-conscious, thinking about him for almost an hour. The dogs were sprawled across the bed, but by 6:10 a.m. they started to stir, a clear signal they needed to go outside for their morning constitutionals. With the dogs in sight of the kitchen window I waited for my first pot of coffee to brew. The scent of water beckoned to the dogs and they scooted down the path to the docks. I wandered outside to the edge of the hill to keep an eye on them. Ten minutes later our soaking-wet golden retrievers bounded up the hillside, eager for breakfast.

It was 6:45 a.m. when I finished toweling off the dogs and began the routine of filling their food dishes. Once they were fed, I had just poured myself a cup of strong coffee when the phone rang. After a few seconds' delay on the line, I heard, "David, this is Mohini Raghunath. Am I calling too early in Canada?" My heart began to pound. I assured her any time of the day or night was a perfect time to hear from her.

"David, we have a little boy that I would like to talk to you about. He came into our care three weeks ago. He is a healthy, happy boy who is very considerate of his playmates in the orphanage. He wouldn't tell us his name, so we temporarily named him Tomi. I think he would be a good match for you," she said, pausing until the echoing on our line ended.

"Yes, yes," I said, "He sounds delightful. What else do you know about him? Please tell me everything," I pleaded.

"We don't know his real age, but a dentist and our doctor have examined him and by the size of his teeth they estimate he is four and a half years old. He is a tall boy for his age. He is darker skinned and circumcised. Would you want a son who was circumcised?"

"Of course, circumcised or not circumcised, it doesn't matter to me. I am circumcised, as are half my peers in North America. I just want a son!"

She told me that being circumcised indicated Tomi was likely Muslim by birth. Children of the World, Delhi, is a Hindu orphanage and being circumcised negated any chance he'd be adopted by a Hindu family. Being darker skinned would also make him undesirable to most Indian families, who want children to be lighter skin tones than previous generations. "Tomi is being offered to our international families, who won't care as much about his colour. David, you are at the top of my international family list and I wanted to offer him to you first." There was a pause as if she wondered whether I would say yes or no to her offer.

Without hesitation I said I wanted him and asked, "How long until I can bring my son home to Canada?"

"Probably another four months, if the paperwork goes smoothly. But there is a lot to do before that may happen. You must first get a Letter of No Objection completed by the Canadian immigration authorities. This must be in our hands before I can present Tomi to the central adoption agency for its approval of this application. There is still much to be done by your authorities. I will send you a list of documents you will need to proceed. Call Mrs. Johnston, your home-study social worker, and tell her I will send the documents to her address. I will enclose a photo of Tomi and all available information in our file on him. Knowing how slow the mail can be, you won't receive this package for a few weeks. Once it arrives, you will be able to discuss the details with the Canadian authorities and start sending us all the necessary documentation to process your application. I think you and Tomi will like one another. I remember you told me you would name a son Nicholas. We will consider Tomi to be your Nicholas from now on and we will change his name on this file and he will be known as Nicholas McKinstry." She paused again to let the echo on our line catch up with the silence.

"I have waited a lifetime to hear those words from you, Mrs. Raghunath. I want him, and I will do everything possible to get the paperwork done in two months. I don't want my son to stay in an orphanage any longer than necessary."

Mrs. Raghunath said she'd fax me the details immediately regarding Tomi, but the original documents she would put in the mail along with the colour photograph of Tomi. I could tell she was smiling on the other end of the phone and I thanked her profusely again and again, much to her amusement.

"You have waited a long time for the right child to come into your life. I hope it will be this little boy. Please call us if you or Mrs. Johnston has any questions about the documents we require from your immigration officials."

I yelled, "Oh, thank you, Heavenly Father!" and the dogs came running to me, sensing my excitement. I immediately remembered lying in bed a few hours ago and thinking about Nick. Had this been his sign to me that a child was coming? I had to call Michael and tell him the news. It was 7:30 a.m. and he'd be driving to school. I called the school's math office and left a call-me-quick message on his voice mail. It took twenty minutes for me to stop walking around in a daze. I poured another cup of coffee and silently told Heavenly Father that I was the happiest man in the world and how thankful I was for His faith in me.

When Michael phoned at 8:10 and asked what was wrong, I told him about the telephone call from India about a son for us to adopt. He was thrilled to hear this long-awaited news and I could tell he was relieved to hear *we would be* parents. He often had a cautious edge to his enthusiasm, as if not wanting to rejoice too soon in case something went wrong.

I was already celebrating Nicholas' arrival into our family, but risk-averse Michael wanted all the T's crossed and I's dotted before letting his excitement bubble over. No matter, I thought, I have enough excitement and confidence for us both. I spent the next hour calling family and friends, which included leaving a score of excited announcements on the voice-mails of my DiCicco clan.

I drove to the Lakehurst General Store to get the mail and told the owners, Marlene and Harry, that I had finally received good news from India. They had been watching the mail for me and every time I got a letter from India they would call to alert me. I knew that word would spread once they knew my good news. I didn't mind: I was eager for everyone to know my good fortune, as the more positive thoughts I had coming my way, the better. I knew Nicholas would be coming home to Canada; it was just a matter of how long until the paperwork could be finalized. No one could have prepared me for the bureaucratic homophobia, fumbling and delays I experienced over the next eleven months. Initially, the federal Liberal government seemed to be encouraging me to become a test case for gay adoptions; however, officials failed to expedite my son's immigration paperwork, so he could come home. India was ready to send Nicholas to Canada within a few months but, yet we waited and waited for the Case Processing Centre in Mississauga to provide a Letter of No Objection to the Indian officials and to fill in forms the Indian officials had sent to Immigration Canada officials. The immigration law firm we hired was based in Ottawa, though it turned out the lawyer we were dealing with had been born and raised in Peterborough. He and his wife both worked in the firm and they were exceedingly supportive of my quest to adopt. They were very experienced and were tenacious when dealing the government officials because they wanted to be part of my story. Although they knew I was gay, my sexuality was never mentioned in any paperwork between their office and India or the Canadian government. It just seemed so cruel that our Nicholas would languish in an orphanage for longer than reasonably necessary, all because of bureaucratic delays and oversights. This file was about a five- year-old child, yet no one in the federal government seemed to give a damn.

Sadly, by mid-May, Jenny joined Nick in the land beyond. Prior to Nick's death I had planted a maple tree overlooking the lake. Nick wanted his ashes buried at the base of this tree, so he'd have an eternal perch over Sandy Lake. We buried Jenny's ashes under the maple tree where his ashes lay.

'Gay Innkeeper catches high profile bank robber' became front page news across Canada in June 1998. By chance, one of Canada's Top Ten Most Wanted criminals wandered up to Woodhaven's door early one Saturday morning in mid-June 1998. He and his gang had attempted to rob the Buckhorn Foodland. Their attempt was foiled and with police in hot pursuit, they drove down a rarely used cottage road, abandoned their car and got lost in the woods surrounding Sandy Lake. After opening the trunk of this vehicle, the police soon discovered the identities of these robbers. Within hours every available OPP swat team and helicopter support personnel descended on Buckhorn to catch this well-known gang. I answered the doorbell that morning at 7 am to find someone soaking wet and wearing a black t-shirt and shorts. Intuitively, I sensed this fellow was the robber from the day before and calmly welcomed him inside the lodge. This robber asked to use a phone to call a friend to come and pick him up after explaining that he had become lost in the woods the night before and just needed to call a friend. At the end of the phone call, I asked if he wanted to clean up and shower in one of the available suites while waiting for his ride. The robber agreed and once hearing the shower come on, I called the OPP and said, "I think the robber you're looking for is in my shower." Forty tactical swat team converged on Woodhaven within 15 minutes and without incident, quickly apprehended the gang's ringleader as he sat down to a breakfast of eggs. This unexpected celebrity was terrific for business and within days the phone was ringing off the hook with people wanting to check us out. A few months later I was given an OPP commendation for assisting in the apprehension of one of Canada's Most Wanted criminals! Instantly, we went being from the gay blades at the end of the lake, to becoming 'those good guys who caught the robber.'

At the end of June Michael started summer holidays. With Woodhaven having more reservations than ever before, we looked forward to a profitable season. Somehow, despite the painful bureaucratic delays, I awakened every morning knowing we had a son and eventually Nicholas would be coming home. Every day felt special—Michael was becoming more excited daily by the prospect of becoming a parent and likewise I, too, felt super-charged over what lay ahead for us. News of Nicholas in India had spread around the lake quickly and we were inundated with inquiries about the progress of our adoption.

In early July our neighbours Joyce and Sandy Gammie called to invite us for supper at their home across the lake. We assumed it was just to be a quiet, casual barbecue for the four of us. Upon arriving, though, we found ourselves being the center of attention for a baby shower attended by sixty of our Sandy Lake neighbours, my Mum and families from Grace United Church. Some we'd met numerous times and others we hardly knew. It was as overwhelming to see this gathering of well-wishers as it was delightfully silly to be told to wear funny hats of ribbon—the kind usually worn by expectant moms at baby showers. In absentia, Nicholas received all manner of toys, books and clothing. People had spent a fortune buying wagons, videos, OshKosh clothing, teddy bears, skates and water skis. We were so blessed to have these wonderful people in our lives.

We were at maximum capacity for guests every night that summer. I'd barely get rooms cleaned and changed when another group of guests would arrive. July was spent preparing for the Woodhaven Mile Swim and the summer regatta held annually, as I had dreamed it might be, on the long weekend in August. We'd cancelled our real estate listing and taken Woodhaven off the market because money was flowing as guests clamoured to have holiday time on Sandy Lake.

Meanwhile, I'd was receiving unsettling faxes and phone calls from Mohini Raghunath, who was extremely concerned by Immigration Canada's tardiness in responding to her letters regarding the documentation her office needed to have processed by the Delhi judiciary. By late July she had telephoned to say that the courts had closed for holidays until early September and Nicholas's file hadn't been submitted for approval because it lacked necessary papers.

The Case Processing Centre, based in Mississauga, is every international adoptive parent's nightmare. All documentation for overseas adoptions must be approved by the CPC. This office doesn't have a phone number and the only mode of communicating with staff there was by fax. I would send urgent messages daily, hoping someone would respond personally to me. And eventually they would phone, but I'd be outside or doing chores, so they'd leave a message saying, "Sorry we missed you, but we'll try another time." And the cycle would begin all over again. The CPC didn't give out its mailing address, other than a box number, so when I sent a letter by courier it was returned address unknown. I called Laura Wen at the provincial Ministry of Community and Social Services in Toronto and begged her to find me a phone number for anyone on staff inside the CPC. She told me her boss had a number, but he wouldn't release it to me. I was irate. Laura politely listened to me rant on about how frustrating it was to never be given voice to voice contact with the authorities who controlled the processing of paperwork needed to complete this adoption. She was on my side but said her hands were tied by both provincial and federal bureaucrats.

CHAPTER EIGHTEEN

AUGUST 1998 SUSAN'S LEGACY ARRIVES

THE DAY BEFORE THE SANDY Lake Regatta I received a phone call from Paul Landers at the People with Aids Foundation. The executive director of PWA, Laurie Edmiston, and I had connected months earlier when she stayed at a Sandy Lake cottage just down the road. I was headed to town one afternoon to do a grocery run when I came across Laurie and a friend jogging on the road. I stopped to say hello and we got into a discussion about the serenity of the lake, which led her to ask me what I did for a living. I explained I owned Woodhaven and gave her a quick rundown on our business philosophy and our benevolence program, wherein we offered free visits to caregivers of the terminally ill and the terminally ill themselves. Laurie told me about her background as the executive director of PWA and asked if I would offer free holidays to some of her clients. I told her to call anytime, handed her my card and drove off. The chance meeting would have a profound outcome: the client Paul was calling about would change Michael's and my life forever.

Paul told me about a woman with AIDS with a young son who wanted to have one last holiday together before she became too ill to travel. PWA had tried to send them to Disney World via the Children's Wish Foundation but the American authorities wouldn't allow her to enter the USA as a tourist because of her HIV status. Did we have any immediate vacancies? A cancellation a few hours earlier created a vacancy and

I was able to book them in for a complimentary three-day weekend. Paul explained that Susan was the mother of three children in their late teens and early twenties and one who was only four years old. I told Paul if she wanted to bring all her kids we would accommodate them in a two-room suite. He said the elder son was estranged but that the two teenaged daughters would probably love to come along.

Regatta weekend was a hoot, as usual. Record numbers of neighbours participated in the early-morning cross-the-lake swim and the afternoon canoeing, swimming and paddleboat events of the fifth annual Sandy Lake regatta. A corn roast and barbecue followed the awards ceremonies and I was thrust back to happy childhood memories on Stoney Lake watching all my friends proudly exhibit medals and ribbons. I yearned for the moment our son, Nicholas, could participate in the regattas and be a part of this community.

The long weekend had been full of activity around Woodhaven, so when ACT called with an ETA for Susan I was in the process of slowly regaining my energy level. Susan wasn't well enough to drive her own car, so her friend Sylvia had volunteered to bring the family up.

Shortly after lunch I lay down to read a book in the library. It was sweltering outside, and I had cranked up the air conditioning to freeze and was just dozing off when I heard a car beep its horn in the parking lot. Susan stepped out of the car, looking exhausted and gaunt, with dark circles under her big blue eyes. Regardless, it was obvious she was an attractive woman in her early forties. Her light brown hair hung in a ponytail down her back past her waist. She smiled at me as I walked toward her and asked, "Are you David the famous bank robber catcher?" I smiled and said yes. "I read about you catching that guy in the news and now we're at the place he got captured."

I introduced myself and Michael and in turn Susan introduced Sylvia, her two daughters, Emma and Courtney, and finally Kolwyn, her young son, holding tightly onto the collar around his dog's neck. It was so hot that we didn't waste time chatting outside before Michael and I carried their luggage inside and checked them into their suite. We left their dog Patsy, a fourteen-year-old English setter, outside to become acquainted with our dogs, who had already begun to lavish her with sniffs and happy whines of 'hello and follow me.'

Kolwyn

Susan shuffled as she walked around the lodge. I apologized that she had to share a suite with her children, but Susan replied that she was absolutely thrilled with their accommodations and the opportunity to be out of the city for three days. Her daughters had changed into bathing suits and were ready to go for a swim, while Kolwyn was thrilled to be the centre of the dogs' attention. Sylvia said she had to get back home and that she'd be back in a few days to retrieve Susan and the kids.

With Kolwyn in tow, her daughters headed down to the dock, while Susan sat down to rest in the library. She wrapped a cozy quilt over her shoulders, obviously feeling the chill from the air conditioning, and chatted while the children were off with Michael swimming. I asked her about Kolwyn's unique name.

Susan told me she'd been born in Colwyn Bay, Wales, and when he was born she decided to masculinize the name with a K rather than a C. Laughing, she said he'd probably never meet anyone in Canada with that name. She told me about being raised in England and then immigrating to Canada as a young adult, and was very chatty about her life, marriages, children and travels.

Five wet goldens suddenly ran into the room, followed by Kolwyn; Patsy was in hot pursuit of Kolwyn, and his smile of delight told us he preferred Woodhaven to Disney World. Susan wanted to take a nap, so I suggested I take her kids to Bobcaygeon for a Kawartha Dairy ice cream cone, the best cones anywhere.

Kolwyn was quite unruly in the car, causing me to wonder if he ever got disciplined at home. I had to tell him three times each way just to sit in his seat and remain buckled up. Then he discovered the electric window button and persisted in dropping his window, letting my precious cold air escape. He spilled his ice cream cone on the car seat and tried to pick it up, which only smeared it deeply into his shorts and the seat. By the time we arrived back at Woodhaven, Susan was up from her nap and talking with Michael and a few other guests who had assembled to watch him prepare supper.

I reported that the ice cream trip had been a success and when she asked if Kolwyn had behaved, I told her, "He was a normal four-year-old in the car, all hands and feet." Everyone laughed and continued to watch Michael's culinary expertise unfold. Kolwyn asked for a cookie and I said it was too close to supper. He immediately went to his mother to ask and she reached into her sweater pocket, pulled out a wafer and handed it to him. Pleased by his efforts to get what he wanted, he ran off to find out what was on the television upstairs. Susan noticed me staring. I must have telegraphed my disapproval by the look on my face, as she said to me, "Being tired and sick, I find it easier just giving him what he wants."

Knowing Courtney and Kolwyn were upstairs watching a video, Susan went outside to have a smoke with Emma. The other guests dispersed to the library to enjoy an impromptu cocktail party. I looked at Michael and he smiled and asked, "How rough was the trip to Bobcaygeon?" I said Kolwyn had been a real handful in the car and how he had only finished half his cone when Courtney egged him on to throw paper around the car.

"That little lad has a mind of his own," I said, "and what he really needs is to be taught that no means no. I was ticked off watching Kolwyn manipulate Susan into giving him a cookie after I'd said he couldn't have one. Considering the state of her health it probably was easier for her to just give in to his demands," I conceded. "But it must be so hard for Susan to temper her need to discipline him with just holding him close, knowing it won't be long before she dies. Did she say anything about a present husband or lover to you?"

I could tell Michael was preoccupied with making supper, but he managed to answer my question, saying simply Susan hadn't mentioned anyone. Michael was marinating ribs, boiling a big pot of corn on the cob and was creating his famous pad Thai salad. Mum was being dropped off at Woodhaven within the hour and would be bringing a dessert.

"Why don't we put on some hamburgers and hot dogs for Courtney and Kolwyn and let them sit upstairs and watch videos while we eat supper?" I suggested. I asked Susan if Kolwyn and Courtney would prefer to eat earlier, and she agreed.

Kolwyn was very fussy about his supper. I put a hot dog and some salad on his plate. He didn't want any salad and asked instead for potato chips. Susan told him he could go into her room and get a bag of chips if he ate two hot dogs. That seemed to appease him somewhat and off he and Courtney went to finish their movie.

At 7 p.m., after wine and cheese in the library, everyone filed into the dining room to have supper. I asked Susan to sit beside me at one end while Emma sat at the opposite end to help Michael dish out the food. Susan was chatty, and I hoped I could find out more about her over dinner. She had a look in her eye that gave me the impression she wasn't a small talk kind of woman. Several of the guests had heard bits and pieces of my recent trip to India, and they peppered me with questions about that country, the orphanages and the difficulties I was encountering as a gay man wanting to adopt. Susan listened intently to my saga about attempts to adopt being thwarted by the Children's Aid Society I briefed them on the demeaning interviews Nick and I had experienced in Richmond Hill with various social workers. We'd have a social worker assigned to us to interview us on myriad subjects relating to care and development of children that might be offered to us to adopt. Being asked on three separate occasions, "'Who is top and who is bottom in your relationship?" or "At what point in sex do you put on a condom?" But worst of all was the fellow who appeared as queer as a three-dollar bill, and asked us, "Why do you want to adopt a boy? Is that so you can home-grow your own play toy?" The indignity of these questions had to be challenged. Feeling these queries were unconscionable by anyone with half a brain, we'd ask these supposed professional social workers how knowledge of a couples preferred sexual positioning would help them assess our parenting skills? Every time we'd be shut down with a simple retort, "Answer my question, and remember, I determine if you will get a child."

Susan didn't say a word during my account of India, meeting Mrs. Raghunath and now waiting for Nicholas's paperwork to be completed so I could go back to Delhi and fetch him home—hopefully by Christmas. I told our guests about the recent baby shower the neighbours had organized for us and how open and receptive Sandy Lakers had been toward us and our plans to adopt.

While coffee was being passed around, Susan asked me quietly if Michael liked children. I smiled and told her that I wouldn't be with him if kids and dogs weren't highest on his priority list. "Michael will be a superb role model for our kids." I laughed and said that without a doubt our children would be computer literate, considering Michael was the computer science and mathematics department head at a boys' private school.

Other than Mum, Michael, Susan and me, everyone else scattered after finishing dessert and coffee. Susan seemed quite content to just sit and watch dusk envelop the lake from her perch in our dining room. Emma had gone off to check on Courtney and Kolwyn.

"Susan, how long have you lived with HIV?" I asked her.

"I became infected back in '83 or '84 from a guy I was seeing at that time," she replied candidly. Then she asked, "How long did your Nick live with full-blown AIDS?" She was very interested in talking about Nick's health and the deterioration he experienced prior to death. Michael asked Susan if she had a boyfriend in her life currently and she laughed and said, "Before Kolwyn was born, I was quite a babe. Never had any trouble finding good-looking men, but since Kolwyn's birth my health has steadily worsened. I'm only ninety-five pounds soaking wet—you should have seen me at one hundred and twenty." She smiled naughtily. "I could have had any man I wanted. But now I look like an old woman about to die. Who'd want me now? Besides, I wouldn't be interested in a man at this point. I know my days are numbered and I just want to be around my young son and the girls as much as possible."

Susan's candour made Michael flinch. Mum asked Susan if she had a faith to fall back on and Susan said she was a reformed Catholic no longer into formal religion. "I have my own thoughts about God and I'm comfortable knowing God will look after me when the time comes," she said.

Susan asked me about Nicholas' health. "There is lots of HIV in India, isn't there? Do you know if he's been exposed to it or leprosy?"

I told her a police officer had discovered Nicholas clutching the corpse of his mother along an alleyway and that his health background was completely unknown. The Canadian High Commission had put him through a battery of tests to determine if he was adoptable by international standards. Other than that, I told her, "We know nothing about his health history." I went on to say that his health really didn't matter. I felt I had waited so long for a child that I was letting God do most of the paperwork and I had to trust that everything would work out as it should. Susan asked if not knowing about his exposure to various diseases worried us and I told her no.

"Nicholas is our son, with or without whatever health issues may crop up in his future," I said. "No point in worrying about what might be. I just want to get him home on Canadian soil."

Kolwyn came running into the dining room and I instinctively looked at my watch and saw that it was 10 p.m. Susan greeted him with a big hug and kiss and said, "It's time for bed, Kolwyn," and excused herself from the table and took him upstairs. I soon followed and called up the stairs after her to say the coffee urn would be on by 6 a.m. if she was an early riser. She smiled back at me and said thanks for a great day and she'd see us in the morning.

It was obvious from the noise coming from upstairs that Susan wasn't having an easy time putting Kolwyn to bed. Mum wryly smiled at Michael and said, "That is typical behaviour for a stubborn four-year-old boy. I should know," she said, "David was the most stubborn child I'd ever encountered. Just hope that Nicholas isn't stubborn or that noise could just as easily be the two of you trying to put a five-year-old to bed."

Michael looked over at me and said, "If Nicholas is like Kolwyn then we'll be in big trouble." I just laughed and told the two of them that no child of mine would be allowed to act up like Kolwyn had that day. I was tired and said goodnight to Mum. Michael said he was going upstairs to watch a sci-fi show he'd videotaped a few days earlier and would be to bed in an hour or so.

Michael nudged me awake at 6 a.m. saying he could hear someone out in the kitchen clanging pots. "It must be one of the guests trying to make coffee so you had better see what's up," he said. I threw on my shorts and a T-shirt, brushed my teeth, and let the dogs out through our bedroom door and followed them onto the lawn. Then I walked with the dogs around to the main entrance and briskly strode in, hoping that whoever was in my kitchen would think that I'd been up and out for a walk with the dogs.

Susan was at the coffee bar making a pot of tea. "Sleep well?" I asked.

"I never seem to be able to get more than a few hours sleep at one time. I've been up for two hours waiting to see the sunrise and talk to you," she said, continuing to make her tea.

"Would you like something to munch on with that?" I asked. Susan said she was going to have one more smoke outside and then she'd come in for a piece of toast. I made a pot of coffee and joined her on the front lawn. She was in a talkative mood and told me about her life and her husband's, her family back in England, and she shared some of the horrors of being a mother about to die of AIDS. Her openness, under different circumstances, could have been unnerving but I sensed her deep need to speak about her health and impending death.

Susan asked me many questions about why Nick and I had moved to the country. Did I enjoy operating a bed and breakfast and how long had Michael been in my life? I could hear rustling inside the dining room, so I excused myself and went to see who was up. It was 7:15 a.m. and Mum was making toast when I opened the screen door to the kitchen. She asked if Susan was all right, having noticed us sitting on the lawn talking.

"I didn't want to disturb the two of you. I went to bed thinking about that girl and her children. How horrible it must be for Susan's older children, watching their mother's health deteriorate like this." Seconds later Susan followed me into the kitchen, greeted Mum with a warm hello and said she would be back for a cup of coffee after she had taken her meds.

When Susan came down she wandered over to where I was sitting beside Mum at the coffee bar. A few other guests had begun to mill about the coffee room, too. One couple asked if they had enough time for a canoe ride before breakfast. As I got up to pour myself a third cup of coffee Susan asked if she could talk to me in the living room. Mum started to wander away to give us some privacy, but Susan said, "Dorothy, why don't you join us? I'd like you to hear what I have to say."

Once seated in the living room Susan reached over and put her hand on my knee, turned to face me and said, "David, I couldn't sleep all night. I just know that there was a reason God didn't let me fly to Disney World with Kolwyn. I was meant to come here and ask you to adopt my son and make him a little brother for Nicholas. I am going to be dead in a few months and I'd love for you to adopt Kolwyn, so he could live here with you, Michael and Nicholas at Woodhaven."

I wasn't sure I'd heard her correctly. I am sure my face had a look of incredulity. Before I could say anything, Susan saw that she needed to repeat what she'd asked.

"I am serious, David. What about you, Dorothy? Would you like to have another grandson?"

Mum's face broke into a smile a mile wide and she said, "Susan, I'd feel fortunate to have Kolwyn as my grandson." Susan looked at me with worried eyes, waiting for me to answer.

I sensed in my soul that this was to become one of those once-in-a-lifetime moments. I desperately wanted to believe in angels and destiny. I considered grabbing Susan firmly by the arms, looking deep into her eyes to say, "Don't mess with me." I couldn't afford to have her wind up my emotions only to have my hopes quashed by bureaucrats shouting, "Never on my watch!" and her acquiescing. I was bruised and beaten, having lived every day with an anchor of skepticism around my neck regarding anything to do with government adoption officials. Disappointment could turn into rage whenever I recalled the string of dodgy social workers who had taken my money and repeatedly walked me down the garden path, only to leave me stranded and alone under an arbor of devastation.

"Susan, if you're serious, you don't have to ask me twice. The answer is yes. I'd love to adopt Kolwyn and have him live with us here on Sandy Lake. Are you really sure about this?" I asked cautiously, feeling my heart rate accelerating rapidly.

"I knew at supper last night that God brought me here for this reason. I'm very sure about this. If you and Michael agree, then I'd like to discuss it with the two of you before lunch." Her eyes were smiling in relief.

I could tell a weight had been lifted off her shoulders. Susan told me that none of her siblings had agreed to adopt Kolwyn without him first having an HIV test, and she wouldn't hand over her son to anyone with attached conditions. Susan's mother lived in England and was too old to start parenting all over again. Susan said that when she asked me about Nicholas' health last night and I'd said his status was unknown and wasn't a concern to me, she knew I'd be right for her son.

"It upsets me so much to think of Kolwyn calling anyone else Mummy. But having two fathers would preserve me as Mummy in his memory for all time." Susan barely finished speaking when her hands rose up to cradle her face and she began to sob uncontrollably. I reached over and hugged her close. My heart felt like it was being ripped apart. After a few minutes of being consoled, she sat back in her chair and looked me in the eyes. "I never thought I'd have to find a home for my little son. I don't want to die but I know in my bones it's going to happen soon. I can't die before I make arrangements for him."

Susan gave me a further autobiographical sketch while Mum left the room to get us all some juice and tissues. She had been just as maverick and strong-willed in her approach to life as I had been. She'd come to Canada from England as a teenager, married young and had her first two children, Austyn and Emma, back to back. That marriage ended, Susan said, because her husband walked out on her into the arms of another woman. During the late 1970s, she took her two children to Jamaica for a holiday. While there she met a wonderful Jamaican, who fathered her third child, a daughter she named Courtney. After three years of living in the hills with her Jamaican lover, Susan and her three children returned to Toronto. She had had many careers, and it was while working in real estate that she met and fell in love with the man who gave her HIV. He died of AIDS eight months afterward.

Mum returned with a tray of juice and settled down in the sofa beside us while Susan continued to tell her story. Over the next few years of returning to Toronto living, Susan had several long-term affairs. In the early 1990s, through real estate friends, she met a successful Toronto mechanical engineer who was also HIV positive. She fell deeply in love with him, yet he remained on the sidelines, unsure about committing to a full-time relationship. In February 1993, Susan found herself eight weeks' pregnant with twins. Her lover and some of his medical friends badgered her endlessly, finally convincing her this high-risk, HIV positive pregnancy was wrong. Eleven weeks into the pregnancy Susan succumbed to his demands and had an abortion. The abortion devastated her for months and she clung to her boyfriend for whatever occasional scraps of love he'd throw her way. Their hot-cold relationship continued to sustain her into the summer of 1993, but when in August she found herself pregnant again, her boyfriend abandoned her and flew to Thailand to work on an international engineering project. Susan said she felt the child growing inside her was more about God giving her a second chance than about her having been irresponsible regarding birth control measures. At this point in her life Susan still hadn't told her family about being HIV positive.

Her son Austyn thought she was stupid to have a baby at her age. Susan said he called her a slut and a whore and refused to have anything to do with her for months. He finally came around but was never again someone she would rely on. Predictably, after Kolwyn was born, Susan told us that her health quickly declined, just as her team of caregivers had warned her. Susan worked hard to mask the signs of HIV ravaging her body. Steadily losing weight, she'd jokingly tell concerned family and friends that having a baby at forty was the easiest way to regain a great figure.

Two years passed, and Susan was frequently ill, and for longer periods each time. She finally had to tell her children, mother and extended family. Twenty-two-year-old Austyn was furious and told her she deserved to die for being such an embarrassment to the family. Emma, twenty, and Courtney gave her comfort and were much more forgiving. Susan said she wrote in her diary that night that she no longer considered Austyn to be her son, vowing that she wouldn't let him upset her again.

Fifteen minutes had passed since Susan began sharing her life story with us. The three of us sat in silence, gazing out the window at the mourning doves at the bird feeder. I broke the silence and asked what provisions she had made for the older children.

"My older children will be fine. Emma and Austyn are out on their own now and Courtney will be taken into the home of a friend of mine. I just can't imagine leaving Kolwyn alone at four years of age," she said. "I think that is why I've ended up here, to ask you to be Kolwyn's fathers and adopt him into your family."

Just then Michael came out of the bedroom. He didn't seem startled to see me holding Susan's hand in mine. He sat down beside us and put his arms around her shoulder. I gave Michael the short version of what Susan had just asked. His eyes watered as he looked at Susan and said, "We would be honoured to continue raising Kolwyn." Like an experienced grandma, Mum moved across the room to sit on the stool in front of Susan and pat her forearm reassuringly.

We could hear Courtney bringing Kolwyn downstairs and his familiar yell "Mummy" as he searched the kitchen, dining room and library. Susan wiped her eyes and broke our huddle by standing up and walking to greet her son with a kiss and a hug. I followed her and began to prepare breakfast for the guests, hardly able to concentrate on chopping the red peppers for the frittata. Was this happening? Could I be dreaming? I was watching Kolwyn with his mother and sister out on the lawn throwing tennis balls for the dogs.

Michael joined me in the kitchen looking out the window at Susan and her children. "Imagine this," he whispered. "You're denied the right to adopt children for two decades and within three months we have two sons being offered to us. I'm speechless. I can't imagine how good you must feel." I told Michael that I was in awe of Susan's strength to do what she had done that morning.

"I can't even begin to fathom how gut-wrenching that must have been for her. Imagine Susan knowing she's about to die and searching desperately to find the best possible replacement parent and home for her little boy. I hope I'm never faced with that dilemma. I don't know if I'd handle this same situation with the grace and dignity Susan just did. Nick must be looking out for us upstairs, Michael. This sort of thing just doesn't happen spur of the moment. God's involved in this somehow, I just know it," I said.

Susan, Michael and I sat down later that morning and further discussed what she had proposed. Susan said she didn't have the physical strength or the money to find a lawyer to make this legal. We told her not to worry about a lawyer and adoption fees, that we would handle all costs. I told Susan how thankful I was for this opportunity to be her son's father and that I hoped knowing Kolwyn would be well loved and cared for might give her some peace. Several more times that day we spoke about Kolwyn, his biological father not wanting anything to do with Susan once he found out she was pregnant, and how Susan had lived her life as a nonconformist who enjoyed every hour to its fullest.

I was curious to know more about Kolwyn's father and asked Susan if he'd ever inquired about her or the child she'd given birth to in April 1994. It was sad hearing it took two years for him to make contact during one of his vacations back to Canada. They arranged to get together in a Toronto waterfront park one afternoon, so he could meet Kolwyn. The visit hadn't lasted long, and they parted as strangers. Susan said that she'd heard he disappeared mysteriously in Thailand and his parents and the Canadian authorities presumed he had died in solitude of AIDS.

Susan asked Emma to join us in the living room later that night and told her that she had asked Michael and me to adopt Kolwyn. Emma appeared unemotional and simply said, "Oh, that's good for Kolwyn," and sat beside her mother expressionless. I wasn't sure if she was stunned by this news or if she simply couldn't let herself think about her mother's impending death.

Friday morning Sylvia arrived to drive Susan's family back to Toronto. Emma and Courtney wanted to go for one last swim before leaving and Susan told them to take Kolwyn down to the dock with them. Once the kids had left the house, Susan explained to Sylvia that she had found a home for Kolwyn with Michael and me. Without hesitation Sylvia grinned and said she thought this would be a great place for Kolwyn to grow up. As Susan got comfortable in the car I told her I would call a lawyer to finalize our arrangement.

"Just let me know when and where, but we should do this real soon," she said. As I closed the passenger side door, Susan smiled at me and her eyes penetrated mine. She blinked, and tears streamed down her face. Then she turned to Sylvia and said, "Get me home."

Sylvia's car had only been out our laneway a few hours when my dear friend Halldor arrived for a two-day visit from Vancouver. I couldn't wait to share the news about Susan wanting us to adopt Kolwyn. He was barely out of the car when I let him know. Halldor, a lawyer himself, told me to hire a lawyer and get a joint custody agreement signed by Susan as soon as possible.

"If her health is as precarious as you say, then it's imperative you do this on Monday." I told him a friend of mine had a family law practice. He urged me to call her at home to make an appointment with Susan. Flabbergasted by this news, my friend Sandy agreed that a joint custody arrangement should be done quickly before anyone could contest it by suggesting Susan wasn't of sound mind when she agreed to Kolwyn being adopted by us.

Five months earlier I hadn't had one child despite my two-decade fight to adopt children, yet within a span of twenty weeks we now had two sons being offered. While I was in awe, Michael remained in a state of total shock. I'm sure I had more confidence in his ability to be a fantastic father than he had in himself. It was both humorous and sad to watch him shake his head in disbelief over how we were on the threshold of adopting two sons. Humorus because Michael obviously hadn't been prepared for the moment when my quest would come to a happy conclusion, and sad because Michael was such a super human being, so kind and so loving, yet went through life blanketed by insecurity. Michael was a strong, handsome man of character with an enormous heart, yet it seemed to me that he was walking through life without the confidence to step up to the plate and at least try to hit a home run. Now on the verge of having two little boys arrive in our home, I sensed he would be a home-run father.

My parents had made every minute of parenthood count for something. Likewise, I couldn't recall a moment in my life when I wasn't preoccupied with thoughts of the children I'd parent. Being a father was just something I knew I'd be someday.

Had someday just arrived?

CHAPTER NINETEEN

SUSAN'S FAREWELL TO KOLWYN

SEPTEMBER AND OCTOBER WERE BUSY months for Kolwyn. Besides adjusting to junior kindergarten and his new classmate at Buckhorn Public School, he attended swimming classes two nights a week and his weekly appointments with child psychologist Brian Nichols. Two times every week I'd drive him to visit with Susan. Every second weekend Michael would leave work Friday afternoon at Crescent School and pick up Susan and bring her to Woodhaven to spend time with Kolwyn in his new home. I kept wondering how I'd handle the situation if Kolwyn were my son and I'd handed him over to strangers before I died, hoping I'd done the right thing for my child. Susan wrapped her arms around Kolwyn and held him close to her the entire weekend, and she cried uncontrollably every night after he went to bed. Michael found it enormously upsetting as he sat on the sofa consoling her. Her visits were gut-wrenching for me, too. Mum often spent weekends with us and frequently ended up on the sofa being hugged by Susan who cried unconsolably for hours on end. Listening to Susan's pitiful and agonizing lamentation was excruciating for us but it cemented our resolve to be strong for her …and for Kolwyn.

Sylvia drove Susan up for Thanksgiving weekend, accompanied by Courtney, who was so happy to see Kolwyn. Most of that time we just spent being with one another, going to the local fall fairs – Courtney or me pushing Susan in a wheelchair and Kolwyn riding in her lap. It was Susan's last good weekend. Shortly after returning from Woodhaven, she became seriously ill and was admitted to Casey House, Toronto's AIDS hospice.

I made the six-hour round trip to Toronto two or three times each week to sit and talk to Susan. Sylvia arranged to meet me for a late lunch most days I was in Toronto. She was very interested in all that Kolwyn was doing and asked constantly about Nicholas. These lunch hours with Sylvia gave me a chance to get to know Susan through Sylvia's eyes and understand her better. I wanted to learn about her personality, her friendships, her attitudes and foibles. I remember Sylvia telling me that as much as she adored her friend, there were times that Susan was all about Susan to the point of being narcissistic. I'd never really experienced that side of her—but Sylvia said she was headstrong when it came to something she wanted. Sylvia lamented that it was apparent Courtney and Emma were also a bit like that. Knowing their mother was ill and didn't have much money never stopped her older kids from dipping into their mother's bank account to buy clothes or cigarettes or go to concerts—leaving Susan broke at the end of the month, unable to pay rent. Susan's mother had frequently transferred money from England into Susan's bank account, so she could pay rent and have money for food.

By mid-November it was clear to everyone that Susan was slipping away, though when Kolwyn and I visited she'd rally and present herself remarkably clear-headed. The last day we visited her, Susan weakly hugged Kolwyn beside her and they talked about all the things he was doing at Woodhaven and in school and how he was enjoying having all the dogs around him, including his own pet Patsy, whom we had adopted when Kolwyn moved in. This visit was short, as she was exhausted, and it was a huge effort for her to sit up in bed to talk to Kolwyn. As we left, Susan grabbed something from the side of her bed: a teddy-bear she had asked one of the nurses to buy for her son to remember her by. Kolwyn was so excited with this gift from his Mummy that he just hugged and kissed her and thanked her. Every nurse on the floor was in tears watching Kolwyn kiss his mother goodbye. Susan lapsed into a coma later that night and died two days later.

I deliberately chose not to interfere in the planning of Susan's wake and funeral. Sylvia called to see how Kolwyn was handling the news and she encouraged me to keep Susan's other children at arm's length. She knew Austyn had made disparaging remarks about gays and that he was angry with his mother for having made guardianship arrangements with me.

"Susan made it clear to me over the last year that she only had one son, that being Kolwyn. Austyn wouldn't show up to help his mother, and when he did he always got into arguments with her and she'd spend hours crying on the phone telling me about his cruel remarks. She had disowned him many times because she loathed the person he'd become."

I asked Sylvia if she would support me over Austyn if he took me to court regarding Kolwyn.

"Oh, for sure. Susan told me she wanted Kolwyn with you. She said she could die happy knowing you and Michael would be his forever dads. I was Susan's best friend and she confided in me. I'd be glad to tell a judge who Kolwyn needs to be with and who his mother wanted him to be with. Susan would cause thunder in heaven if Austyn were ever to get custody of Kolwyn."

Susan's mother, Joan, had just arrived from England and was staying with her sister Molly in Scarborough. I called hoping to be able to speak with Joan. She answered the phone on the first ring and began inquiring about Kolwyn and his reaction to Susan's death. Joan wasn't keen to have Kolwyn attend the funeral or the wake. She felt it could be disturbing long-term for a four-year-old to see his mother's lifeless body laid out in an open casket. I argued that seeing his mother in a casket might help Kolwyn understand that Mummy's soul had gone up to heaven and that only her body was left behind to go into the ground. Joan acquiesced, saying, "Well, go ahead and bring him and let's just watch his reactions. If he doesn't handle the wake, then he shouldn't come to the funeral service."

Joan said she was exhausted from her six-hour flight but that her sisters and brother had been wonderful to her, especially Molly. I told

Joan that Molly and her son Michael had bluntly told me a few weeks earlier that they weren't pleased Susan had given Kolwyn to me.

"Under these circumstances don't be too harsh with them, especially Molly. As the eldest of my siblings, she can appear bull-headed as the matriarch of our Canadian family. But I couldn't manage Susan's funeral without her. She has a great heart, but sometimes she can be frightfully blunt if she feels loved ones are in jeopardy. Give her time. I think you'll like her more as the two of you get to know one another." Joan paused to gather her thoughts again. "I really don't think you should stay too long at the wake tomorrow. Two days in a row experiencing grieving family might be too much for little Kolwyn. What time do you think you'll come to the funeral parlour?" I told her we'd come early in the afternoon so Kolwyn could see Susan without too many others around. I sensed Joan still wasn't convinced Kolwyn should see his mother's body in a casket.

"Austyn is bringing the girls to the funeral parlour around three o'clock. It might be best if you get there earlier and leave before he arrives. I can't stand the bugger. He was so mean to his mother. I don't know if I can ever forgive him for the way that he treated her. Kolwyn is where Susan wanted him to be and don't you pay any mind to Austyn's ranting." Joan's words were deliberately chosen, and I felt her full allegiance squarely behind me and Michael.

The next afternoon Michael, Kolwyn and I arrived at the funeral parlour just a few minutes before the 2 p.m. visitation for Susan. Joan and her siblings had come half an hour earlier to view the open casket and to say prayers with the priest. Looking shell-shocked, Joan saw us enter the viewing room and came up and hugged us all. The rest of Joan's siblings, whom I'd not yet met, came over and introduced themselves one at a time. Courtney suddenly appeared behind us, knelt and hugged Kolwyn. She clasped Kolwyn's hand in hers and headed toward the casket. I excused myself from the small congregation of Susan's family and walked quickly to catch up—I wanted to observe Kolwyn when he saw Susan's body in the casket. Courtney started to cry and put her hands to her face to cover her tears. Kolwyn seemed unsure what to do.

I lifted him up and said, "Remember what we talked about last night, Kolwyn? This is just Mummy's body. She isn't in there. God already took her soul up to heaven a few days ago."

Kolwyn looked puzzled and remarked, "But it looks like Mummy. See Mummy's long fingernails," he said pointing to Susan's clasped hands, exposing her trademark long nails.

"Well, this is Mummy's body, but she isn't in it. Remember, we talked about the turtle shell and how an empty shell looks like a real turtle except the insides have already gone up to heaven? Well, that is what Mummy's body is like. We can see her body, but all her insides have gone up to heaven."

I needed to choose my words carefully. I had attended the wake of a favourite great-aunt when I was only seven years old. I had been fascinated by the body lying there and watched closely to see if the chest rose to show signs of her being alive. I'd asked my mother if I could touch the body and she said it was fine to touch the hands. The cold feel of my deceased great-aunt's hand had reassured me she wasn't in her body any longer and it felt better imagining her being warm up somewhere in heaven's clouds.

So, I said to Kolwyn, "Do you want to touch Mummy's hand? It won't be warm like when she was inside her body. She took the warmth to heaven with her." Kolwyn, quite mesmerized by every detail of Susan's body lying before him, nodded to me that he wanted to.

"You first, Dad," he said as he almost touched her and but then pulled back. I put my hand on Susan's folded hands to show Kolwyn there was nothing to be nervous about. Without hesitation he reached out and touched Susan's hand with his fingers and held them there until the coldness of her hands registered in his mind.

"Her hand is cold. I guess she isn't inside, because Mummy has warm hands," he said looking up at me for some assurance.

"That's right, Mummy went to heaven, so she could always look out after you. She is feeling good and warm up there with God. What colour wings do you think she has on today, Kolwyn?" I asked, trying to change the mood around the casket.

Kolwyn's eyes brightened up. "Orange. I bet she has orange wings. That's my favourite colour," he said with a smile. I prayed that this experience of touching his mother would be as positive in his memory as it had been for me when I was his age.

We stayed long enough for Kolwyn to be greeted and fussed and cried over by numerous relatives. Austyn walked into the room and I could sense the mood of Joan and her siblings change the moment they noticed his arrival. Emma came over and gave Kolwyn a big hug, followed by Austyn. Emma gave me a warm kiss on the cheek and asked how Kolwyn was doing. Austyn brushed tightly up behind Emma to avoid any eye contact with me and lifted Kolwyn up into the air and hugged him. Kolwyn gave him a big hug back but then wanted down, so he could continue to visit with one of his young cousins. Without acknowledging my presence, Austyn proceeded up to view his mother's body with Emma in tow. Courtney joined them, and a hush fell over the room.

I determined that we'd get the hell out of there within a few minutes. I didn't want Kolwyn being exposed to scenes of defiance by Austyn. I winked at Michael, who moved close to me and said he'd get the car and wait for us out front. A few minutes passed before Susan's three older children turned around and left the casket. They dispersed around the room to talk with friends and family and to be comforted. I whispered to Joan that we were going to take Kolwyn home. She hugged me and quietly suggested we meet tomorrow at Molly's prior to the funeral and we'd all drive over to the funeral home together. I whisked Kolwyn up in my arms and said it was time for his Happy Meal at McDonald's, hoping he wouldn't make a fuss about leaving. Thankfully, the word McDonald's did the trick and he gleefully raced ahead of me to Michael in the waiting car.

Kolwyn didn't seem too bothered by the day's events at bedtime. I talked to him about the funeral service the next day and how it was a time for people to think good thoughts about Mummy and to celebrate her life. I told him there would be a fun party with lots of children after the funeral service back at Aunt Molly's house. Michael couldn't get out of a meeting to attend Monday's funeral, which meant I'd be alone.

The small chapel attached to the funeral parlour was barely occupied when we arrived at 1:45 p.m. The priest was waiting upstairs with Susan's open casket for her family to have one last viewing, a prayer and the closing of the casket lid. As the lid was being lowered, Austyn, Emma and Courtney ran up the stairs and the closing was delayed giving them additional time with Susan's body. I took Kolwyn downstairs to the chapel and we sat two rows behind the front pews. Joan accompanied the priest and Susan's casket into the chapel.

The service began five minutes late. Joan wept openly in the front pew while being comforted by Molly and Emma. Suddenly, Joan lurched out of her seat and stood rigidly straight to the left of Susan's casket. Seconds later she uttered a guttural, mournful cry and fainted. Once revived, she sat slouched over and wept inconsolably in the pew as the final prayers were said. Courtney and Emma were greatly affected by their grandmother's fainting spell and their grief-tinged faces caused a swell of crying from the pews behind me. Courtney and Emma came over to Kolwyn and hugged him tightly. Although looking frightened and confused, Kolwyn didn't cry, nor did he take his eyes off me. I smiled reassuringly, and he squirmed away from Courtney's embrace and back into my arms.

Just as the funeral had been hours before, the reception at Molly's was emotionally charged. Susan's death had hit home with her forty-something friends and cousins: death could come at any age. To the elders of Susan's family, her death signified a young soul being laid to rest forty years prematurely.

Kolwyn ran around the house playing with a flock of young second cousins. Joan suggested I help pass around trays of finger sandwiches, which gave me an opportunity to introduce myself to many of Susan's extended family. I noticed many eyes watching me as I worked the room, passing platters of food. Courtney and Emma were convivial. Austyn refused to look at me. An hour into the reception, Joan whispered that this might be a good moment to make a quiet exit with Kolwyn. I gathered Kolwyn's things and told him we had to go. He resisted and ran off to chase one of the toddlers he had been teasing. Joan gave him a hug as he ran past her and she said it was time for him to put on his coat and boots.

I was holding my breath hoping that we would get out of this house without Kolwyn crying or making a scene. He grabbed hold of Courtney and said he wanted to stay with her, the primary caregiver he had known for most of his young life. Courtney, to her credit, told him she'd visit him soon at Woodhaven. This didn't calm him down much, as he wanted to stay and play with the other children. Courtney sat with him and put on his boots and helped to button up his coat. Kolwyn was crying and kept repeating he didn't want to leave, and everyone in the house seemed to have gathered in the kitchen to witness him being torn from their midst. I imagined a million dagger-eyes looking down on me as I struggled to pick Kolwyn up, squirming and resisting any comfort from Courtney, Joan or me. I managed to raise him in my arms; Joan was standing on the top step of the stairwell leading down from the kitchen and waved me out. She said, "Just get him in the car and go. I'll phone you later tonight."

Watching me carrying Kolwyn to the car, while he cried and struggled to get out of my arms, caused many of the relatives to sob openly over Kolwyn's grief and loss. I wondered if one of his relatives might suddenly challenge my guardianship. I just wanted to get Kolwyn strapped into his car seat and drive away as fast as possible. Joan had grabbed her overcoat and was following me to the car. She handed Kolwyn a cookie and told him she loved him and would see him soon. As we huddled together at the car with Kolwyn choking back tears and eating his cookie, Joan looked at me and said, "Take good care of my grandson and don't let him forget how much I love him."

Just then Austyn ran out of the house toward us. Was this going to be the confrontation I'd anticipated? I braced myself for whatever might happen. As Austyn approached the car, he had tears in his eyes and said he just wanted to say goodbye to his little brother. I felt sorry for him—maybe he wasn't so rotten after all. Maybe the death of his mother had brought him to his senses. He kissed Kolwyn on the cheek and said goodbye. As he passed in front of me he said, "Thanks for bringing him to the funeral today."

Joan was waiting in the cold to wave us goodbye. She leaned in the window and said, "Don't be fooled by Austin's tears and don't trust him. It's time to do what Susan wanted. Take Kolwyn home where he belongs at Woodhaven with you and Michael." She then opened Kolwyn's car door, leaned in and told him to give her a big hug. As we drove up to the end of the street and turned north, I looked at Kolwyn whimpering in his car seat. I couldn't begin to imagine the bewilderment and grief this four-year-old must be experiencing. I felt so helpless. A few blocks later I asked if he would like to go to McDonald's and get a Happy Meal. Instantly his tears stopped, and he smiled brightly. Two hours later he was sleeping soundly in his bed and I was very relieved to have survived the past four days.

The first few days after Susan's funeral I was busy on the phone trying to get a flight booked to Delhi. I was in contact with Mohini Raghunath at the orphanage by fax around the clock to make sure all my documentation was in order. I hoped that my adoption case would be heard in the Delhi courts before the judicial offices closed for six weeks starting December 5, 1998.

Brian Nichols, the psychologist we found months earlier to help Kolwyn adjust to his new home and life suggested we double our appointments during those first few weeks after Susan's death. Kolwyn looked forward to his sessions with Brian and was apparently processing his suddenly changed circumstance and transitioning well to his new life as Kolwyn Irlam Rattenbury McKinstry.

At Trent University Kolwyn was becoming not only comfortable but proficient in the water, easily capable of swimming unassisted for one length of the twenty-five-metre pool within weeks of starting his lessons. It was a proud moment watching him smile at me from the pool, indicating he was enjoying himself.

On December 2, Mohini called to tell me that the Canadian officials hadn't forwarded my documents in time for the courts to process them before they closed; this meant that I'd have to wait for the next court session, which wouldn't begin until late January 1999. Nicholas wouldn't be home for Christmas. I was more devastated than angry. From the moment Kolwyn arrived, we had told him about his older brother, Nicholas, who would be coming home from India soon. I loathed the idea of Nicholas spending another day separated from us and I considered the possibility of going to India to wait alongside him until his documents came through. I faxed Mohini about this idea. Within hours she responded with a phone call telling me not to waste money on accommodations and food for what could be two to six months until Nicholas's paperwork was completed. I was so sick of hearing patience, patience and more patience.

A few weeks later, while wrapping gifts for the upcoming women's shelter Christmas program, a strange late-model car drove into our lot. As the driver got out of the car and walked toward the house with a woman and several toddlers in tow, I could see it was Austyn. My first impulse was to yell upstairs advising Kolwyn to stay there with his Lego and be quiet. I had a feeling this unscheduled visit might be confrontational.

Austyn asked if his girlfriend and her two young kids could come in, too. I beckoned them inside. Austyn wondered where Kolwyn was and I told him he was playing upstairs.

"I want to take Kolwyn home with me for a week or so. I have friends in town who want to see him again and I've got time to take him around with me," he announced. His manner was combative and high-handed. Looking him straight in the eye I said, "That's not going to happen, Austyn. I have legal custody of him, as per your mother's instructions. He isn't going anywhere with you unsupervised. Besides which, he is in school three full days a week and it's important for his stability that he continue with his new routines here in our home."

Just then Kolwyn came racing down the stairs, having heard the dogs barking upon Austyn's arrival. Austyn smiled and opened his arms to signal Kolwyn to run to him for a hug, "Hi, Kolwyn, I've come to take you home with me," he said and began walking toward Kolwyn. I firmly placed the flat of my hand on his chest and stopped his movement toward my son.

I looked at Kolwyn and said firmly, "Kolwyn, I want to talk adult-talk with Austyn, so you go to your room until I call you." He didn't argue, and an unsure frown spread across his little face as he followed my orders and walked away from us to his bedroom.

"He's coming with me, David. I'm his family," Austyn said.

I told him to get his girlfriend and children out of my home and under no circumstances was he to think of visiting Kolwyn without our permission.

"I have only to call the police and they will have you arrested on the spot for trespassing. But before the police get here I'll have rearranged your face. This isn't an idle threat; it's a promise. Now get yourselves off my property."

Austyn's girlfriend tugged at his jacket and Austyn nervously laughed. "All right, I half-expected this from you. I got something from the sheriff for you in my car." Austyn helped his girlfriend and the two toddlers out to his car. It didn't take long before he came back, sneered at me, threw an envelope at the door and said, "See you in court, asshole."

I grappled for a second with whether to call the police, so they would have a record of this trespassing infraction on file. Instead, I stared out the library window, watching Austyn's car quickly fade out of sight. I retrieved the papers he had thrown outside the front door. It was a legal document telling me I had to appear in court on December 18 to defend my right to have custody of Kolwyn.

A few hours later, when I had calmed down, I called Joan, still in Toronto trying to clear up Susan's estate before heading home to the U.K. I told her about Austyn's surprise visit and she cursed him for being so stupid.

"He mustn't get Kolwyn. Susan would turn in her grave if you lose Kolwyn to them. You must fight this. Do you have a lawyer?" she asked. I told her I would mount a defence through a good lawyer in town, but if she had any damning information on her eldest grandson that would help my case, she should put it on paper and courier it to me. Joan said Susan had written in her journal that she had renounced any claims Austyn might have as her son. Since the day Susan revealed her AIDS status to Austyn, he had been cruel and belittling. She'd been devastated by his embarrassment about her "catching AIDS."

Sylvia called the following day and I told her about Austyn's visit. Immediately she offered to write a letter to the court indicating her close friendship with Susan and how in ten years of knowing Susan she had only heard Susan mention Austyn's name a few times.

"I only ever met him in person around the time Susan got sick."

Michael had come home the night before, so he could be in court with me on December 18. I was nervous and dreading having this case heard in Peterborough, a town not known for its liberal-thinking judiciary. Our Toronto lawyer arranged for local counsel, Catherine Blastorah, to take on the case.

Austyn, accompanied by Emma, began by telling the story of his little half-brother and his mother's recent death to Judge Alan Ingram. "The only way, Your Honour," he said, "for two fags to get custody of Kolwyn was to take advantage of our dying mother. I just want what is best for my little brother."

Before my lawyer could interject, the judge looked down over his glasses at Austyn and said, "I've read all the relevant material and submissions in this case. First things first: Your mother was of sound mind when she arranged for co-guardianship and in doing so demonstrated her choice of custodial surrogate parents upon her death. We will honour her wishes. Secondly, young man, don't ever try to use a gay offence in front of me. This is 1998 and that won't be tolerated in my courtroom."

Firmly, Judge Ingram spelled out the facts to Austyn: that he could fight me for custody, but it could end up being a lengthy and costly battle, which would be difficult for someone unemployed. Austyn argued back on several points, but the judge refused to entertain his ramblings about two gay guys not being fit parents and how his mother must have been out of her mind to give us custody.

Ten minutes later the judge announced to the courtroom, "Kolwyn is to remain in his custodial home and I declare this petition to cancel interim custody by Austyn denied. I further order that any visitations by Austyn, Emma or Courtney be requested in writing to David McKinstry at least forty-eight hours before any proposed visitation occurs, and visitations will be at David and Michael's discretion. This case is adjourned."

Kolwyn had stayed with Mum that morning in case Austyn tried to kidnap him from school or Woodhaven. Neither Austyn nor Emma looked at Michael or me. As the court emptied, they walked to their car and drove off without saying a word to us.

"Hopefully that is the last we see of them," I said wistfully to Michael.

A few days later our first group of mums and children from the women's shelter arrived for the annual Christmas event at Woodhaven. I had just returned from taking Kolwyn to the dentist for the second of two root canals resulting from a diet of pop and candy the first four years of his life. We had really gone all out this year in terms of buying presents, and donations from Disney Canada and a host of other groups had risen fivefold.

Huge snowflakes fell on Woodhaven all Christmas Day. Inside was warm and the smells of turkey and pies in the oven made it seem like paradise. Outside, the falling snow made us feel like we were at the North Pole. Kolwyn's first Christmas at Woodhaven was spectacular. Not only did our Christmas guests and their children get piles of gifts under the tree, but so did Kolwyn. It seemed like every person we had ever met was visiting us with a gift for our new son.

We served supper to our guests and after successive rounds in the hot tub, the children were so sleepy by 8 p.m. Christmas night that there was no fuss when their mothers suggested they go to bed. Kolwyn was just as tired and I was very strict about his 7:15 p.m. bedtime. He was asleep within minutes of his head touching the pillow. Michael was going to drive him to Toronto, so he could have a few hours with his half-siblings the following day. I worried about letting them have anything to do with Kolwyn, especially after their attempt in court to challenge the custody arrangement, but I didn't feel good about denying them access, especially since this was the first Christmas without their mother.

Kolwyn returned home in emotional chaos after his Boxing Day visit with Austyn, Emma and Courtney. Austyn had told him not to refer to me as Dad or Michael as Daddy. It took several days for Kolwyn to return to his new self. We were determined he would not have unsupervised visits with any of his half-siblings from that point onward. It was too disruptive for him—he was a little boy adapting to new home and school routines and dealing with unprocessed and very disturbing memories. How disturbing we didn't know.

We arranged for Brian to have an extra session with Kolwyn a few days after New Year's. The great strides Kolwyn had made were nullified by his Boxing Day visit to Toronto. His anger was back, and he just couldn't deal with all these resurfacing feelings. Besides, four months shy of his fifth birthday, Kolwyn was still not toilet trained. Our poor little boy had been through enough in his young life and potty training was low on my priority list. Like Brian, Mum reassured me that once he felt love, comfort and stability in his new home toileting would follow soon afterward.

A few days later Brian asked to meet with Michael and me alone. Brian opened Kolwyn's file, put his reading glasses down on the pages and said he had something very important to discuss with us. What came next was a total shock.

"Kolwyn is sexualized far beyond his years. He presents as a little boy too aware of both male and female sex organs. I have observed him frequently putting male dolls on top of female dolls and demonstrating a humping action. This clearly indicates that he has either observed adult sexual behaviours or has been a participant. He told me about putting his hands on a female relative's genitals and touching her breasts. I will put this in a report for you to give to the judge," he said quietly.

I felt my guts begin to knot. Thirty-nine years previously I had been forced to lie nude with and touch the body parts of a man and woman, neighbours, and the memory of it hung like an anchor around my neck. I could still summon those familiar feelings of shame, fear and lost innocence I had felt as a helpless six-year-old. How ironic to adopt a son who had probably experienced the same sexual abuse at the hand of a woman. The thought of our son having to deal with this overwhelmed me with sadness.

Brian told us to talk to Kolwyn about private body parts and how they are private.

"Reinforce in him that he must never touch another person's body parts with or without their permission nor should he allow anyone to touch him. Kolwyn is sexualized to about the level of an eleven- or twelve-year-old boy. You will need to be vigilant and keenly aware of this fact as he matures and develops peer relationships outside of the family."

Not that we hadn't suspected something, but Michael and I were dumbfounded at the confirmation. Brian suggested that Kolwyn was an intelligent child and he would learn quickly once boundaries and limitations were set on his behaviours. Brian stressed the need for consistency and setting rules as cornerstones in our effort to help Kolwyn accept limits and respect the rules in our home.

He had lived without consequences, without much supervision, and it was time for him to learn social skills that would set the stage for happy interactions with others in his home, the classroom and sports.

CHAPTER TWENTY
BRINGING NICHOLAS HOME TO CANADA

KOLWYN ENJOYED HIS VISITS WITH Poppa and Nana, so it was a happy event when Paul and Clara arrived to have supper and stay overnight. I found it odd that during the first hours of their visit they hadn't raised the subject of Nicholas's impending adoption, nor my upcoming trip to India. As I cleared the supper dishes, I provided an unsolicited update on my travel plans.

Clara looked at Paul, sighed, and then said point blank, "Why don't you put off the adoption of Nicholas. You have a real gift in Kolwyn: a very happy, healthy son. Aren't you better off to stop while you're ahead? Adopting another child, especially one from India who has no health records and is a different colour from Kolwyn, could spell trouble. You don't know what kind of health problems he'll have as he grows, and Nicholas will stand out in the classroom. Kids learn prejudice early and he'll be teased about being different. You know how mean people can be," she said. Paul nodded, silently echoing her sentiments.

My hackles rose at the suggestion of leaving Nicholas behind in India just because Kolwyn had appeared in our lives. Recently, several newer friends had asked if I'd considered not completing the expensive India adoption now that we had one healthy son. I was swift to anger at their blatant insensitivity and made it clear those remarks had no place in our home or circle of friends.

From day one, Clara and Paul had been attentive, loving grandparents to Kolwyn. It was vital to our ongoing relationship that I have faith that they would be just as loving and wonderful to Nicholas.

Still, I said heatedly, "Never, never again suggest I reconsider Nicholas' adoption. He isn't yet in Canada, but he is our son just as Kolwyn is our son. As far as I am concerned, you have two grandsons here— one white and one brown. If you were in my shoes now I know you would be fiercely protective of Nicholas. After all," I softened my tone and smiled, "your genes are in me, so I come by this tenacity legitimately!" Clara and Paul's grimaces told me they didn't appreciate any inference that they might be prejudiced. I wondered if I had been too harsh with them. I wanted to freeze this moment in time, so I could find a different way to articulate my feelings on this matter. Obviously, my sharp response had stung them as much as their remarks about leaving Nicholas behind in India had stung me moments earlier.

I had lots of thoughts racing around in my mind. Clara and Paul couldn't bring themselves to tell their friends that their biological son was gay. Why would I expect them to immediately embrace having a brown grandson being raised by their biological son and his male lover? Why would I be loyal to those who would deny my identity? For obvious reasons I preferred not to think about this too much. I didn't want to push them away, but I needed my position to be clearly understood. Michael and I had already discussed how we'd deal with prejudice from within our family circles. We decided everyone would have a chance to play a role in our sons' lives as grandparent, aunt, uncle or cousin, but there would be no place for those who challenged the dignity of our nuclear or extended-family portrait.

Still, weeks earlier Michael had voiced concerns about how this adoption had seriously compromised us financially and he wondered aloud how he didn't know if my returning to India was best for us, especially having the added expenses of one son already. Without hesitation I told him I loved him 200% but that affection would sour overnight if he ever again hinted that it made better financial sense for me to abandon Nicholas in India. I understood Michael felt stressed over our continuing financial distress, but for me Nicholas already was our son and he was coming home – with or without Michael's backing. So, when Clara and Paul raised their concerns about completing Nicholas's adoption and said, "Be happy with what you have and forego the trip to India," my rage resurfaced unfairly. I remained positive and steadfast in my determination to bring Nicholas home. I thought to myself, "Why the fuck can't these pessimists get on board and be my cheering section? Imagine looking into my 5 yr. old son's eyes and telling him "oh, well it doesn't make financial or social sense for us to continue with your adoption".

Clara assured me she wasn't being prejudiced, just trying to be realistic. "You live in the country and the boys will go to a rural school. Kolwyn will have enough to deal with having gay parents. Imagine all the problems Nicholas could face dealing with two gay fathers and being the only brown boy in school, in the entire county. I just don't know if it's fair to Nicholas," she said. I knew Clara was kind and loving, genuinely worried about all the adjustments that lay ahead for our sons. Nonetheless, I didn't budge, and the subject of cancelling Nicholas's adoption ended.

There was another issue: I hadn't been feeling well over the Christmas holidays and my lungs felt like soggy bags of mush. I was beginning to wonder if I had persistent pneumonia, so I made an appointment to check my lungs again in early January. The physician on duty said he would do some tests and call me with the results in a day or two, sent me for a chest X-ray and then ordered me home to bed. A few days later, my doctor called to say that I did in fact have a bad case of pneumonia. It took a few days on heavy medication for me to begin feeling better. I lay low, doing minimal work while Kolwyn was at school, so I'd be alert and mobile when he got home. By the third week of January I was feeling much better and had resumed most of my normal routines.

Impatient for news from India, I would fax Mohini each morning. I longed to tell her about Kolwyn but knew the Ontario government wouldn't allow me to simultaneously adopt domestically and internationally. I had kept knowledge of Kolwyn from our social worker to avoid changes to my home study, which would cause further delays. If Mohini learned that I had custody of a Canadian boy who I was in the process of adopting, then her government would immediately halt placing Nicholas with me for eighteen months, until Kolwyn's adoption was finalized. I decided to tell Mohini I had been named joint custodian of a little boy whose mother was dying of cancer. I claimed this boy's mother was still very much alive and hopefully would live another few years. I wanted Mohini to receive photos of Kolwyn to share with Nicholas, without any alarms going off. I fibbed and told her Kolwyn was staying with me a few days each week, to give his mother respite. I didn't want Mohini to know too much but I did want her to be aware that Nicholas would have a possible sibling down the road. She said she was indeed pleased to hear Nicholas would eventually have a brother.

Then in early February, Mohini called and told me to book my flight: "Nicholas has been given clearance for adoption by the High Court in Delhi."

Thrilled at the news, I said I'd be there in a week. She giggled and replied, "You have waited this long. Don't be impetuous. Book your flight for early March. It will take me another three weeks to get his health certificates in order and have the Canadian doctor check him over and do blood work. As of this moment, Nicholas is yours. It's only a matter of weeks before you may come and take him home." I could tell Mohini was thrilled, too. I asked her to book me into a small hotel near the orphanage, so I could walk from her house to my hotel. I had been prepared for months to return to India at a moment's notice. My ticket was bought, and I paid extra to be able to change departure date without huge financial penalties. When I told Mohini I had already booked my flight she laughed and said that was no surprise. "You have lived with hope in your heart for so long and it has finally paid off for you. Congratulations, David."

I left Michael a message at school to call me *urgently* to hear some good news. I was on the phone spreading this thrilling information to interested friends and family within the hour. Then I called Mum to let her know another grandson was finally coming home.

The tone of Michael's voice convinced me he really was delighted about Nicholas. I had been worried for weeks that some last-minute glitch would arise and postpone my trip again. I worried the Indian courts would say that I hadn't filed the documents in the proper order, or that the Canadian officials had forgotten to stamp the right day of the week on something.

Michael would be home for his two-week March break beginning March 9, so I booked my flight out of Toronto on March 10. This would be a good time for Michael to have Kolwyn alone and for the two of them to spend quality weekday time together. Mohini said I should only have to stay in Delhi about fifteen to twenty-five days before bringing Nicholas home.

I called my social worker to share this news. Barbara was happy for me and said she would inform the immigration law firm in Ottawa to expect me and Nicholas back at the end of March or in early April. Another secret: I had not been able to tell Barbara about Michael, which bothered me terribly. Since my home study had been modified to indicate I was a widower, I hadn't mentioned Michael coming into my life. The cost, both in time and money, to have the paperwork updated would be onerous. This duplicity that each level of government forced me to engage in was undignified and so unnecessary and did nothing to promote the integrity of the adoption process. I supposed it would take a politician experiencing the system first-hand for sanity to prevail and common-sense methodology and compassion to become the norm for all people caught up in the politics of becoming adoptive parents.

Mohini said her office would courier the court documents to my immigration lawyer so they could prepare the necessary paperwork for Nicholas's entry to Canada. The firm in Ottawa told me that as soon as they got the court approvals from Delhi it would only be a matter of a few days until they'd have the paperwork stamped and, in my hands, to take along to India.

I was overjoyed. Nicholas would soon be home in Canada. But financially I wasn't sure how we'd accomplish this. I needed more than the $4,500 left in my account. The plane tickets for Nicholas and me alone had cost $4,100. There was the $2,500 U.S. to pay Mohini for the final adoption expenses. Food, local transportation, incidentals and accommodation would cost another $9,500 U.S. or more if I stayed three to four weeks.

At the same time, my health had continued to worsen. Since Christmas I'd had two bouts of pneumonia. One-night Kolwyn and I were horsing around in the living room and he jumped on my back and pleaded for a piggyback ride around the room. He wrapped his hands too tightly around my neck. I couldn't breathe, and with that plus my constant fatigue, I fainted on top of him. Kolwyn was frightened and asked me if I was going to die.

I managed to see the doctor the following noon hour and over the next few days I had a battery of X-rays, MRIs and bloodwork. I had been told initially my problem must be pneumonia-related and thought these additional tests would confirm a worsening case of some resistant pneumonia. It was surreal to have the doctor tell me I could have lymphosarcoma, lung and heart cancer.

"You mean I could die?" I asked. The doctor told me my lung X-rays didn't look good and that if it was as bad as they suspected, this lymphosarcoma would be terminal.

Getting to India took on a heightened urgency. My immediate thought was of Nicholas waiting for me to bring him home. Also, that I had lots of life insurance for Michael and the boys in the event I died. I informed my medical team that I needed enough puffers and steroids to keep me going until I got back with Nicholas—I was leaving in seven days and nothing was going to deter me from bringing my son home from India. I told Michael I had a manageable but deep-rooted pneumonia that was slowly getting better. My health, as far as Michael was aware, was a non-issue as I packed and prepared to fly to India.

My dear friend Deb Reid called a few days later to inquire about my pneumonia status and the adoption of Nicholas. She and I had gone through high school together. Then she moved west, married, had two children and finally left her bad marriage and returned to Peterborough as a single parent. We had reunited at church a few years earlier, just after Nick and I had moved to Sandy Lake. Deb had often stated that if she had been a few years younger, she would have gladly been a surrogate to give us a child.

I fibbed about my health—fine, I said—but confessed I was still $6,000 to $10,000 short and joked that I'd have to sell my body on the streets of Delhi to rich gay Indians to finance the remainder of this adoption. She asked how I was going to raise that kind of money and I said, "God has helped me this far and he won't desert me now."

Later that afternoon Deb telephoned again. "David, I have two credit cards with a combined $6,000 credit limit sitting in my freezer for just such an emergency. If $6,000 will help bring Nicholas home, I could get you cash tomorrow and you and Michael could pay off my credit card and the interest monthly."

She was like an angel come to give me good news.

The next day Mum and I went out for lunch. Mum asked me how my money was holding out and I told her we were really worried about having enough for the adoption.

"I don't have much money, David," she said, "but if it's a matter of needing a few more thousand dollars to get Nicholas home, I just qualified for another Visa card with a $10,000 limit. In fact, I spoke to the bank and am having a second card made up with your name on it. It should be at the bank tomorrow and you could take that along to India." I was stunned: between Deb's offer and now my Mum's additional credit card, we had the cash required to bring Nicholas home.

Throughout February, Woodhaven had been at full capacity on weekends and empty during the week, just the way I liked it. Kolwyn was feeling very much at home with us. He loved to play computer games with Michael on weekends and during the week I took him for swim lessons, out for lunches and to sessions with his child psychologist; for weeks he had helped me to pack four suitcases full of clothing for the kids in the orphanage. I had borrowed a camcorder with which to video my first meeting with Nicholas, had cash in hand, American money orders tucked into safe hiding spots, stashes of necessary drugs. Daily I telephoned Ottawa about my immigration paperwork and Delhi inquiring about Nicholas. One morning when I called Mohini, by luck Nicholas had been brought to her office by one of the orphanage workers to attend another child's going-away party. Nicholas uttered a high pitched "hi" over the phone to Kolwyn and me. I told him I would be there in a few weeks, knowing full well that he didn't understand a word I was saying.

I had enjoyed having Kolwyn to myself for the past seven months. It gave us a chance to bond and learn lots about each other. As my departure got closer I became remarkably calm yet saddened knowing my time alone with Kolwyn had almost come to an end.

Finally, I was only twenty-four hours away from leaving for India. That night I could barely get through Kolwyn's story time without huffing and puffing. I snuggled up beside him as we said prayers. We both knew tonight would be our last night together before he got a brother and Michael and I got another son. I felt sad that this chapter of our lives was about to end but my excitement over bringing Nicholas home outweighed the melancholy. Kolwyn hugged me tight. It was a very special father-son moment for me.

I put the dogs out for one last pee. Twenty minutes later I was in bed, propped up on pillows, reading Rohinton Mistry's novel *A Fine Balance*. I'd started it during my first trip to India and I was determined to have it finished before I returned in a few days.

I read for over an hour, then decided it was time for sleep. I put my pillow at the bottom of the bed and made myself comfortable under the duvet. The nightlight by the door cast a dim glow on a photo of Nick I kept on my dresser. It was a handsome shot of a robust Nick taken in 1989. I paused and stared at his photograph for several moments before my eyes welled up with tears. I missed him terribly. I knew intellectually that I had to move forward with my life and emotionally I was 200% committed to Michael, but after three years in the grave, Nick was still a constant spiritual force in my life.

CHAPTER TWENTY-ONE

WHAT A DIFFERENCE A YEAR MAKES

AS THE PLANE TOOK OFF, I quietly thought about the past seven months. Kolwyn's adjustment to life with us on Sandy Lake, away from his mother and older half-siblings, had been like 'trial by fire' and given me an informal master's degree in parenting. Kolwyn had so many issues, especially his anger over the enforcement of the rules in our family versus the loosey-goosey approach he'd experienced with Susan. Although he'd had no male role models in his first four years of life, our son's adjustment to having two dads appeared surprisingly easy, according to his psychologist, Brian Nichols. Kolwyn appeared to have made a fast study of us and accepted that this was his forever-home. And from day one, we told him that he had a brother named Nicholas, who was anxiously waiting in India to come home and join our family.

We had explained what adoption was all about: how God knew his mother wasn't going to stay on earth for a long time, so He had us waiting to take over when Mummy got sick and returned home to heaven to be with God forever. I explained in story form how God wanted Mummy, Daddy and me to raise him, but since Mummy would only be down here on earth for a few years, God decided to let her have him all to herself until she got sick, then his two fathers would take over for Mummy. We provided him with simple explanations about how his life was unfolding and Kolwyn responded better than we expected. He completely trusted my explanation of what was happening to his mother and life in heaven before his earth life, and the description of Michael and me being parents-in-waiting appealed to his simple view of the chaos in his midst. Kolwyn understood his mother was in pain, and when she got to heaven she wouldn't hurt any longer. "She will watch down over you for the rest of your life, just like she does from your picture of her at the head of the bed," I'd tell him.

In the days and weeks following Susan's death, Kolwyn and I would sit at the dining room table drawing pictures of Mummy dressed like an angel in heaven. He enjoyed this drawing game as he got to choose the colour of Mummy's wings, which were most often blue, pink, orange or green. We tacked up pictures of Mummy with wings all over his room, the refrigerator door and the bathroom mirror. Gradually, a noticeable peace enveloped Kolwyn whenever Susan's name arose.

Kolwyn could spend hours being challenged by puzzles. Without using the instructions or being guided by us, he could put together puzzles far advanced for his age. It was obvious that Kolwyn had inherited his biological father's artistic and mechanical engineering genes. We bought him paints, crayons, art paper and Lego, with which he'd amuse himself for hours. I would watch him in total awe as he got lost in his own artistry. I wanted desperately to reach inside his mind to find out how he was feeling about all the life-altering adjustments he'd been through.

We had designed our new kitchen with a huge laundry tub built into the counter beside the double stainless-steel sink. We could use it as a soaker sink for dirty pots and pans or employ it as a bathing tub when we were busy in the kitchen and Kolwyn decided it was bath time. He loved bubble baths in his private kitchen tub, where he splashed safely while I worked at the kitchen counter beside him. Kolwyn also spent hours each week in our six-person hot tub, a place he remembered his mother had enjoyed during her five short visits to Woodhaven.

He attended junior kindergarten three days a week at Buckhorn Public School. We would walk down our long lane to catch the bus each morning and I'd be there to meet him at 3:40 p.m. Being an outgoing and friendly child, Kolwyn adored school and his teacher. Having no immediate neighbours, I found it was crucial to import children for him to play with. Calling classmates' parents, I'd introduce myself and suggest they bring their son over to play with Kolwyn one afternoon each week. This meant Kolwyn always had friends over during his non-school days.

Kolwyn loved to show off the big hot tub. Invariably, when he'd have friends over for an afternoon, I'd let them all go in and splash around if an adult was supervising, and non-swimmers wore life jackets. I had grown up in a YMCA and in those days, boys never wore bathing suits and swimming nude was the norm, so it didn't faze me if a child arrived for an afternoon of playtime but had forgotten his suit. I would tell him he could wear a spare bathing suit, his underwear or go in the hot tub naked. It wasn't a big deal to any of the parents who regularly sent their children to play with Kolwyn for an afternoon.

A few months after Kolwyn arrived, a social worker from his school called to introduce herself. She wanted to make herself available to me, as a new parent, should I need any help or suggestions during the first months adjusting to parenthood. We had a long chat over the phone, during which I told her about Kolwyn and his four-year-old friends having just streaked through the kitchen and into the hot tub. She asked why they were naked. I said I wasn't fussy about them wearing bathing suits because most of the time they took their suits off anyway while in the hot tub.

"It's no big deal for us or them," I said.

"I'd rethink your position on them choosing not to wear bathing suits," she urged. "The last thing you want, as a gay man who has just adopted a son, is for someone in your community to start gossiping about the gay guys at Woodhaven who invite little boys over to swim naked in the hot tub with their son."

I was speechless and taken completely off-guard by this comment. It astonished me to think any sane human might twist something so innocent into something so vile. I wasn't happy to hear these words of warning but quickly realized the social worker was just doing her job and most probably was right to caution me. Still, I wondered if she would have warned someone heterosexual under the same circumstances?

Regardless, from that point onward, I enforced the wearing of bathing suits. This was a poignant and startling awakening for me as a new parent and I wondered how concerned I should be about letting other people's issues become headaches for us.

I subscribed to every parenting magazine I could find, seeking to give Kolwyn and Nicholas the benefit of the best current child-rearing advice. I would discover an article Monday about a new parenting technique, only to discard the advice by Friday in favour of something better or newer. Kolwyn would be given a time-out one day; the next time I'd employ a totally different punishment.

I remember feeling duped, many times, by Kolwyn during those first few months into his first school year. Because he had arrived with no sense of consequences, he was very mad when reprimanded. Kolwyn was an angry little boy and he had good reason to be angry. Three weeks after meeting us for the first time this four-year-old had been wrenched out of his familiar environment and transplanted to Woodhaven, where he suddenly lived with two fathers and six dogs. I marveled at the ease with which he had moved in, immediately referring to us as Dad and Daddy and adjusting to JK.

Considering the trauma, he'd experienced, it was remarkable he wasn't emotionally wounded beyond repair. Instead, Kolwyn's ability to quickly adapt to his new family and home was astounding to everyone. He had detached emotionally from Susan before he'd even arrived at Woodhaven. He rarely raised the subject of his half-siblings or his mother—it appeared he was quite happy with his new life and was adjusting well to his new fathers, grandmothers, cousins, aunts and uncles. I wondered if this was due in part to Susan having spent more of the past two years resting in the hospital bed in their living room than she had actively parenting—a task assumed by his half-sisters, Emma and Courtney, and the daycare staff. I remember an incident one day when we visited Susan at Casey House being a clear indication Kolwyn had detached himself from his old life. Susan was lying in bed anxious for her little boy to arrive, so she could give him a teddy bear. She looked ashen and almost limp from the pain medication. A few weeks before going into Casey House, and while visiting Woodhaven, I had driven Susan to a local hair stylist, so she could have her long hair cut off. She explained, "There is no point in this hair going into the grave with me, and the Cancer Society will take it and have wigs made for women going through chemo treatments." Kolwyn peaked into her room and appeared not to recognize his mother at first without her long hair, but her trademark long fingernails signaled to him that she was still alive.

During her first few weeks in Casey House, Susan called me at all hours to chat about Kolwyn, as she had done from her house in those initial month and a half after he had come to live at Woodhaven. Often in tears, Susan would wail repeatedly that she'd never expected to saddle her baby boy with this kind of emotional upheaval. Susan worried it would have a lasting impact on Kolwyn, so I spent considerable time telling her about his daily routines, swim lessons at Trent, his love of Sunday school, his new circle of JK friends who regularly visited us for play dates. She was particularly happy hearing he had transitioned well into our home with the dogs, and often Kolwyn would tell her on the phone that his brother Nicholas was coming home from India soon. But the tears of a dying mother wanting nothing more out of life than to hold her child in her arms would stream down Susan's face. I heard her painful sobs during each of those many phone calls in the middle of the night when she couldn't sleep and just wanted to hear news about Kolwyn and his adjustment to life without her.

While he had settled in well, Kolwyn could become out-of-control angry when I'd admonish him for naughty behaviour, to the point that several times I had to give him a controlling bear hug to stop him from hurting me or himself or tearing apart his room. One morning, just before school, he had a fit of rage after being told to get dressed quickly or we would miss the school bus. I didn't want another thirty-minute bear-hugging session on the floor. Instead, I walked briskly into his bathroom and turned on the shower to cold. It ran through my head that if I cooled him off and diffused this situation in thirty seconds he might regain his composure and we'd be able to get to the bus in time. He was shocked into silence by me carrying him into the cold shower. I hugged him tightly while the cold water soaked every inch of us. Within twenty seconds his body relaxed, and he sobbed in my arms. For the first time since he'd arrived, he said, "I'm sorry, Dad, I'm sorry."

I told Michael about this incident later that day and he was concerned this cold shower technique bordered on child abuse. Shocked, I immediately called Brian Nichols, our child psychologist. Brian calmly listened to me recall that morning's incident in the shower. Being both a father of grown children and a child psychologist, I could count on him for good advice. Brian recapped what we already knew. Kolwyn came to us with anger issues and he had only known rules and consequences since moving in with us. Because this had been a major shift in his young life, Brian felt he was simply testing boundaries. Brian didn't think cold showers should be the norm; however, the fact that I had gone into the shower with him and Kolwyn had seen that it wasn't just him getting wet and cold made my actions non-abusive. Relieved to hear that the cold shower acted to diffuse the tantrum, Brian said it was better to cool him off that way than to have let him hurt himself or the dogs. He felt that Kolwyn saying he was sorry was a breakthrough in his level of trust and love for me as his dad.

"This morning you saw him respond to you like a parent. He just wanted to be consoled by you after admitting he had misbehaved. Just keep telling him how much you love him every hour of the day and you'll be fine." Thankfully, this became a learning lesson for Kolwyn about governing his anger impulses. Slowly, as he came to trust in our love, Kolwyn's rage diminished and his angry outbursts fell into the normal range.

Another lesson was about me maintaining my own composure while addressing or admonishing Kolwyn. Aware that his first instinct was to yell when he tried to talk his way out of a situation, one day I'd had enough and told him not to yell as it was disrespectful and unnecessary. Kolwyn pursed his lips together, put his hands on his hips and stood his ground; then, looking up into my face, he said, "Why can't I yell? You yell at me!" What a revelation this was. I did in fact get louder the madder I got with him. What a lesson to learn from a four-year-old. I became vigilant about the pitch and tone of my voice whenever I reprimanded Kolwyn, and lo and behold, Kolwyn stopped yelling back at me.

Kolwyn enjoyed Sunday school at Grace United Church. My parents had been members of the original congregation of Peterborough residents who had built the church fifty years earlier. Kolwyn became a bit of a celebrity at church, as most of the older congregation had watched me grow up. They were happy to see their friend Dorothy McKinstry finally becoming a grandmother. Kolwyn was quick to introduce himself as Kolwyn McKinstry and it was heart-warming to see him connecting to his new family name. A huge oil canvas of Christ in Gethsemane had been painted by a long-time friend of Dad's and then donated to the church in honour of their friendship. One Sunday just before the processional began, Kolwyn whispered into my ear, "Since that's Grandpa's painting, why can't I take it home?"

Giving Kolwyn a spiritual grounding like the one I'd had growing up in a faith-based home was a high priority with me. Michael had attended the Unitarian church with his parents during his formative years, but he wasn't into any organized faith or church. However, he was supportive of my desire to have our children raised Christian.

Patsy, a fourteen-year-old English setter came along with Kolwyn when he moved from his mother's house to Woodhaven. Since Susan was no longer capable of looking after their family pet, she suggested Patsy should stay with Kolwyn in his new home. This delicate, sweet-natured canine had the eyes of a kind grandmother. Kolwyn and Patsy were inseparable, and she helped him to acclimate into his new life. Patsy got along well with Mylo, my beloved black Lab, and our golden retrievers. There was something peaceful and spiritual in Patsy's doe-like eyes, an omniscient wisdom that made me wish she would live forever. Ten months later, though, in the middle of the afternoon, while Kolwyn was at school, Patsy slipped away to be with Susan. When he returned from school, Kolwyn helped me bury her under a flowering shrub next to the maple tree where I had laid Nick's ashes. Burying Patsy beside Nick at Woodhaven gave me hope this would further anchor Kolwyn to our family.

Meanwhile, Kolwyn's siblings fought us for permanent custody.

Though they lost their first bid they kept us in the court system, it delayed finalization of Kolwyn's adoption for two years. They tried to get alternate-weekend access and after that failed, they sought joint custody. In each case the judge deemed them unsuitable, as not one of them had a full-time job or the financial ability to look after the needs and demands of a little boy. Prior to meeting us, Kolwyn's very Catholic maternal grandmother in England told Susan she wasn't at all keen that some gay man would be raising her grandson. But after speaking to her priest and several respected church friends who explained to her that homosexuality wasn't acquired through osmosis, she quickly became our most ardent supporter in and out of the courtroom.

The daily drive to and from Toronto wasn't feasible so during the school year we maintained an apartment in the city for Michael. During the week I was alone with Kolwyn and it gave us plenty of time to bond. Kolwyn found my childhood picture Bible, given to me by my grandmother, and quickly decided he preferred Bible stories at bedtime. With him curled up beside me on the sofa, I'd read to him every night before bedtime prayers. Kolwyn was a good sleeper but occasionally experienced bouts of insomnia and around 2 a.m. he would awaken, start singing, progressively getting louder until I awakened and came to his bedside. It only took a few minutes of quiet talking to lull him back to sleep, but then I'd be awake the rest of the night.

Friday afternoons Kolwyn would sit by the library window colouring pictures or doing a puzzle but watchful for any sign of Michael coming down the laneway. Before the dogs heard the car, he would have spotted the headlights and jump up and down at the window yelling, "Daddy's home, Daddy's home!"

We tried to make his mother's death a celebration of her life and talked about how happy she was up in heaven with all her relatives playing on the clouds and watching over us at Woodhaven. Kolwyn liked this explanation and although he had been incredibly stoic during the weeks prior to and just after her funeral, within a few months we began to witness him experiencing behavioural setbacks. During this period, I parented using the time out method of discipline for naughty behaviour.

I'd stand quietly outside his closed bedroom door to monitor his reactions. Sometimes during these time outs I'd hear Kolwyn crying for Mummy. It broke my heart and I'd immediately go to and comfort him. He learned quickly about apologizing for bad behaviour and he would hug me tightly and whimper that he was sorry for being naughty. Those moments were what I'd waited a lifetime to experience as a parent. It was impossible for me to stay upset with Kolwyn. His big smile exposed white teeth and through his grin he'd look up at me and say, "You're not cross with me, are you?"

Frequent weekly trips to Peterborough for groceries, to pick up lumber or paint or visit Grandma McKinstry gave us ample opportunity to laugh and talk together. I taught Kolwyn songs I had learned in my childhood; songs only seasoned campers would know. I'd sing them to Kolwyn, as I had done to Nick's nieces and nephews over the years. He learned every word within a matter of weeks and merrily we'd sing these songs together as we traveled in the car, walked to the school bus or when it his bath time.

Kolwyn continued to see his child psychologist on a weekly basis. Brian wanted to monitor his anger management and discover the triggers that launched his anger into outer space. The absence of his half-sister Courtney, a primary caregiver for most of Kolwyn's early years, seemed the only difficult adjustment for him. Unfortunately, due to her serious bouts of teenaged seditiousness, Brian recommended we not maintain any direct contact with either of Kolwyn's half-sisters. I had mixed emotions about cutting off contact with them, but Michael and Brian felt it was imperative Kolwyn not feel pulled between two worlds.

By Christmas, after only four months with us, it was obvious Kolwyn was feeling loved and secure in his surroundings. Our pack of canines adored Kolwyn and had unreservedly welcomed his dog Patsy into their pack. We often joked with him that he was the King of Woodhaven. Forever curious about who owned what, Kolwyn would ask, "Do I own the dogs if you die? Do I own the hot tub?" This was a turning point in his psychological development and adjustment to us. According to Brian, this was a sign Kolwyn was adjusting to his new life and all the things associated with his new identity. It was humorously obvious that Kolwyn felt he had hit the jackpot by coming to live at our house, considering that guests and friends who met him for the first time often brought him a gift. His bedroom looked like an advertisement for the Gap, Toys 'R' Us, and OshKosh.

Kolwyn's first Christmas

*

I was two hours into the flight to India when an attendant jolted me back to the present, asking what I'd like for supper. After a quick meal I leaned back in my seat and again my thoughts were of Kolwyn. Had we prepared him well enough for the changes that were about to happen to our little family?

Kolwyn had been very clingy and wanted all my attention. Even at his young age, he understood that my leaving meant things would never be quite the same around our home. I regularly made a point of sitting him down to talk about how neat it would be when I returned with Nicholas.

I'd say that Nicholas would love to play hide and seek with him when Dad and Daddy were busy with guests. I explained gently that Nicholas would need lots of patience and understanding from us when he came home because he wouldn't know how to speak English. I'd ask Kolwyn if he thought it would be hard to learn a new language and we'd discuss how he could help his brother learn English. I wasn't sure Kolwyn was old enough to understand how his parents' attention would be divided between him and his new brother.

Fourteen months ago, my first encounter with India had not been positive, other than meeting Mohini at Children of the World. Now, thoughts of Nicholas energized me. I hoped I would be able to capture on film the precise moments when I'd meet our son face to face. I wanted to chronicle those special moments for Michael and Kolwyn and have a celluloid memory for Nicholas in the future.

I yearned to share the truth of my life with Mohini, but I knew it wasn't yet possible to reveal the reality of Nicholas having a brother and a second father. This deception weighed heavily on my heart, but I understood the importance of maintaining secrecy to ensure the successful outcome of this final leg of my journey. I was prepared to do whatever it took to get my son home on Canadian soil.

My health hadn't been good all winter and Michael's heightened concern over my fatigue was worsening. I kept telling him it was just a nasty bit of pneumonia deeply embedded in my lungs. One afternoon as we sat talking on the sofa watching Kolwyn put together a puzzle, he had become serious and said that if my health was bad then maybe we shouldn't go ahead with a second adoption because of the strain on me. Half-joking, he added that if I was going to die, he felt that one son would be enough to raise as a single parent.

I hadn't revealed that initial tests indicated I could be terminally ill with lymphosarcoma. However, if the worst happened, I knew that he had inner emotional strength that he hadn't tapped into yet. I felt that whatever the outcome, he'd handle parenthood like an expert. My Doctor made sure I had medication and puffers to combat the effects of extreme heat on my soggy lungs. I dreaded arriving in Delhi and sucking in those first few breaths of diesel fumes and hot, humid air. At least I wasn't stopping over in Bangkok this time. The smog and oppressive heat of that city would have done me in.

There was still so much to do before I returned home with Nicholas that I didn't want to focus on what could lay ahead of me with my health. It wasn't denial; to get Nicholas home to Canada I just had to devote what little energy I had left to this endeavour.

As the jet touched down on the tarmac of the Delhi International Airport, I wondered if my luggage and all the clothes I'd brought for the orphanage children would arrive, or be lost, stolen or redirected to another port. It was just after 1:15 a.m. Walking off the plane I had mounting anxiety and a growing apprehension about having to deal with Indian officials, airport personnel, taxi drivers.

My luggage arrived intact. I changed $2,000 U.S. for rupees and hailed a cab, giving the driver the address of the small hotel where Mohini had suggested I stay. After getting lost multiple times, the taxi driver finally found the hotel. I checked in at 3:45 a.m. and was shown to my room by a very sleepy front desk clerk. I threw off my clothes, slipped into the bed and fell asleep instantly.

I awoke to someone knocking at my door. As if in a stupor-state, I could barely open my eyes. My watch read 8:15 a.m. The knocking continued. I opened the door and looked out to see the clerk.

"Your guide from orphanage will be here in fifteen minutes. You meet him outside or he come here?" he asked. The orphanage was sending someone to walk with me to the nearby office for my appointment to meet our son face to face.

"Fifteen minutes! Okay, tell them I'll be waiting outside." I needed to shower and shave. My hair felt like a greasy mess. What would I wear to meet Nicholas? I scolded myself for not having thought about the clothes I'd wear the first time my son laid eyes on me. Was the video camera ready? I scrambled through three pieces of luggage to find my clothes hidden beneath the piles of children's clothing I'd brought along for the orphanage. It had been thirty-seven degrees Celsius when I'd landed and the thought of wearing long pants was unappealing, but I knew from my first trip to India that wearing shorts was a sign of poor manners and so I slipped on khaki trousers.

The phone beside the bed rang.

"David, this is Raghu, Mohini's husband. I am in the lobby and will wait for you. We will walk together to meet Nicholas at the office." I thanked him for coming to meet me and said I'd be just a few more minutes. Oh my god! Walking in thirty-seven-degree heat would have me in a lather of sweat. I slipped on my favourite cotton Brooks Brothers short-sleeved shirt and headed out the door.

Raghu was a distinguished light-skinned man, about seventy years old. An aura of kindness emanated from him the moment I looked into his eyes and shook his hand. I told him I was nervous and hoped my first encounter with Nicholas would be memorable.

"I'm sure my eyes tell you I've been awake through two days of travel time. Poor Nicholas will wonder what he's getting into if he sees me like this. I arrived in Delhi five hours ago and I haven't even had one cup of coffee yet. Do you have coffee at the orphanage?" I asked, half-joking. Raghu assured me that if I liked strong coffee I'd enjoy the coffee he would make before we met Nicholas.

We walked through lovely treed streets lined with cows chewing grass and leaves off vines attached to the walled enclaves of Delhi's rich. Now retired, Raghu had been a senior executive with the East Indian Railway Company. He and Mohini lived in a very wealthy, gated area of Delhi known as Vasant Vihar. Mohini had transformed the top floor of their home into offices for her orphanage. Raghu pushed open the tall iron gates leading into his yard and I followed him along the path I'd walked just a year ago. The thick-walled house was cool inside, and it took a few seconds for my lungs to register the refreshing air streaming into them. As we passed the stairwell leading up to the third-floor offices, I asked Raghu if Nicholas had arrived from the orphanage.

"Oh, yes. He was delivered an hour ago to meet his new father. Your son is waiting upstairs with Mohini," he replied.

"Never mind the coffee, Raghu. I want to meet my son." I began to fumble in my bag for the video camera. "Do you know how to operate a video camera?"

Raghu said he was a semi-professional videographer since it was most often him who stood back and filmed the introductions of children to parents. I handed him the camera and we headed upstairs. I wanted to race ahead of him and call out "Nicholas," but I had to keep my unbridled enthusiasm in check. Raghu smiled as I turned and waited for him to join me at the top of the stairs. When he stood beside me at the top of the landing, he appeared winded but smiled and said, "You new parents are alike. I'm sure you're anxious to meet your son." Like a father, he put his hand on my shoulder and looked into my eyes and assured me that this would be a day I'd never forget.

I could hear Mohini's voice around the corner. Raghu told me to keep walking down the hallway, which led to her office. Several people were milling about at the end of the hallway. Raghu walked up beside me and the two office assistants bowed their heads in respect as he passed.

"Mohini, David's here," he said as we neared her office door. I was looking around to see Nicholas but apparently, he wasn't upstairs yet.

She came from behind her desk and greeted me warmly. "It is so good to see you. Are your accommodations all right?" I gave her a thirty-second synopsis of the past five hours and she asked if I would like cup of tea or coffee before meeting Nicholas. I said I'd love a cup of coffee. My mind was in overdrive, but my body needed a caffeine kick-start. We entered her office and sat down. Several of the staff stood in the hall smiling at me and talking softly in Hindi. I recognized two of them from my first visit.

The coffee arrived and gave me what I needed to calm down and enjoy the moment at hand. Mohini said another family was arriving today to adopt Ruby, one of Nicholas' favourite playmates. I heard commotion from the next room. Mohini said something in Hindi to her staff and they smiled and nodded.

"Are you ready to meet your son, David?" she asked with a smile that filled her face.

"I certainly am, but just a moment," I said as I remembered the video camera. "Raghu would you please film me meeting Nicholas, so we have a permanent record of this moment?" I handed Raghu the camera and he fiddled with it for a few seconds before investigating the viewfinder and finally said, "Ready when you are."

I walked around the corner of the office and out into the hallway before entering an adjoining office. As I crossed the threshold I could see the shadowy outline of a little boy hiding behind the legs of one of the staff. The female staffer pulled Nicholas from his hiding spot and pushed him toward me.

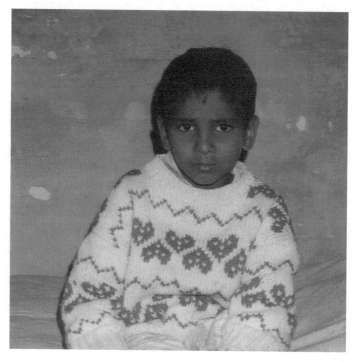

First picture of Nicholas we received

I looked at Nicholas in total wonderment. He appeared frightened, curious and excited all at once. For so long I had wondered if it was possible to love this little boy in the instant we met, or would I have to grow into loving him? Was it reasonable, let alone sane, to expect that fate would snap its fingers and instantly an orphan and his new adoptive parent would look into each other's eyes and love one another? What were this little boy's expectations? Standing there in front of him, tall, fair-skinned and fair-haired, was I what he expected? He still probably had strong memories of the life he'd known, albeit briefly, with his family, and now this white stranger was going to be his father and take him to a far-away place. In that split second, I prayed, "Heavenly Father, give this little boy the armor to survive this."

Everything was happening too fast. I wanted to freeze-frame this special moment in time—I had lived most of the past year of my life waiting for it.

Nicholas looked like the boy in the photographs I'd been receiving from Mohini, but different enough that it momentarily startled me. He was extremely thin and lanky. I noticed the absence of two front teeth as he smiled nervously up at me. Nicholas's eyes were dark and piercing, which for a brief second almost unnerved me.

I tried to imagine what he must be thinking as I walked toward him, this white foreigner, towering over him. No longer were either of us just some impersonal photograph in a file. I hoped with all my heart Nicholas wouldn't be permanently affected in some negative way by the experience of meeting me for the first time. I was petrified he wouldn't like me.

I knew Mohini and her staff had tried to prepare Nicholas for this day. Whenever I'd raised my concern about how Nicholas might react to me, Mohini would gently say, "Just give it time. Children are much stronger than we adults think they are. Nicholas knows he is one of the lucky ones to get a family."

Knowing children were dying on their city streets from disease, malnutrition and abandonment, Mohini wasn't going to worry too long over any fears Nicholas might have of a future in Canada with me, far from the life he'd known as a beggar and street urchin in the back alleys of Delhi.

Mohini had often said to me during our many telephone calls that Nicholas had watched longingly as his young friends celebrated the arrival of new white adoptive parents from foreign lands. Nicholas told Mohini how he longed for the day he'd get parents and have his going-away cake at the front of their classroom. Finally, the time had arrived for him to leave the orphanage, his friends, his interim family, and go to some distant land in the arms of a white man. I couldn't imagine the myriad feelings he must be experiencing. Our eyes locked onto one another and we just stared wide-eyed. I was only half-aware of huge tears avalanching down my cheeks.

Twenty seconds after first laying eyes on each other, Nicholas stretched out his hand, walked up to me with downcast eyes and said, "Hello, Poppa."

If ever words were heaven-sent it was what I heard from his lips. I stooped to his eye level and hugged him and whispered, "Yes, Nicholas, I'm your father."

Nicholas looked at me with a nervous half smile and then ran back behind the skirt whence he'd come. Mohini was watching us and I could see a few happy tears on her cheek.

"This is incredible," I said with tears constricting my voice. "You can't imagine how happy I am to finally meet my son." I ached to bring Michael and Kolwyn into this celebration. I desperately wanted to share news of Kolwyn and Daddy with Nicholas but knew it couldn't happen now and wouldn't until we arrived on Canadian soil.

Mohini and Raghu hugged one another in the doorway and smiled sweetly at me. Mohini said, "We have all become so fond of you, David. I am most excited by your reaction to Nicholas. He will love you. Give it some time. He will be a good and dutiful son."

Just then we all became aware of Nicholas sobbing in the corner of the room. I walked over to hug him, but he wanted nothing to do with me. Mohini told me to give him time to get used to me; after all, I represented not only his future but the end to his past and present. She said he would need time to mourn the loss of everything he'd known, and it might take a while for him to warm up to me. Mohini put her hand on my arm and said, "Be patient. It has taken a year for the two of you to meet. Give him a few weeks to adjust. Every child from here must pass through these same experiences. We have seen it happen many times before. It will pass, and you'll have the loving son you always wanted."

The staff took Nicholas to another room while I followed Mohini back into her office. Raghu said he would go downstairs and prepare breakfast. Mohini suggested that I wait in her office until Nicholas returned and then just sit with him and let him adjust to my presence. Alone to process my thoughts while waiting for Nicholas to reappear, I was numb with feelings of fear, insecurity and immense happiness. I had loved Nicholas from afar and seeing him in person was one of the happiest moments of my life. We would survive the adjustment period that lay ahead of us. I had such a mixture of thoughts running through my head during those minutes. Was it fair of me to take him away from his orphanage home, his culture and his country? Was my adopting him more a selfish act than an act of selfless parental love? Finally, though, I knew in my heart this was *my* son and he was coming home with me.

Nicholas re-entered the room where I was sitting and came toward me but stopped a few feet away. With his deep, dark eyes cast downward he slowly shuffled forward and stood purposely centimetres away from my knee. I wanted to grab him tightly, hoist him onto my lap and hug him. But I realized he had to come to me when he felt comfortable and I couldn't force him to jump into my arms and smother me with the hugs and kisses I'd hoped to receive.

Before breakfast, cake and candy were served downstairs in the living room. This had been the moment Nicholas longed to experience. This was his celebration and he was the centre of attention. It was his "birthday" cake to cut and share with his playmates. Nicholas slowly warmed toward me. He'd bring one friend after another over to meet me. He wouldn't come too close, but he would point to me and say, "Poppa." My fears began to fade as I watched him interacting with his friends. I felt in my soul a reassurance that everyone in heaven was cheering me on and destiny was unfolding just as it should. Ruby, Nicholas' closest friend in the orphanage, and her new Spanish family joined us and over the next 5-6 days we spent most of our time together visiting Temple sites, markets, the zoo, ice cream shops and the Taj Mahal.

Unfortunately, I had purchased airline tickets with fixed return dates. My options were to stay on in the hotel for another fourteen days at $250 U.S. per day or purchase new tickets. Ruby and her family left for

Spain. It was an emotional goodbye for every adult in the room as we watched Ruby and Nicholas hug one last time – hopefully neither of these children understanding the finality of this moment.

Mohini told me we should leave quickly once Nicholas' paperwork was properly notarized at the local court office. She felt that the pain of separation from her and the others in the orphanage would be hard on Nicholas and we might just as well get it over with as quickly as possible, so he could begin the process of adjusting to his new life. I called the airlines but couldn't get two economy seats on any airline for two weeks. However, one unscrupulous agent, recommended by the front desk clerk, suggested he might be able to get me two tickets out of Delhi in first class. He made a few calls and spoke in Hindi, so I couldn't know what he was talking about.

"There are two seats in first class out of Delhi late tonight. A cancellation just happened. These tickets will get you to Frankfurt, where you can use your Air Canada economy tickets from Frankfurt to Toronto. It will be easy for me to get you on a connecting flight to Toronto on Air Canada within hours of landing in Frankfurt. But if you want them I must call my friend back immediately. He has other people who want these tickets. It will cost you $4966 U.S. for two First Class tickets to get out tonight as far as Germany." He smiled and waited for me to answer.

I did some mental math and realized that it would cost $3,500 for Nicholas and me to stay in the hotel for another two weeks. I calculated it would probably cost me another $1,200 just to eat, do some sightseeing and keep purchasing toys and clothes for Nicholas. These tickets sounded like a bargain.

"I'll take them," I replied. I hadn't even factored in a bribe for this agent but figured it would only be a few hundred dollars.

The travel agent spoke again for several minutes on the phone to his connection with the two First Class tickets up for grabs. He kept looking up at me and shrugging while talking in Hindi.

"Sir, my friend has to pay so many people to get his hands on these tickets for you. He needs $2,500. US funds on top of the ticket prices to make sure I can get these tickets for you. If you still want these tickets, I must tell him quickly."

As mad as it made me to pay bribes, I knew I was out of options and I'd become manic about getting Nicholas home on Canadian soil. I agreed to pay his price, knowing it left me with an emergency fund of only $800 in case of a glitch between Frankfurt and Toronto. Two hours later a delivery person came to my hotel room door and discreetly placed the tickets in my hand.

Nicholas had been pulled away from the corpse of his dead mother in a back alley of the Behar refugee section of Delhi. The neophyte police officer, prompted by his humanity, cradled a sobbing and inconsolable Nicholas, and took him to a police station rather than simply ushering him off into the unforgiving world of the streets. Nicholas was inconsolable once again when transferred from the familiarity of Mohini's arms into mine. Then we climbed into the taxi for the forty-five-minute ride to the airport. Destined for some faraway place with this unfamiliar new dad, he stood on the seat beside me and looked out the back window of the taxi, desperate to cling to all he had known, tears streaming down his face as Mohini and Raghu waved to us. It was a moment I'll never forget, being unable to soothe my son. For an instant I felt like I was back in the final stretches of my first attempt to swim Lake Ontario, unsure how it would end. At that exact moment, I somehow summoned the courage and determination I'd need to get Nicholas home to his new life and family in Canada.

At the departures area, he became hysterical, determined that he wasn't leaving India with me. Thirsty from all his crying, he reluctantly drank the apple juice I gave him, unaware I had crushed two Gravol pills into his juice. He was sound asleep in my arms as we were escorted onto the jet, bound for Frankfurt. At that moment the cost of those tickets was the furthest thing from my mind.

Awakening shortly before we touched down in Frankfurt, Nicholas was offered a bowl of strawberry ice cream. His shrieks of delight could be heard from one end of the plane to the other. My son had become the darling of First Class; passengers and flight attendants surrounded us fussing over a child enjoying hand controls for the TV in front of him, eating ice cream and consuming fruit drinks. Nicholas had become quite animated by this attention, which seemed to give him some respite from the anxiety of hours ago.

Deplaning in Frankfurt, Nicholas having become somewhat of a celebrity on Lufthansa, two of the flight attendants accompanied us to the Air Canada boarding lounge. One of them talked to an employee at the boarding desk, who smiled and nodded to us. We were immediately taken aboard, and our seats changed so we could sit in the bulkhead— this way we would have more leg room and Nicholas could easily get out of his seat and stretch without having to walk far. As if still in first class, he was given lots of attention by the flight attendants. One came by and said that his sister and brother-in-law had adopted a child from Romania a few years earlier and he remembered working on their return flight, watching his new nephew experiencing this adventure. He put his hand on my shoulder and said, "It will all be worth every dollar and every tear once we land in Toronto."

An hour out of Toronto, Nicholas indicated he needed to go to the bathroom. Within a minute it dawned on me that toilets were something new for Nicholas and I discreetly opened the door and there he was crouching in the corner to defecate. I realized we had a long road ahead of us to acclimate Nicholas to North American life. Coming from a background of abject poverty Nicholas was bound to be in sensory overload in a land of books and TV remotes, of microwaves that make popcorn, of having his own bed and his very own bathroom, pets, a bike, school, plus the love of two fathers and a brother and a huge extended family.

The day after Nicholas arrived home, he met his Grandma McKinstry, learned how to ride a bike on training wheels and discovered the need to discard his sandals in favour of wearing warm winter galoshes in the snow. After he opened his belated Christmas gifts that first morning at Woodhaven, we wanted to take Nicholas and Kolwyn outside for some playtime in the sun. We encouraged Nicholas to put on his new winter boots, but he stubbornly refused. Michael had already assembled the boys' new bikes and readied them with training wheels for their first lessons. The parking lot was a patchwork of gravel and snow under the heat of the late March sun. We agreed to let Nicholas learn the hard way and sensed that once his feet hit the snow it wouldn't take long for him to want warmer footwear. Ten minutes later with lots of snow between his toes Nicholas humbly indicated he wanted to ditch the sandals, slip on thermal socks and *his* winter boots.

All we could do is guess what this chatty little boy was saying. He just rambled on in Hindi, as if we understood every word he spoke. I had learned a smattering of Hindi phrases, so I could ask if he was hungry, thirsty, had to go to the bathroom, or was tired. Other than that, we just hoped he would learn English quickly. His first two days at Woodhaven were filled with us nodding and smiling at he as he explored everything — especially the pool table and the TV.

I had no way of knowing Maureen Gallagher, from the days of the Peterborough YMCA swim team, was about to check-in for the weekend with her boyfriend, Nosh Pestonji—a Persian who spoke Hindi! It was wonderful to reunite with Maureen after many years, but even more exhilarating was hearing Nosh conversing with Nicholas. We immediately surrounded the two of them, asking questions that Nosh would translate, then relay Nicholas's answers.

"Ask him if he likes the snow?" Michael asked. Nosh laughed when Nicholas responded, "Nah." Kolwyn wanted to know if Nicholas liked him and his dogs. Nosh again laughed as he relayed Nicholas response. "He says he really loves you and the dogs and he wants you to be his brother." Kolwyn beamed. I doubt that this is what Nicholas said, but thankfully Nosh took the liberty of embellishing the response, which thrilled Kolwyn. He walked over, and hugged Nicholas and Nicholas hugged him back. It was magical to watch.

We were able to finally get some answers about Nicholas' reaction to different foods: what did he like, what didn't appeal to him, was he okay with the dogs (he had been scared stiff of Mohini's little Bijon back in Delhi, but since he *owned* these dogs he was fine with them). Nicholas loved being in the hot tub with Kolwyn. He had no fear as long his feet were touching the bottom. Maureen and I looked at each other and in unison said, "Time for swim lessons."

That first weekend in Canada went so quickly. I'd been thrilled to reconnect with Maureen and meet Nosh. Nosh left us his phone number and said to call him anytime we needed clarification about what Nicholas might be saying or thinking.

Boys at indoor play centre.

Shortly after arriving home, I finally told Michael about my tentative diagnosis of lymphosarcoma. It was an emotional moment for us as I shared the potentially devastating medical news Tony had given me before I left for India. Michael's face was ashen at the thought of becoming a single parent to our two young sons. I had told Mum only days before leaving for India; now the three of us could talk candidly about the situation. Mum, in her usual way, didn't waste time on what-ifs but was anxious for me to get in touch with my doctor so conclusive tests could be done quickly. As it happened, I wasn't home more than a few days before Tony and his wife came to meet Nicholas. Tony said he had arranged for me to see a top lung specialist within a few days. Helping Nicholas adjust to his new surroundings and making sure Kolwyn didn't feel like he'd been knocked off his single child pedestal was paramount —but so was getting my medical status clarified. I remember feeling I had my family under one roof and I couldn't be happier—I didn't want this bubble of 'utmost happiness' to burst and a part of me didn't want to think about more tests and what they could mean to us. However, I couldn't play 'the ostrich with its head in the sand' and I needed to attend to this matter as soon as possible because my new reality was that of husband and father of two sons.

Mercifully, there was a reprieve. After numerous invasive tests at the hospital, what I expected to be a death sentence was commuted to a serious but curable fungal infection in my lungs called Sarcoidosis. It would take months of therapy involving puffers and high doses of prednisone, but I would become healthy again, and live to see my sons grow.

Nicholas continued to be wary of me and seemed to gravitate to Michael more easily. On the one hand I was thrilled for Michael, but envious Nicholas chose him over me. I'm sure Nicholas had lingering thoughts of me being the bad man who had stolen him from his country. About a month later, Nicholas gave me my first hug one night at bedtime and within a few months he was giving me unprompted hugs and kisses.

The joy in my heart the first time he reached out for me was indescribable. Patience isn't my middle name, and the long wait for Nicholas to show his affection toward me was difficult.

Kolwyn was frustrated that he couldn't communicate easily with Nicholas. He had waited so long for his brother to arrive and desperately wanted to be able to talk to him in English. Those first weeks in Canada, our days were filled with the constant, high-pitched squeals of delight from our Hindi-speaking son.

Boys dressed for Easter

He had other habits, too. From the day he arrived, he began to hoard things in his room. Wrappings from chocolate bars, pins, dog collars, fruit, banana peels, bunched-up used tissues, brochures, juice cartons. Nicholas had a keen eye for anything he could snatch and hide away. We gave him an empty pillowcase into which he stuffed all his treasures. He kept everything in this and carried it around the house, refusing to let it out of his sight. It accompanied him to the bathroom and under the covers of his bed at night, and rarely was it out of the tight grip of his hand.

Nicholas took his Billy sack to his first day of school. When he proudly shared the prized contents of his pillowcase with his senior kindergarten classmates, they laughed at the garbage he thought was valuable. Confused by their reactions, he became even more possessive about his secret treasures and wouldn't show them to anyone but Kolwyn. By his third week of school, Nicholas would go to school reluctantly without his bulging pillowcase. Every afternoon when he returned home, he'd run to his room to open it and count everything to be sure not one item had been stolen in his absence. If I'd removed rotting banana peels, soggy used tissues or mouldy apple peelings, I'd be reproached in Hindi and he'd shake his finger at me. It was a grim reminder of the street life he'd known in India.

At school, Kolwyn became fiercely protective of Nicholas, frequently scolding classmates if they laughed at or made fun of Nicholas's inability to communicate in or understand English. I attended school with Nicholas for the first week, just to be sure he was comfortable. His kindergarten teacher was made-to-order for our two sons. Herself an adoptive parent, Barbara became a valuable source of information for us and had just the right mix of maternal mothering and gentle discipline that our sons needed. Nicholas was trying so hard to learn new English words every day. The first word we taught him was "no" and he would walk around the house saying, "No, no, no, no," to dogs, people and inanimate objects like doors and pillows. It was obvious Nicholas would be a fast learner: each new day he would acquire two to three new words.

In fact, every day in Canada was twenty-four hours of firsts for Nicholas. He learned it was important to use the indoor toilet rather than squat outside while on the school playground or on our laneway.

Our first family photo"

Both boys were enrolled in swim lessons at Trent University. Nicholas cried pathetically as I carried him onto the pool deck for his first swimming lesson. I had arranged for private lessons, so our boys would be together and hopefully inspire one another. Kolwyn soothed Nicholas's fears by jumping into the water and showing him how enjoyable it could be. After ten minutes of squirming, Nicholas allowed himself to be carried into the water, holding tightly onto the neck of his instructor. By the end of that first class, Nicholas was bobbing under the water, laughing and squealing with delight over the joy of being submerged. Unfortunately, his paper-thin body provided little insulation from the cool pool temperature. His brown skin turned almost blue by the end of those swim lessons at the Trent pool and he'd huddle under the warm spray of the hot showers until thawed.

The boys could see I was passionate about them, their Daddy, our dogs, their schooling, providing our guests with a great vacation and loving life in general. I was forever ready to take someone to task over any comment, look or action I perceived to be mean-spirited, racist or homophobic, forever acutely aware of people's reaction to our family. It wasn't easy for Michael to live with someone whose passions were always ready to strike their mark.

EPILOGUE

10 PM ON FATHER'S DAY, 2017. I'd given up hope of hearing from Kolwyn and Nicholas.

Our sons had once again gone tree-planting for the summer, north of Dryden, Ontario. They'd only get into town, where there was internet and phone service, every five days, but other than two quick calls from Nicholas in seven weeks, we hadn't heard from them. This had upset Michael more than I thought it would, and I remember feeling like the world's worst father with two sons who apparently didn't want to communicate with us. That wasn't how I envisioned fatherhood.

My goal in life, from a very young age, was to be a father—not just some ordinary dad but a *great* one. I'd had a wonderful role model in my father, someone all my friends thought was a terrific dad and who some wished he was their father. My dad was someone I could count on for love and support, encouragement and discipline, in equal measure. I wanted to be like him to my children, which I believed would make him feel immense pride in what he'd accomplished as a father, despite his having died of lung cancer when I was in my early thirties. Is this evidence of my always wanting to validate my parents' decision to have chosen me to adopt? Funny how that issue still creeps into my psyche.

During my young adult years and into my late thirties, this yearning to be a parent developed into an obsession. When I applied to become a Big Brother in Vancouver, I lied on the application form when asked if I'd ever had homosexual thoughts. I saw too many examples of poor parenting by absentee fathers and fathers who weren't making their kids a top priority and vowed, "I'll never be like them." A few of my friends who'd become dads really put their kids first and I dreamed of the day I'd be like them, with kids of my own. I'd had relationships with women and men but by age thirty I had come to terms with being gay. I hadn't met many other gay men who wanted to be fathers, other than Jason and Nick. I began to reconcile myself becoming a single parent.

Instead, I was blessed to find Michael—someone who also committed to be a father. And of course, the arrival of Kolwyn in 1998 and Nicholas in 1999 finally realized my decades-old dream of being a parent.

After Nick's death, my dear friend Henri Nouwen, regularly spent a week each month at Woodhaven, in a retreat from his busy world at L'Arche, north of Richmond Hill. We'd spend hours talking by the fire, Henri counseling me and offering advice about my pursuit of parenthood. I remember how he would pepper me with questions about my fervent desire to adopt children. He challenged me to vocalize my motivation, and I told him I wanted to have something of my own—a child who needed me and vice versa. We would fulfill one another's needs, a child for a home full of love and encouragement and mine to provide parental guidance and offer my child a future of hope. Henri forced me to dig deep into the pain I'd felt over abandoning Drew, the child I fathered while in university, who was given up for adoption. Never knowing the boy I'd created, considering I'd dreamed of being a dad since an early age, was more devastating to me than I'd realized. I was driven to make up for that mistake: I'd given up my responsibility for one son and would have to make up for that with future children.

I'd frequently catch myself daydreaming about the children I'd end up adopting – would they be academics, musicians, actors or athletes. I'd encourage them to be athletic, non-smokers and conscious of their health. Maybe swimmers and skiers. They'd go to summer camp. I'd take them skiing in the Rockies, they'd become lifeguards. I wanted them to live on or near a lake, so they could enjoy summer activities as I had done in my youth. Most of all I wanted to replicate what my parents had done for me. If I could give my children a quarter of what I'd had, they'd do well in life. I envisioned my kids thinking I was a cool dad, bringing their friends home to our house and it being a hangout for them. I'd hand out fair discipline, as my father had done. I hadn't been afraid of my father, but I knew there were rules, and my kids wouldn't be afraid of me. We'd be respectful of one another and I'd always be there to build up their self-confidence; they'd know they could count on me to be their greatest supporter. I'd felt such shame over creating a child in my teens put up for adoption, that I would do whatever I could to make life heaven on earth for my children. Was that penance for my sin? Was there some underlying need to provide my kids what my parents had given to me? Whatever it was, I had to be the best dad I could be.

In practical terms, once the boys were settled with me and Michael, I had a lot of ideas about raising them that were heavily influenced by my own upbringing. Church, for example. Every week I would take them to Sunday school at Grace United in Peterborough—I loved to dress them in matching outfits—hoping to instill a sense of spirituality. And from the day our sons arrived home, we taught them, as we had been taught by our parents, never to address adults by their first names but respectfully use the honorifics Mr., Ms. or Mrs. I beamed with pride when others would comment on our sons' good manners. I remember one occasion when Nicholas had an overnight at a new friend's house and his classmate's father called to ask what kind of politeness pills we gave our son!

Boys off to Bayview Glen School

On week-nights we spent family time talking over supper, playing cards or board games, having 'semi-controlled' water fights in the kitchen or bathroom, or reading books—no television. Once in bed, Kolwyn and Nicholas had another twenty minutes for personal reading time and then we said bedtime prayers.

There were chores. As I noted in 2003, "Kolwyn cleans out the kitty litter every day for one week, then switches with his brother. On alternate week's they must vacuum. Twice each week one of them must go outside to the yard and poop and scoop up after the dogs. Both boys have learned to load and unload the dishwasher and unload groceries from the car. By the time they are twelve, they'll be doing their own laundry and by the time they turn fifteen years old, I expect both boys will know how to change a tire and do an oil change on the car." They were paid an allowance for the daily and weekly chores and we encouraged them to put a significant percentage into a savings account. Kolwyn spent every cent of his money whereas Nicholas became the banker in the family, his pockets bulging with savings.

One aspect of the boys' lives that was different from my own geographically stable childhood and adolescence was the number of moves we made, starting in the fall of 2000, when Michael's stress over our financial instability was affecting his health. The court battles and adoption costs had pushed us to the edge. I could handle hanging on by my fingertips, but it wasn't possible for Michael. The adoption saga had cost us every cent we had saved and managing our debt was an onerous task.

Heartsick, I agreed to sell Woodhaven. Our move to a modern farmhouse an hour away was a disaster. My notion was to create another Woodhaven, but on a smaller scale. However, the reality, a four-thousand-square-foot bungalow situated on flat farm fields with a one-acre pond we'd dredged, hardly had the charm of our previous place. It soon became apparent we had jumped too quickly to buy this property and had wasted any profit from Sandy Lake on unnecessary renovations. Ultimately, after eighteen months, we declared bankruptcy and began an odyssey during which we moved four times in six years. The boys attended local public schools but also spent four years at Bayview Glen, where Michael teaches. And then in 2006 we repurchased and moved back to the Sandy Lake property—establishing Woodhaven once again.

Twelve years later, now twenty-four and twenty-five, Kolwyn and Nicholas are accomplished young men. Kolwyn is a promising young artist and finishing his degree in philosophy and English at U of T – he may take a second degree in art/film studies. He is passionate about English, reading, painting and film. Nicholas graduated last year from Trent University with a degree in Business/Entrepreneurism. He has a passion for financial matters, the stock market and investing his summer income – at last count he had tripled his summer earnings in just 4 months of buying and selling stocks! Of our two sons, Nicholas is more of a homebody, likes stability and routines, and tells me he wants 3-4 children. He will be a wonderful dad someday. Still, if Kolwyn chooses to be married and become a parent, I know he will put his children at the center of his universe. Both our sons have steady girlfriends and a nest of truly warm-hearted friends.

If the past 20 years of parenthood had highlights, what would they be? The first time our sons said I love you would be at the top of that list. Other achievements would be that we provided a home with faith and values at its core; a large extended family including the McDowell's, the DiCicco clan, Michael's brother David and his wife Deborah (our Vet), Jill, Joyce, Barbara and my maternal biological half-siblings. Grandma McKinstry was a huge asset to our sons, becoming a strong female influence in their lives, someone they came home from school to see, someone who would mend their clothes, tell stories of the way it was many years before in 'ancient history' when there weren't phones in homes, kids walked 5 miles to school in a blizzard, no indoor toilets, no electronic devices, tv or winter weekends spent snowboarding. Being able to send our boys to Bayview Glen School and inspire them to learn good sportsmanship values through competitive swimming, soccer, snowboarding. The Peterborough Rotary Club chose Nicholas to go on an international student exchange to Australia after his Grade 9 year and we grew as a family by hosting both Australian and Indian rotary exchange students in our home. We have great memories of traveling to Canada's east coast and dipping our toes in the ocean off PEI's brown sand beaches. Likewise traveling on a train, weekend ski holidays, annual summer regattas at Sandy Lake. Every Christmas the boys played a huge role in our family sharing Woodhaven with women and children from women's shelters – an opportunity for us to provide a hand-up to those going through a tough time. Guests who came to Woodhaven and then became dear friends and became part of our extended family circle. God-mothers Lindalee Tracey and Margaret Donnelly provided guidance, daily "motherly" phone chats and encouraged our boys to dream big and not take life or good health for granted. Sadly, both our sons god-mothers died too early and their deaths left a huge emotional void in Kolwyn and Nicholas' lives. Our sons were lucky to have had Grandma McKinstry, Grandpa Doug (Rattenbury), Grandma DiCicco, Nani-ma Mohini Raghunath, Poppa and Nana as grandparents. I'm so thankful our sons have familial anchors to their DiCicco cousins. Our boys have been blessed with an abundance of life-lessons that continue to shape their view of the world and give them hope for an exciting and challenging future.

Over the years I've been particularly vocal about raising the adoption option to guests embroiled in expensive fertility treatments. These impromptu discussions would occur frequently around our dining room table early in the morning, sharing coffee with early risers watching the sun slowly peek over the horizon. We were fortunate to have facilitated several adoption's by linking couples with good social workers licensed to do government approved home-study documents. My hope is that in writing this chronicle of my life and struggle with adoption it will inspire others to adopt children, domestically or internationally, who are languishing in foster care/orphanages without forever homes. The United Nations currently states that 8 million children around the world are presently living in orphanages or foster care without the love and support of permanent 'forever' families. The limitless potential which single people or couples could provide to a child – love, security, family – and to understand that the moment you hold that adopted child in your arms, he/she might just as well have your blood coursing through their veins and they will become YOUR child. Biological determinants can't be ignored when raising any child, but you can influence biology by providing a healthy, happy environment for your child. After all, when someone gives birth to a child, there is no guarantee what you'll get biologically– autism, delayed speech or motor skills, introvert or extrovert, ADHD – but as a parent you must celebrate it and deal with it. You don't have a choice. I recall walking through the orphanages of Thailand and India and I'm reminded of the vivid "PLEASE TAKE ME" facial expression of the many children, ranging in age between sixteen months and eight years old, watching as I walked by, their eyes pleading with me to carry them home. The large numbers of children and young teenagers who have only known Foster Care facilities as temporary homes, never being offered a forever-home, are waiting for young/older single men/women or couples to adopt them and give them a sense of belonging. Imagine a young teenager entering high school having been bounced around between ten foster homes and just wanting to tell his/her high school friends that he/she has a family to call their own. So much money is spent on fertility issues but, so few dollars go into publicizing the adoption option for the childless single/couple desperate to have a family. The adoption option, for those children already born into this world, is lacking prominence in the minds of those yearning to become parents.

Reflecting on the past twenty years of parenthood, the question to myself is, have I been the dad I hoped to be? I recently asked the boys about their upbringing and recorded the conversation. Listening to my sons talking about their lives with their two fathers was eye-opening. I had desperately wanted to keep them young forever. I loved how they used to look up at us with wide-eyed excitement when we'd give them hugs, new books or toys or take them on trips. I didn't want this stage to end and in trying to stop the clock, I alienated them when they became teenagers. We were adversaries during those years—the antithesis of the relationship I'd had with my parents. Part of my motivation was to spare them my own teenage follies: smoking and drinking and doing dope, engaging in stunts like sneaking drunk into the Bethany Ski Club and skiing down the darkened slopes at age sixteen. Of my parenting approach Kolwyn would say, "I was angry that you did things as a teenager, but you tried endlessly to prevent us from doing the same things you did."

Michael was much more laid back. He gave Kolwyn and Nicholas a lot of latitude and worked hard to convince me to ease up. It's obvious, now, that I should have bowed to his judgment more than I did. I had memories of an idyllic childhood and my teen years were full of careless abandon– often we would do such stupid stunts such as driving our parent's big cars at breakneck high speeds on country roads trying to set land speed records. We were all driving our parents ski boats from the age of 10 and our summer gang was proficient at fast turns and maneuvers around Stoney Lake, known for its hidden shoals. So many nights spent water-skiing under a full moon or brazenly driving our ski boats full throttle through the shallow 'duck pond' passages separating Upper Stoney from Lower Stoney Lake. The most stupid stunts involved jumping into the wake of the 150 h/p ski motors, missing the propellers by mere feet and thinking this was just dare-devilish fun … a potentially fatal stunt. We all knew if our parents ever witnessed these activities we would be grounded for life. I vividly recall those wild times and believe it was a miracle we lived to tell these stories. That is probably why I seemed such a cautious prude to my son's during their formative teen years. I knew what death-defying stunts I had experienced as a teenager and didn't want them replicating my stupidity. It must have been a difficult journey for Michael, as he tried to back me up in front of the boys, but behind our bedroom door he'd do his best to persuade me to consider a different way, one that would give the boys a heightened sense of control over their own lives.

I realized that our boys felt they'd been cheated out of some experiences, such as staying in the same home, having the same friends and school, being allowed to be more like their teenage friends and generally having more freedom, but I had no idea the depth of their antipathy toward me during their teen years. It hit me hard to hear their bitter account of life with me as their dad.

Kolwyn: "We were never allowed to watch TV or play video games during the week and only got five hours of TV on weekends. Our friends had unlimited access to electronics. This made us feel different from other kids, which in the end may have had a non-silver lining, in that I then had huge cravings for TV that I later satisfied to excess in my teens.

And in high school we were never allowed to go to parties if there was drinking. Getting drunk was the norm for my high school parties. Not being allowed to go alienated us. Even though it now sounds reasonable, at age twenty-four, your demands that we not attend parties with drinking in Grades Nine and Ten meant we missed out on essential social activities. Eventually we stopped asking if we could go to parties because you'd insist on calling the parents to see if the party was adult-supervised and if there would be alcohol. So, we became estranged from our peers by being on the fringe and then out of the social circle. I was angry that I felt stunted socially because of you and felt I could have been a leader in those groups. I felt caged up and couldn't express myself because I wasn't at those parties and not privy to the stories of those parties where all my friends met and had fun. I only knew those kids in a classroom context or at lunch. That's why I skipped as many classes as I did to hang out with them at the mall and do cool stuff."

Nicholas: "Which made us feel like we were observing life from a distance rather than being part of it. You wanted open communication with us, but we knew how you felt about some things, so we would just do it and not say anything to you. Like going to a party, having sex or whatever. But when we were eighteen you would say to us that no matter the time of night, just call us and we will come and pick you up. You should have done that in Grades Nine and Ten. That would have influenced us more and been more crucial to us during high school, whereas when we were older we'd already learned how to deal with those situations, like calling a cab. You should have started letting go of us much earlier."

David: "I was worried about you. You both had baggage. Kolwyn, you had a gene pool that included serious drug and alcohol dependency. The racial card was always in my mind, Nicholas. I knew you bottled things up inside. You saw yourself as white, English and Canadian from the moment you landed in Canada. You wouldn't admit to being bullied or tell us that classmates were being mean toward you, so I was the one who tried to prevent potential rough issues from becoming a reality for you."

Nicholas: "But I didn't care about all that. It really didn't matter if kids were my casual friends or best friends – just that I was part of the group. Even if they only called me friend temporarily- I didn't care. It was that or be alone. I rode the wave without questioning. Kolwyn was rebelling against a lot of things. He was okay questioning everything, wanting more freedom, whereas I was just trying to be part of the crowd and blending in.

High school family picture on the dock.

Kolwyn: "Yeah, Nicholas took the blows and said nothing. That wasn't me."

Nicholas: "I was trying to follow the norm. I was always involved in sports and did well. That became my calling card. I also tried hard to keep a low social profile."

In April 2011, at age seventeen, Kolwyn ran away from home and stayed away for five months, having virtually no contact with us. Years later he told me, "I just didn't think it was right of you to restrict my freedom. I was away from my jail guard."

His estrangement from us became an important life lesson for him because only having Grade Eleven and seasonal employment earnings, his pay cheque would barely cover rent for a shared dingy basement apartment on the outskirts of town. He became isolated because he had no money to pay for transportation, enjoy supper out with friends or to go to the movies.

I was completely absorbed in the sorrow I felt over my son running away. Michael retreated into himself, becoming angrier with each passing day that Kolwyn refused to connect with us. I wouldn't talk to Michael because he didn't want to discuss Kolwyn—it was too painful for him. Michael was as sick with worry as I was, yet he tried to let on that Kolwyn would not return home to live with us again. But I wanted our family intact. Kolwyn's desire to distance himself from us was a dagger in my heart. I pressed Nicholas to communicate with his brother often to keep a line of communication open. Nicholas could see the distress his brother's absence was causing us and he was mad at Kolwyn for staying away. He thought our family was imploding and felt he was losing his brother.

It was gut-wrenching to read the few messages Kolwyn sent us during that summer. They said we were the worst people he knew and that we had killed his spirit. He swore he was never coming back to our "jail." I don't think I had a good night's sleep that entire summer.

It was Mum who admonished me and Michael for unintentionally neglecting Nicholas that summer; he was about to start engineering studies at Ryerson University. At the end of July, I phoned Alpha Delta

Phi, my U of T fraternity, and asked if they had any rooms to rent out to Ryerson students. They did and suggested that Nicholas consider joining Alpha Delta Phi. As fate would have it, he was given the same bedroom I'd lived in thirty-five years earlier. This diversion helped me to get through Kolwyn's fifth month away. We moved Nicholas into the fraternity house the last day of August and he was set to start life at Ryerson and become a member of my fraternity. I was so proud of him. With Michael back in Toronto and Nicholas at university, I started to consider the possibility Kolwyn might be gone forever. His remarks to us in emails certainly led me to consider he wanted nothing more to do with us. Melancholy hung in the air around me. Maybe it was time for our youngest son to tough it out on his own.

On the first day of September, I went to bed as usual surrounded by our dogs. Around 2 a.m. I felt someone jostling my arm. I thought at first it was one of the dogs having a nightmare beside me. In a sleepy fog I heard someone saying, "Dad, it's me, Kolwyn. I'm home, Dad." We hugged each other and spent until 6 a.m. talking about his estrangement from us. He'd been kicked out of his apartment for non-payment of rent a few days earlier. Our wise family friend, psychologist Brian Nichols, discovered where Kolwyn was working and dropped by to ask him out for supper. Kolwyn and Brian spoke until midnight. Finally, Brian asked where he was going: would he live on the streets, go to a shelter? Kolwyn said he had burned most of his bridges with friends over the past few months and had no one he could rely on. Brian asked if it was now time to go home. Kolwyn reluctantly agreed. I called Michael around seven a.m. to tell him the news of our prodigal son returning home. I sensed immense relief in Michael's voice, but also apprehension as he said, "What is he going to do now? Why did he come home? He must need money! You really think he came home because he wanted to come home?" (As Kolwyn later told me, it was true—if he'd had the financial means he wouldn't have come home.)

But whatever his motivation, he was back and needed a plan for the school year, the start of which was days away. The solution was spending the upcoming year living with Michael in our apartment in Toronto and finishing high school back at Bayview Glen. A year later he was accepted into U of T's Victoria College and six months after that he won the best actor award in the Hart House Drama Festival. His charmed life seemed back on track.

Today, the boys look back on the experience of their teenage years more philosophically. For example, Nicholas notes, "We have an appreciation for chores and manual labour that our friends don't have, and I think we are as good at tree planting as we are because we learned teamwork at a young age and to do chores and get the job done. We don't complain about chores in rough conditions like some of our entitled peers do."

Kolwyn agrees: "Without the way we were raised we wouldn't be the great tree planters that we are."

Nicholas also says that he and Kolwyn, "were different from our peers. We could spend time alone or together. Relentless socializing was boring, and we came to rely on each other and on ourselves." And to my considerable surprise, Kolwyn says he might emulate my child-rearing approach: "As bad as some of my teen years were, I'll probably do the same to my kids because I think I'm stronger for what I endured. It gave me character, and I want that for my kids. Look at the daily news. Everything is framed in negatives. They never say a thousand planes around the world landed safely today! Instead they only talk about the one plane that didn't land safely. Through it all, you and Daddy taught us to see the positives and the bigger picture."

For me, the bigger picture included challenging provincial/federal laws which were prohibiting gay couples from co-adopting. Prior to our precedent-setting case, one father was the legal parent, while the second had no authority to sign for an emergency operation, take the child out of school or cross the border on a vacation. I found it unconscionable that I would have legal status and Michael would not. We were equal partners under the law but prevented from having equal legal status in terms of our children. In 2000, we went to court and became Canada's first gay couple approved to co-adopt. Our precedent-setting win influenced other provinces to follow Ontario's lead.

In 2017 during Canada's 150th birthday celebration, our precedent-setting success was the reason our family story was chosen to be one of thirteen photo essays produced by the National Film Board of Canada for its Legacies 150 sesquicentennial project. As the NFB announcement said, "These first-person stories explore where we come from, who we are, and what kind of nation we are becoming." I heard from a lot of people who were touched by our story, but perhaps the most moving response was the card I got from a woman in London, Ontario who wrote,

"I have long-held the belief that families are built in our hearts, not by blood connection. It looks like you and your husband have built a wonderful family with your two sons." And she concluded, "I just wanted you to know how special you and your husband are, and that you have the undying admiration of a stranger."

Our story, "A Portrait of a Family," finishes with "Love always wins." Three years before same-sex marriage in Canada became legal in 2003, we held a wedding ceremony in the loft of our barn at the farmhouse, attended by 120 family and friends. Kolwyn and Nicholas were our ring-bearers and witnesses. Since then we had considered ourselves married. But in May 2010, while reviewing our Wills with a lawyer friend, we learned that only if we were legally married could the estate automatically go to our children without lengthy delays. The next week we stopped by Grace United Church and were married in the minister's office. Five minutes later, as legal husbands, we were back in our respective cars – Michael heading to Costco and me driving to Home Hardware.

A few months later I took Kolwyn and Nicholas to India for the summer. It had been a dream of mine to return to India someday and show our sons the birthplace of Nicholas. After a month of traveling and exploring, I left our sons in the capable care of Mohini Raghunath at Children of the World, Delhi orphanage to volunteer their time at the orphanage, delivering clothing and food to the poorest neighbourhoods as part of the outreach program Mohini had established years earlier. The juxtaposition of poor VS middle class in India is extreme and it left a lasting impression on Kolwyn and Nicholas. They both returned to Canada feeling there was no need for poverty in India if that government *really* wanted to fix the problem. Nicholas commented soon after returning to Canada that he could never live there as India was just too hot and crowded – spoken like a true Canadian!

India trip 2010

Meanwhile, Michael remains at Bayview Glen School. A few years ago, he completed his Master's in Education, which reinvigorated him in the classroom. He has really enjoyed implementing twenty-first-century technology into his math classrooms. During the school year he stays in our apartment in Toronto, returning home to Woodhaven every Friday night. Our sons enjoy spending time with him and he is learning to express his point of view to the boys more often. He no longer waits to be asked for his opinion, whether they want to hear it or not.

Mum died at age 102 in March 2017. I miss her greatly. To the hour she died, she was first a mother and second a non-judgmental friend. She loved Michael as a son and supported us unconditionally. She doted on her grandson's and some of her happiest life-moments were as a Grandma. She lived independently in her own apartment at Woodhaven for nine years and enjoyed fellowship, wine and interesting conversations at supper with Woodhaven guests. When some of our many special repeat guests would call to make reservations they'd often ask, "How is Dorothy doing?" She left this world as she lived day to day: on her own terms. She fought arthritic pain for years and at age 101 started using medical marijuana and became a 'weed crusader' for geriatrics. I remember she organized a luncheon for some local friends a few months before she died. During dessert, I spoke to one of her friends about Mum being on weed and how well it managed her arthritic pain. Mum's friend asked if it was working and Mum replied, "You know how constipating the codeine in Tylenol 3 can be for seniors. The effect of codeine on my bowels was constant and very uncomfortable." She pulled out her bottle of weed tincture from her pocket and said for the past year, since using weed, she wasn't as dependent on Tylenol 3's and her bowels were "as regular as clockwork" and the weed managed her pain. That lunch conversation influenced several of her elderly friends to get prescriptions for medical weed. As one older friend of Mum said to me at her funeral, "Thank God for your Mum telling me about the weed. My great-granddaughter thinks it's wild that in my 90's I'm baking weed brownies!"

Grandma McKinstry

Mum loved her family and never lost sight of the bigger picture. "Don't worry about yesterday. You can't change the past," she would advise us. "Live in the moment and concentrate on today. Don't fret over what might happen tomorrow—you may not wake up tomorrow."

It's advice I consider when the days after Father's Day 2017 passed and still we hadn't heard from the boys. Eventually Nicholas called, and upon being gently rebuked for not calling on Father's Day he protested, "Gee, Dad I was out of range. We just got back to camp, and I made the call as soon as I could." I ask where his brother is and there is a sheepish pause before he responds, "What do you want me to say?" Kolwyn just didn't think it was necessary to communicate until he arrived home later that summer. His lack of attention to the emotional needs of others is troubling, as it will set him apart from friends if he isn't prepared to go out of his way to keep in touch, especially when it isn't convenient for him. I hope this trait is just part of his growing-up phase and won't become habitual. Still, Kolwyn is charming and has a good heart and is more deeply affected by the world around him than he'd ever let on.

Suddenly, twenty years have sped by and it's 2018. It's part of normal family dynamics that what doesn't break you makes you stronger in the end. When Kolwyn and Nicholas are home from university, we have lots of laughs, raucous games of crib, hearts or euchre. We still adore and visit regularly our DiCicco side of the family in Guelph. Our extended small circle of dear friends and family congregate frequently at Woodhaven for meals, special occasions. Christmas and Easter holidays are especially memorable when we sit and discuss career options, politics, difficult decisions, girlfriends (and how I hope they will let me choose the right wives for them). Our sons now confide in us and seek our advice and counsel on issues affecting their hearts and finances. We have moved on from the rough times and I'm adjusting to life with two grown sons, the next generation of Rattenbury-McKinstry's.

What family is a dream family? Ours isn't. I've come to believe that every family has its element of dysfunctionality …we're no different. By today's standards, I think being a bit dysfunctional means you're normal! Nonetheless, we love one another and we're learning not to judge one another too harshly. We are evolving into adults who consider our emotional baggage before pouncing down each other's throats. Like my father said, "Family is family. When all is said and done, friends may come and go but family is always there for one another regardless of the circumstance." I think my Dad would be proud of the father I've become and immensely proud of my husband and our two sons. I have no doubt Dad would be the first to say that I over-reacted to some of the boy's shenanigans and I was a slow-learner at the parenting game. He would have told me to stop controlling my son's lives and let them fall and skin their knee's. He'd say that my intentions came from a loving and good place but the execution of my game-plan needed tweaking and for me to lighten up. If my Dad were alive I'm sure he would have cuffed my ear and said, "David, for goodness sake, let my grandson's do what boys do and quit being such a prude and control-freak! You should have acquiesced to Michael's advice on dealing with hormonal teens more often."

I regret I didn't have the trust and courage to tell my father I was gay—oh, to go back in time and correct all my wrongs. It gives me pause to think of Mum's legacy and advice about leaving the past in the past and concentrate on living today to the fullest. As a parent I suppose I learned too late that what doesn't destroy you today makes you stronger tomorrow. I am so thankful to the universal God for being born with an abundance of character and tenacity, enabling me to grab hold of the vision of a future with children in my life.

Achieving this goal was fraught with emotionally tortuous twists and roadblocks. Barriers instigated by bureaucrats and politicians wanting to appease the religious judgmental right-wing voting fringe of society rather than using their political celebrity and sway to silence naysayers whose religious doctrines would rather have a child stay in foster-care or an orphanage instead of in a home with parents who happen to be gay. Thanks for the many celebrities, such as Oprah, Elton John, Rosie O'Donnell, Ellen DeGeneres, Mark Tewksbury, Tom Harpur, Henri Nouwen, Justin Trudeau and The Obama's who purposefully created very public social justice platforms against racial hatred and homophobia. Their legacies will be a beacon of hope for future generations but especially those people today barely existing under odious regimes of despotism and for the innocent vulnerable children without parental love and protection who go to bed crying each night, in every corner of this world, wishing for a different tomorrow.

There are so many children without parental guidance and love, no backyards with a dog or heaps of extended family/communities to call their own. Adoption suitability should be less about the <u>age</u> of the adopting parent, and more about their motivation/desire to change/influence the life of a child. No matter the age or circumstance of a prospective parent reading this book, please consider the plight of just one desperate child waiting to call someone Mom/Dad/Grandpa or Grandma. Adopt a young sibling group and, bingo, instant family! As an active, healthy 55-year-old, adopt a teenager lost in the shuffle of Foster Care programs – you'll experience parenthood and that child's dream of a family will finally happen. Life will change beyond your wildest expectations if you truly desire to share your life with a child and become a parent through adoption.

I'm not special – I just did what I had to do to reach my goal. As I had been told as a child, some higher Being foreordained that Kolwyn and Nicholas would be our sons. I was simply an instrument to make it happen; our family *is* because it was meant to be. I explained adoption to our sons as being their unique story of us becoming a family – providentially, the way it was meant to happen. Their mothers were not going to live a long time on earth and had these two lads all to themselves until they died. At that point, we, their Dads, were in the wings ready and waiting to pick up where their mothers left off. It sounds like a fable, but it gave Kolwyn and Nicholas immense comfort, just as it had given me comfort as a young child. I do feel the universe has blessed me ten-fold being raised by the parents I had; maybe being older parents, they had a wiser, more patient parenting methodology than if they had been 22-year-old parents? Their guidance inspired me to dig deeper into my rebellious soul to find the character, courage and persistence needed to optimize my performance and finish whatever I started – especially reaching my goal of parenthood through adoption. Dad and Mum had one condition whenever we entered a race – just do your best, whether win, lose or draw and be proud of your performance. Thankfully my biological birth mother's gene pool included a double dose of resilience – every obstacle I encountered on this adoption journey reinforced my competitive resolve. I am profoundly fortunate to live in Canada and be able to call Michael my husband, and we are so pleased to share with the world our two delightful, charming, talented and loving sons, Kolwyn Irlam Rattenbury McKinstry and Nicholas-Eric Rattenbury McKinstry.

Kolwyn age 21

Nicholas age 22

ABOUT THE AUTHOR

IF YOU'RE SINGLE OR A couple, straight or gay, and you desire to be a parent, this book is for you. If infertility or biology prevents you from parenthood, the adoption option could be a perfect solution to your dreams of becoming a parent for the first time or for adding children to your existing family. Thousands of children languish in foster care and orphanages around the world through no fault of their own. Your inability to parent may be through no fault of your own. Why not match your need for a child with the desperate hope of a child to find a forever family? The tenacity I mustered along this rebellious journey to parenthood, via the adoption option, resulted in me fulfilling a lifelong dream to be a Dad to two boys, aged four and five. People have asked if I felt an instant connection to these two boys and I replied, "the second you hold that child in your arms, it's as if they were born of you." Together with my husband Michael, we are as much a family as our peers who gave birth to their children. I only wish at some point in history the law will require biological parents to go through the battery of inquisitions and intrusive questions every prospective adoptive parent must endure. Maybe in doing so, there would be fewer unwanted children born into this world to parents who really should never have exercised their right to have children. Orphanages around the world and foster care programs in this country are full of children whose biological parents apparently didn't understand the meaning of being the best parent they should be to their children. Our sons have two Dad's and we are a 'normal' family with all the same issues non-adoptive families face as their children grow from children to adults. We are aware of the role biology has in our sons' lives but the environment of love and mutual respect we provided to our children grounded them and they are every bit a Rattenbury-McKinstry as if they had our gene pool mixed into their blood.

It wasn't a cake walk. This was a journey fraught with strife and unimaginable obstacles, but it was worth every moment of pain. We have two sons whom we adore and love, and now look forward to the day we have grandchildren, which wouldn't be possible had we not embraced adoption to become parents.

Printed in Canada